SALVATION FOR SALE:
THE EARLY CATHOLIC CHURCH'S TOLL ROAD TO SALVATION

PAUL L. BURGESS

Professor Emeritus-Economics, Arizona State University

Published by
The Pudding Stone Press
La Jolla, California

ISBN 978-0-9990099-1-8

First Edition, 2017
Printed in the USA

Printed on permanent/durable acid-free paper

Text set in Garamond

Cover design by Lindsay Lutman

CONTENTS

ACKNOWLEDGMENTS

I wish to thank the following persons for valuable comments on earlier drafts, without assigning any blame for the ideas and any mistakes included in this book: Scott Ehrig-Burgess, Jean Francois Godet-Calogeras, Athena Godet-Calogeras, Patti Sills-Trausch, Robert Wallace, and some Roman Catholic priests. I also thank CJ Kempton for meticulously checking the many quotations and sources for accuracy. Special thanks go to Bill Isenberger and his friend, IB, for reading many drafts and suggesting several improvements that included referring to the church's approach to collecting money from its religious customers as a Toll Road to Salvation. But my greatest debt is to my wife, Marie, for her encouragement, support, and willingness to give up part of our retirement years for work on this book.

1

ECONOMICS AND RELIGION

How did the church remarkably rise from its humble roots to become the richest entity in the western world? It did that over many centuries by using a web of seemingly unrelated factors to create a long toll road to salvation for mining the profits of sin from cradle to grave and even beyond. The toll road stops included regulations and payments or fines for: baptism and confirmation; holy services such as masses; confession, penances, and indulgences; tithes and taxes; sexual dreams, thoughts, and behavior; marriage and divorce; saintly assistance; monumental cathedrals; death; and purgatory.[1] Eventually, the church also had to defend its wealth, power, and toll road by subordinating women and initiating a set of reforms. Unfortunately, the church's approach adversely affected not just Catholicism and Christianity but the world in many ways, such as the Inquisition and using religion for worldly wealth and power rather than spiritual ends. Although the book uses the lens of economics to view the history of the ancient Catholic Church, the final chapter discusses 'solutions' for some of its policies and actions that still have important implications for today's world.

At first blush, it may seem odd to examine the first 1,300 years of the Catholic Church's history through the lens of economics, but the historical record provides unequivocal evidence of the importance of economic incentives in explaining the development of the church, its policies, and the actions of its leaders. Thus, the approach taken assumes that church leaders often responded to worldly costs and benefits in making the decisions analyzed—rather than relying on Jesus' message that focuses on the next world, not this one.[2] Nonetheless, it should be emphasized that the approach taken here recognizes that spirituality, rather than worldly costs and benefits, may drive some individual and organizational behavior.[3] Clearly, however, economically motivated decisions and actions of Catholic churchmen explain much about the departure of the church from the early Christian vision that closely followed that of Jesus. That departure grew over the thirteen centuries covered in this book until many aspects of the institutional church were unrecognizable images of the life and teachings of Jesus.

God is beyond full human understanding, so there are bound to be many conflicting explanations of God's relationships with humans and all of creation. We have different views about good clothes or behavior, so surely it would be difficult to agree on exactly what the Ultimate Good is or how God should be explained. Consistent with this idea, early Christians and Jewish followers of Jesus had some different views of what their faith meant and how it should be practiced. Some of the differences were strong enough that one can refer to different Christianities (e.g., Gnostic Christianity vs. the Christianity that evolved into the Catholic Church). And the Catholic version of Christianity is featured in almost all surviving sources, so the history of that version is the one usually discussed by historians and others.[4] These considerations led me to specifically distinguish between Catholics or Roman Catholics and other Christians.

The leaders of what became the Catholic Church claimed that their version of 'truth' was the only road to eternal salvation, and they began a quest for wealth and power. Based on standards of worldly wealth and power, they succeeded, as shown by the church's dominant role in both religion and society well beyond the period covered here. The church and its leaders had amazing power, prestige, and wealth in this world, even though they claimed to be God's spiritual representatives of the next world.

Using economics to analyze the policies and actions of the Catholic Church and its leaders obviously does not provide all the answers. The motives and behavior of humans are too complex to analyze from just one point of view, so the economic approach does not replace prior analyses of the church. In fact, the various approaches taken in explaining the church and its behavior provide an important foundation for this book. But economics can provide some important insights about history, religion, and religious behavior that have not been emphasized in the often brilliant work of those in other disciplines. In particular, the early church and its leaders were masterfully strategic in wearing the mask of Jesus while contradicting his life and teachings in constructing and using their long toll road to salvation for wealth and power.

Some also might claim that economics is not relevant for much of the period analyzed, because custom, gift giving, and kinship relations were so important during that time. But economic motives—especially including the attempts of individuals to make the best of their situations, given their circumstances—are powerful determinants of human behavior in any age. And such motives strongly influenced the behavior and decisions of many church leaders, including popes, bishops, and abbots of wealthy monasteries.

Because the process of creating and using the Roman Catholic Church for wealth and power is such a complex one that now has a history of nearly 2000 years, it is a monumental task to deal with all aspects and its entire history. Thus, the timeline here ends with historical events up to about 1350, which approximately coincides with the end of an economic era.[5] Although the text is self-contained, there are more details and extensive documentation in the notes, including many citations of works by scholars in other areas.[6]

What Focus, What Church?

There are many examples of serious failures by some of the church's highest leaders, but such individual examples are not the focus. Instead, the interest is in factors that fundamentally shaped and, in some ways, still affect the Roman Catholic Church, other religions, and even the world. These include, for example, creating a culture of guilt, attacking dissenters with violence, and using religion for worldly wealth and power.

The church analyzed here is the institutional Catholic Church, especially the Roman Catholic Church (rather than other, smaller versions of the Catholic Church).[7] Its foundation was laid by men who were the forerunners of the Roman Catholic Church hierarchy. And it has ended up as the oldest institution in the entire western world, so it is of interest for that reason alone, even apart from religious considerations. For, how could it survive as an institution, when countless others have not? The institutional church is made up especially of its hierarchy, its property, and its wealth, since it is a non-profit corporate entity that owns worldly goods. Many religious orders and monasteries also became fabulously wealthy. All such entities, property, and their associated hierarchies are included in the institutional church analyzed. It also includes the church's policies, teachings, and actions, many of which contradict the life and teachings of Jesus.

The main persons of interest are those in the command structure that has the pope in the top position, but there are many other leaders in the hierarchical church. Where do individual priests, nuns, deacons, and religious brothers and sisters fit in this approach? They are the links from the hierarchy to the church's religious customers, as they are assigned to carry out many of the doctrines and teachings developed by the hierarchy. Apart from carrying out or sometimes ignoring, even defying, the policies created by the command structure, individual priests, dioceses, and religious orders also are part of an interesting principal-agent problem widely studied in economics. This problem involves how any hierarchy attempts to enforce its views on down the chain of command, despite usually strong incentives for individuals to maximize their own interests rather than those of the organization.

Because the focus here is on how economics influenced the church, its leaders, and its policies, negative aspects of the Catholic Church necessarily are emphasized.[8] That is not to deny there are other, very positive aspects of the church that include many holy

5

acts and people through the centuries. Many of the church's members, nuns, deacons, priests, and teachers carry on the Gospel message of peace, love, hope, forgiveness, and socioeconomic justice. In fact, it seems the good works of such Catholics provide an aura of respect for the institutional church. In light of how often the church hierarchy ignored, contradicted, and betrayed Jesus' life and teachings, an amazing aspect of the Roman Catholic Church is how much good its priests, nuns, religious orders, and lay persons have done through the centuries. But thousands of other books and articles focus on the positive aspects of the church and its members.

Basic Approach

Economists devoted very little attention to religion and religious choices until recent years. But there now has been an upsurge in work by economists and other social scientists who have used models of rational behavior. This recent work assumes that, although religion may be a difficult topic to model with a 'scientific' approach, it still is possible to gain insights into religious behavior by examining it with the tools used to analyze other aspects of human behavior. And that is the approach taken in this study.

Economists and other social scientists use models of rational behavior to explain religious choices and 'religious economies'.[9] A religious economy is like a commercial economy in the sense that it has sets of actual and potential customers, and a set of religious firms seeking to satisfy those customers. And adding to the economic aspects of religion, churches provide some of the same services (e.g., counseling) provided by secular business firms. Religious services and products are complex ones that cannot easily be categorized into any one of the usual categories used in economics.[10] Thus, attempting to model religion in a testable way is extremely difficult, as discussed further by Ekelund Jr., Hébert, and Tollison.[11] Nonetheless, as shown throughout this study, the various tools of economics are essential in better understanding church policies and the behavior of its leaders and customers.

The basic economic approach assumes that economic agents—including the Catholic Church, its leaders, and its religious customers—make their decisions on the basis of expected costs and benefits.[12] In other words, it is assumed that participants in the religious market 'rationally' make choices, as is the case for those in markets for ordinary goods and services. In this context, they try to maximize their net gains, given the constraints and opportunities they face. Some costs may be hard to measure in dollar terms, such as the value of salvation and the enjoyment or distress involved in religious interactions, but 'rational' behavior is based on all (estimated) costs and benefits, not just those that are easy to measure. Further, the focus on rational behavior in the religious market does not deny that any church leader might be motivated somewhat differently for various issues, and many undoubtedly were motivated by a mix of both spiritual and economic concerns. But the overwhelming historical evidence discussed in the following chapters clearly shows that economic incentives were extremely important and often dominant over spiritual ones in shaping so many of the church's policies and actions.

Nearly all previous economic research focuses more on selected actions of the church, and excellent overviews of the economics of religion are provided in three sources—Ekelund, Jr.,

Hébert, and Tollison, Iannaccone, and McCleary.[13] In contrast, this study uses economics to examine a large sweep of Christian-Catholic history.[14] The broader scope has advantages and disadvantages. More narrowly focused work can use more sophisticated economic modeling to examine narrower issues. In contrast, less sophisticated modeling and more reliance on general principles of rational economic behavior are used here to examine more issues in a much broader sweep of history. Because of its scope, this study also relies much more on general history, economic history, church history, sociology, political science, medieval studies, religious studies, and church teachings than is the case for analyses of church behavior by other economists.

Economic Aspects of Religious Goods and Services

Religious goods and services have some characteristics that are essential in analyzing them from an economic viewpoint. The ones most pertinent for this study are:

- Credence Goods and Services.
- Allocating Time and Household Production.
- Team Production, Club Goods, and Religious and Social Capital.

Credence Goods/Services

The value consumers place on many goods and services depends importantly on reputation or credence, and these are referred to as 'credence' goods or services. For example, most people want to know the reputation of the heart surgeon before she operates. Many parents pick schools for their children at least partly on the basis of reputation. Many students pick universities based on their reputations or credence. Actually, the list is a pretty long one, and a prominent place on the list is taken up by organized religion. Eternal salvation is a credence good that involves current payments for future payoffs that cannot be known with certainty. Thus, it can be modeled as an investment since it shares the key characteristic of any investment—present costs for future benefits. In that sense, the ancient Catholic Church offered the hope of 'profits' that were to be collected in the future after life on earth ended.[15] In many cases, parents choose the religion for their children. But even in those cases, most eventually want to know whether the religion has any credence.[16] Does it have a credible program that helps connect one to God in some convincing way? For this study, the key credibility question involves the Catholic Church's claim that the path to eternal salvation runs solely through the church. Thus, the credence of the Catholic Church was essential in trying to decide whether its religious offerings were likely to be genuine.[17] How did its religious customers do that? They observed what trusted friends or advisors did, they observed how church members behaved, and they saw what people were willing to pay for their religious beliefs. Based partly on that information, potential and existing customers implicitly or explicitly estimated the net benefits of belonging to the church. And the importance of the credence of early Christianity is a key factor in explaining the rapid growth of the new religion, as discussed in the next chapter.

Observers from both within and outside of early Christianity have commented that the blood of the martyrs encouraged its growth. The reason is that the martyrs willingly gave their lives for their Christian beliefs, and there were few, if any, pagans who were willing to certify the 'value' of their religious beliefs in the same way. That is, the martyrs provided credence for early Christianity by so willingly giving up their lives for their faith. The early church had many stories of the martyrs and saints that undoubtedly convinced some of the credence of the Catholic faith, and this tradition continued throughout and beyond the period covered in this book. (The importance of using the saints for one of the toll booths on the church's road to salvation is discussed in Chapter 6).

Allocating Time and Household Production

Household production and time allocation were brought to the forefront of economic analysis by Gary Becker's ingenious formulation of the problem.[18] Although Becker did not apply his insights to religion and religious behavior, others have. Within organized religion, most religious goods are 'produced' by combining one's own time with other inputs that are provided by the religious organization. For example, Catholics use their time to attend masses, which are presided over by a priest. Such activities are referred to as 'household' production, because the 'final' good or service is not purchased solely in the market but instead produced by combining household time with externally purchased goods or services, in this case the religious services provided by an organized religion. Of course, household production includes many things besides religious services. For example, one produces a vacation by combining one's own time with other inputs that usually are purchased in the market, such as gas for a car, a plane ticket, hotel rooms, and meals. In short, there is nothing unique about the fact that most religious services provided by organized religions are classified as household production. But that classification emphasizes the importance of one's own time in the production process, rather than just focusing on externally purchased items.

It costs persons at least time and almost always money to participate in organized religions, so the church's religious customers tended to respond to changes in time and money costs by purchasing more or less on the church's services. Also, persons with high time costs would be expected to pay more in money and less in time, and the reverse for those with low time costs. For example, religious practices in the period covered here and in earlier societies were much more time intensive than they are in societies with advanced economies today—the price of time has skyrocketed because individual productivity has, so the time intensity of religion generally has decreased. In any case, the Catholic Church studied here provided a variety of opportunities for its religious customers to pay in both time and money, as discussed at various points in later chapters.

Team Production, Club Goods, and Religious and Social Capital

Almost any group activity involves what economists refer to as team or club production. For example, a symphony is produced by the orchestra working together to produce the final product, a symphony concert. Note that the concert then is household production from the point of view of the consumer who combines time and a purchased ticket for the concert. There are many other examples of team production, such as professional sports and firms in which workers cooperate in teams. In short, team production is a typical mode of production, and religion is a prime example. And most of the religious services of the Catholic Church involve team or club production. [19] Further, the repeated production of collectively produced goods—as especially illustrated by masses in which both priests and religious customers participated—reduced individual worries about product credence for unprovable religious claims, such as eternal salvation.

Related to the ideas of team production and club goods is the fact that the net benefits one gains from participating in a particular religion also depend on religious capital—the accumulated stock of knowledge one has about a religion. Iannaccone emphasizes that religious capital and Coleman emphasizes that 'social capital'—the accumulated socioeconomic benefits of belonging to a religion—are important in determining the net benefits one derives from belonging to a particular religion.[20] For example, the social and economic benefits of belonging to a particular religion tend to increase in proportion to the number of members, because more members increase the possibilities of beneficial social and economic interactions. As discussed in the next chapter, these interactions were important in attracting religious customers to the Catholic Church, especially after it became the officially sanctioned as the church of the Roman Empire.

Economic Concepts for the Religious Economy

Standard economic concepts apply for religious choices and religious economies. The main ones used within the overall framework for this study are briefly discussed below (those used only occasionally will be explained as needed):

- Competition, Demand, and Supply.
- Monopoly Power.
- Bargaining Power.
- Rent Seeking.

- Price Discrimination.
- Economics and Church Corruption.

Competition, Demand, and Supply

Religions operate in a religious market and, with appropriate modifications, the basic laws of supply and demand apply in that market.[21] Thus, the Catholic Church confronted and still confronts a whole host of issues that revolve around the demand and supply of religious services. And incentives for seeking and defending a faith monopoly can be seen through demand-supply effects. Although there are some subtle reasons that give rise to standard demand and supply relationships, the basics are extremely intuitive and encountered on a daily basis.[22] Under ideal conditions for a competitive market—especially including no pricing power by either buyers or sellers and full information—consumers come out ahead in getting what they want at the lowest possible price (that allows firms to make a 'normal' profit). In any case, under such conditions, markets produce efficient outcomes, as explained by Adam Smith in his 1776 *Wealth of Nations*. For example, within a competitive religious market that has no coercion or regulation by secular authorities, substantial religious diversity to match the diverse tastes of religious customers would be expected. Indeed, there were many versions of early Christianity before the leaders of the Catholic Church collaborated with secular rulers to create a legally enforced faith monopoly, as discussed in the next chapter.

Whenever a church imposes an increase in the time or money price of its services, its religious customers tend to respond by purchasing less of the services, other things equal. For example, increasing tithes, mandating confession, and imposing penances all increased the cost of the Catholic Church's religious services—and tended to reduce the quantity of the church's religious offerings its customers would buy, other things equal. Although church leaders had no modern theory of how prices would affect the demand for their religious services, they clearly understood that any large increase in the costs of participating in the church either had to be justified through higher value or imposed as a requirement to continue participating in the Catholic community. Thus, elaborate justifications were made for the necessity of things such as mass offerings (to save one's soul), confession and paying for sins with penances (to save one's soul), death bequests (to save one's soul), and the sale of salvation insurance for purgatory (to reduce suffering there). Further, the church could impose excommunication on those who refused to comply or cooperate (and they could be subjected to the claws of the Inquisition during the latter part of the period studied). The penalty for excommunication included economic sanctions that prohibited offenders from conducting any commerce with other Catholics. These sanctions and other penalties were designed to force reluctant or doubtful religious customers to remain in the church and pay on its long toll road to salvation discussed in Chapters 2-7.

Monopoly Power

In contrast to competition, a pure monopoly is one firm that controls the entire market for a particular good or service. However, more generally, monopoly power exists in less extreme forms, and all such cases distort the beneficial results of a free market by allowing those with that power to tip the benefits of the market in their favor, thus reducing the benefits received by their trading partners, whether on the buying or selling side of the market. Monopoly power means easier profits and less pressure to perform efficiently than is the case under competition. Of course, as monopolists learn, they can be overtaken by firms that provide new products, services, or technologies. But while the monopoly lasts, it can provide wealth and power that cannot be found under competition, as exemplified by the Catholic Church in the religious market, especially up to the time of Luther and the Protestant Reformation in the sixteenth century. In any case, the Catholic Church had substantial monopoly power for the whole period studied here, and that allowed it to mine the profits of sin on its long toll road to salvation discussed in later chapters.

The unique aspect of the church's monopoly position is the nature of its key product, eternal salvation, which gave it the most powerful monopoly imaginable for those who believe salvation can be achieved only through the church. The monopoly power of the Catholic Church allowed it to eliminate competition and reduce the supply of religious services by other religions, so it could charge more for its services than otherwise would have been possible. And on the demand side of the market, the absence of more competition resulted in greater demand for the Catholic Church's services than otherwise would have been possible, again giving it more customers and allowing it to charge more. Further, the elimination of competing or substitute religious organizations changed the shape of the demand curve in a way that gave the Catholic Church more pricing power.[23] These changes in supply and demand curves thus increased the church's pricing power—it could extract more from its religious customers than under more competition.[24]

Although the church did not have unfettered monopoly power, the actions of the church's leaders and the institutional church they created include the following hallmarks of monopoly power that are discussed in the following chapters:

- Charging at every stop along the toll road to salvation it created. The church's monopoly power allowed it to charge higher prices than would have been possible in a market of many competing religions that featured eternal salvation (as began to happen during the sixteenth century's Protestant Reformation).
- Extracting the time, money, and wealth of its religious customers in exchange for the promise of eternal salvation that supposedly could be provided only through the Catholic Church.
- Accumulating the massive wealth and power for the Catholic Church and its churchmen by selling salvation.
- Establishing and regulating franchises to spread the church's market reach through a multitude of churches, monasteries, and various religious orders.
- Abusing consumers with corrupt and incompetent church leaders and priests.
- Developing and implementing strategic moves and counter-moves to advance the interests of the church and its churchmen against their potential and actual competitors, who were labeled heretics.
- Living lavishly by church leaders, especially the papacy, cardinals, bishops, some monks, and some religious orders.
- Creating churches and powerful monasteries that were large employers and acted as quasi-monopolists in the small medieval towns and huge agricultural areas they controlled.

Bargaining Power

The degree of monopoly power of the Catholic Church depended on support by the state's coercive power, and it was masterful in bargaining for the support of a long line of emperors and rulers. But even in the case of a monopoly church backed by the full coercive power of the state, there continued to be more than one Christian religion or sect, as shown by the many schisms and heresies in the history of the church, some of which are discussed in Burgess.[25] It simply is impossible to represent the all-encompassing image of God in any one religious tradition that could be accepted by all of humanity. That is not surprising, given that much about God is shrouded in a mystery for the human mind. (And, 'No one has ever seen God,' the Gospel of John 1:18 reminds us.) If humanity cannot agree on a single design for clothing or cars, how could it ever agree on one explanation of God?

Much of church history involves bargaining and negotiating between church leaders and secular powers. Both parties had some monopoly power and they bargained against each other for gains through cooperation or competition.[26] In fact, the power of the church depended on such negotiations by church leaders with Constantine and many other rulers.[27] Naturally, the outcomes of these situations depended importantly on the relative bargaining power of each party, and that varied between the church and secular rulers through the centuries. Of course, a major cost of the church's monopoly power was that church leaders had to negotiate their positions with their secular collaborators. Part of the cost was that church leaders made accommodations to support or, at least, not oppose secular policies that conflicted with the Gospel message, such as violence, warfare, and murder. Further, the church had to contend with lay powers who sought to gain economic benefits from managing or controlling church property in various ways, including the appointments of bishops and popes.

Churchmen also had to devise strategies for dealing with their supporters-collaborators-competitors, especially the secular powers that made it possible for the Catholic Church to create so much wealth and power. For example, when economic and political arrangements were made with a string of Roman emperors and secular rulers that made Catholicism the official religion of Rome and the West, at least some in the church probably assumed that they were making decisions to further the church's religious goals rather than enhancing its secular power and wealth. Based on the historical record, other church leaders clearly saw the outcomes as more wealth and power for themselves and the institutional church. On the other side of this bargaining game, the emperors and rulers surely were interested in using the church for their own ends of unifying their empires and enhancing their secular power and wealth. For many rulers, the church simply was a valuable partner in furthering their own wealth and power. Nonetheless, even though the church won and lost individual battles with secular rulers, it won in the longer term, at least as an organization interested in wealth and power. It was left standing as a fabulously wealthy and powerful institution at the end of the Middle Ages, whereas many secular kingdoms had come and gone.

Rent Seeking[28]

Rent seeking refers to the transfer of resources from one party to another by simply changing the economic, social, or political 'rules of the game'—but without creating any real production in return. Instead of creating any new wealth, existing wealth is simply transferred from one party to another. Because time, expertise, and other resources are used up in the process without creating any output for society, it is inefficient from society's viewpoint. A classic case of rent seeking is lobbying to gain favorable laws or regulations from governments. These benefits for the church included factors such as regulated prices, market licenses, quantity and quality controls, tolls, territorial charters, and many others. The Catholic Church repeatedly engaged in rent-seeking behavior to increase its wealth and power, as will be apparent in following chapters and as shown in other studies, especially Ekelund Jr., Hébert, and Tollison and Ekelund Jr., Hébert, Tollison, Anderson, and Davidson.[29]

Immediately after its recognition by the Roman Emperor Constantine in the early fourth century, church leaders began currying favors from imperial Rome. And they were remarkably successful in their efforts that began the church on its road to achieving tremendous monopoly power and wealth. Given the importance of rent seeking for the church's wealth and power, many examples are discussed in later chapters, and two of them illustrate the church's mastery of the tactics:

- After becoming Constantine's ally, the church obtained Roman legislation later in the fourth century that made it *the* religion of imperial Rome. Other religious competitors were suppressed or banned, and new entrants into the religious market were prevented or targeted for elimination. And those policies continued through the centuries studied here.

- A large number of laws were passed through the centuries to increase or maintain the power of the church and enforce its policies. For example, the churches of other versions of

Christianity and Jewish synagogues were expropriated and converted into Catholic churches under the authority of secular power.

Price Discrimination

Charging different prices for the same service or product is referred to as price discrimination, which is a common phenomenon. For example, movie theaters sometimes charge different prices, based on the ages of their customers. Bars have happy hours during which they sometimes charge lower prices for women than for men. Lawyers, accountants, doctors, hospitals, and others sometimes charge different prices for the same services, based on their customers' willingness/ability to pay. A firm can increase its profits by engaging in price discrimination, but that requires certain conditions, all of which the church easily satisfied for most of its religious offerings:

- Some degree of pricing power, so different prices could be charged to different customers.
- Market segmentation—somehow dividing either individual customers or groups of customers into different segments, so different prices could be charged. This was fairly easy for the church to do, given the knowledge of its churchmen about the income and wealth of their customers.
- Prevention of resale because, without this condition, those who buy at lower prices could resell to those who otherwise would be charged a higher price. Obviously, the church's major religious offerings could not be resold.

Because the church could so easily practice price discrimination, It was repeatedly used in collecting payments on the church's toll road to salvation discussed in later chapters. This pricing strategy included different amounts expected as regular offerings, different penance prices for the same sins, different sizes in the death bequests 'needed' for salvation, different prices for church-approved annulments/divorces, and different prices to relieve suffering in purgatory. And your priest-confessor was there to help you discover the price needed to pay for your sins. The approach of death was especially effective in uncovering an ever higher willingness to pay for the church's salvation insurance.

Economics and Church Corruption

During the twelfth and early thirteenth centuries, the criticisms against the corruption of the church and its churchmen reached new highs, threatening the economic viability of the church's faith monopoly. In response to these religious and economic concerns, the church implemented reforms during the eleventh-thirteenth centuries that are discussed in Chapter 9. As part of that reform era, the church wanted to deal with concerns about selling sacraments. One response was that the church's Fourth Lateran Council (1215) decreed that all sacraments had to be administered for free, but the same canon reminded lay people to make their customary offerings. Thus, regardless of pious church pronouncements against selling holy services, churchmen continued to expect and receive payments or donations for the salvation insurance they sold. Further, churchmen and the papacy continued to practice price discrimination to increase their profits from sin, even after the sale of holy services supposedly had been banned by Lateran IV.

Prior Research

Recently, a large body of literature on the economic motives and behavior of the Roman Catholic and other churches has emerged. But the roots of this literature go back to Adam Smith who devoted several pages to religion in his 1776 *The Wealth of Nations*, which is considered the foundational book of economics.[30] In recent years, many economists and other social scientists have approached the topic as one that involves the rational choices of both the producers and consumers of religious products and services.[31] [32] And that research provides a basis for much of the analysis in this book. In particular, a fundamental insight of Adam Smith is that organizational structure is crucial in determining individual and group behavior. Many other contributions used throughout this study have been developed in recent years. For example, Smith's insights are developed in the modern theory of industrial organization.[33] Hull and Bold analyze the church as an entity that maximizes profits in order to ensure its long-run survival.[34] Ekelund Jr. and Tollison provide a detailed analysis of the economic origins of Roman Christianity.[35] Iannaccone and Ekelund Jr., Hébert, and Tollison analyze the medieval Roman Catholic Church as an economic firm that focused on rent seeking as a quasi-monopolistic, bureaucratic firm that extracted wealth from its religious customers and engaged in various strategies to defend its monopoly power.[36] All of these and other studies cited above are important as a foundation for this book.

Conclusion

Given the background provided in this chapter, the following chapters look at the specifics of how the church created and used its toll road to salvation for mining the profits of sin. That toll road was a long one, and the church managed to collect payments at every stop along the way from birth to death and even beyond the grave, once it invented the concept of purgatory.

2

INITIAL STEPS IN ESTABLISHING THE CATHOLIC CHURCH AS A PROFITABLE BUSINESS ENTERPRISE

Sine Emptore Nullum Negotium—the door of the dean's office in my W. P. Carey's Business School at Arizona State University used to have a plaque with that or a similar Latin phrase, which translates to, "Without a customer there is no business." The dean wanted faculty to appreciate students as customers, not always a common concept in the academic world. But like business deans and for-profit businesses, many Catholic Church leaders acted as if they fully understood that business adage, even if they claimed to be spiritually motivated and demeaned business/commerce as almost inherently sinful activities.

The monopoly power conferred on the church by imperial Rome—starting with Constantine in 312 and followed up in 381 and other years with laws—increased its customer base simply because other religious choices were made illegal. But there was much more involved in establishing the church's product credibility and developing/expanding its customer base. That customer base and other strategic moves made it possible for the church to create a long toll road to salvation that made the church fabulously wealthy. Some initial steps are discussed in this chapter.

Factors Behind Church's Initial Customer Base: The Rise of Christianity[37]

No one knows the exact numbers of early Christians, but Stark argues that there is no need for extraordinary growth in the latter half of the fourth century that might be attributed to Emperor Constantine's adoption of Christianity for the Roman Empire. Instead, he uses contemporary data for the Mormon religion, which grew at a rate of about forty percent per decade for the one hundred years from about 1898 to 1997. By using this growth rate and a peak population of sixty million for the Roman Empire, he starts at a very small estimate of the number of early Christians and projects their growth on the basis of a growth rate of forty percent per decade. This yields the following estimates of Christians as a percentage of the Roman population:

- .002% (about 1,200 persons) in 50 AD.
- .36% (about 216,000 persons) in 200 AD.
- 1.9% (about 1,140,000 persons) in 250 AD.
- 10.5% (about 6,300,000 persons) in 300 AD.
- 56.5% (about 33,900,000 persons) in 350 AD.

How did Christianity rise from a small, persecuted group to become the official religion of imperial Rome? It involved several factors, such as:

- Socioeconomic justice was a strong theme in Jesus' teachings, and it undoubtedly was a major reason so many from the empire's oppressed masses were attracted to Christianity.

- Life expectancy was extremely low at the time of Jesus and all the way through the 1350 and beyond. Jesus' message of love, hope, and eternal life must have resonated strongly in a world of extreme economic inequality, violence, disease, and early death. The promise of rewards in the next life was a powerful one in such a world, and the church masterfully packaged itself as the only path to those rewards.

- Christians willingly provided help and hope to those in need, even if they were not Christians. The Christian mutual support network, help for others, and the hope for a better life added to the religion's credibility and attracted more members.

- Christians honored work, unlike elite pagans, who viewed work as demeaning. For a society in which all but the wealthy had to work hard for survival, the Christian position on work surely was more credible than the pagan one.

- Persecutions and martyrs were important in proving the worth of the faith. Why would Christians willingly die for their faith, unless its promise of salvation was a credible one? Church writers memorialized the persecutions and martyrs in stories that were repeatedly used through the centuries.

- The new religion had its roots in Judaism, but the population in Jerusalem and the Holy Land provided a limited area for recruitment of new members. St. Paul was especially effective in helping spread the reach of Christianity as a leader in evangelizing the Gentiles throughout the vast Roman Empire.

- Christianity spread rapidly, and part of that success was due to its primary focus on the empire's towns and cities. Christian missionaries and merchants carried the message with them to major urban centers. Word about the new religion spread quickly in relatively densely settled areas.

- Although women ultimately were subordinated by the church's male hierarchy, early Christianity clearly was friendlier to women than the pagan religions of the time. And women were important in convincing their husbands and children to convert.

- Christianity had vibrant worship services that involved the entire community in religious team production. The participation and enthusiasm of Christians in worship services surely was impressive to nonmembers.

- Especially compared to pagan priests, many early church leaders had no pomp, no circumstance, and usually no displays of wealth. Their leadership provided a credible and different model of religious leadership in a society dominated by elite religious leaders, who even included the emperor as the head of his own cult.

- Pagan religions had many different gods and many different philosophies. The more unified approach of Christians to one all-powerful God represented a highly credible alternative that spread throughout the empire.

- Early Christian leaders obviously understood that product credibility in Roman society was importantly related to a religion's ancient roots. Although Christianity was a new religion, it successfully claimed ancient status by taking over Jewish Scriptures as its own (eventually as the Old Testament in

Christian-Catholic Bibles). Christian leaders argued that Jesus was the Messiah foretold in those Scriptures, but Jewish leaders rejected that claim. In response, Christian leaders argued that the Jews did not understand their own Scriptures.

Product Credibility for Wealth and Power

Stark and Eilinghoff each have analyses of product credibility that help explain how organized religions tend to operate in establishing credence and trust with existing and potential customers.[38] Based on their work, several important factors can be identified in establishing and growing a religion, especially as applied to the Catholic Church:

- Since the true value of most religious promises cannot be known with certainty, the credibility of them must be established through observable facts. Thus, the ability to offer credibility is a central feature of developing a religion, as discussed in Chapter 1. The credibility of early Christianities was increased through the production and consumption of religion by the whole community through team and club production. Those community rituals reinforced the 'truth' of Christian beliefs for active and potential followers of the faith.

- Tangible benefits, such as assistance for those in need, increased general confidence in the intangible benefits, especially eternal salvation. Testimonials and repeated stories of miracles were common in the early church.

- Religious leaders usually have greater credibility if their personal compensation is relatively low, and it was extremely low in very early Christianities.

- Voluntary martyrs are perhaps the ultimate sign of confidence in the eternal benefits promised in Christianity. Also, the costs via martyrdom may have been limited to a relatively small number of persons, perhaps only hundreds according to some experts. Regardless of the exact numbers, the accounts of martyrdom were used repeatedly in church services, and they increased confidence in the religious offerings of the church.

- Any collectively produced good has the problem of free riders. Early Chirstianities mitigated this problem by strict codes of behavior for members and strict punishments for violators. In this context, early Christianities were strengthened by rigorous standards that tended to prevent free riders from draining their religious energy. The average commitment level of early Christians was extremely high, compared to the commitment of pagan worshipers. Consequently, the collectively produced worship services in early Christianities must have been extremely satisfying to their members.

- Experts receive extensive training and provide religious services to less well informed customers, who rely on the experts for guidance and advice. The complexity of a religion's theology tends to increase the credibility of its experts, who have to spend years mastering it.

- Religions use the same symbols and practices repeatedly in their services, and it has been shown that repetition in and of itself increases credibility. Thus, as in the Catholic Church, traditional services repeat exactly the same liturgical practices.

- Life is full of rituals that signal major changes, such as marriage, initiation, and funeral ceremonies. Religions attempt to take these over to further certify their credibility by providing 'real' products or services. For example, the Catholic Church asserted its authority over certifications of marriages and divorces during the Middle Ages.

- Elaborate worship spaces and expensive ornamentation strongly suggest 'success' in dealing with past and current customers, as illustrated by select Catholic churches after Christianity became the imperially favored religion in the Roman Empire. Such expensive surroundings are a signal of credibility for some current and potential customers.

- The Catholic religion was used to explain inexplicable events, such as floods, plagues, or natural disasters. The explanations involved Divine discontent.

- The priests-pastors-leaders of some religions, including those in the Roman Catholic Church, must take vows of celibacy to separate themselves from secular society and increase their credibility as honest brokers for the religion.

- Organized religions are strongly inclined to separate the world into two groups, believers and non-believers. There is a strong tendency to declare that any who disagree are unfaithful, deceitful, false, wicked, and dangerous to the credibility of the 'true' faith and beliefs. The Roman Catholic Church did this through the centuries, and it relied on violence and murder in many cases, including the inquisition and the crusades.

From the above summary of ideas about credence goods and services, it is apparent that the Roman Catholic Church eventually came to practice all of them. In fact, much of the history of the church and its leaders revolves around attempts to enhance or certify the credibility of the church's doctrines and teachings or to dispute the credibility of competing views.

Establishing Catholic Church's Domination

How did the Catholic Church manage to dominate all forms of Christianity during the fourth century? What were some of the strategies used to attract and retain its customers? How did it use franchise licenses to spread its market reach? This section looks at these questions.

There were many varieties of Christianity during the early period, including Arianism, Gnosticism, Docetism, the Marionites, and the Donatists. But Catholic Church leaders successfully used strategies to dominate the emerging Christian religion and use their church as a vehicle for wealth and power. These strategies included factors such as the following:

- The collaboration with and support of the rulers—starting with Constantine in 312—who granted the church immense monopoly power in return for its religious sanction of the rulers' secular power. The rulers supported the church with laws, lavish support and gifts, property confiscations, and executions or banishments of the church's opponents.
- The fact that rulers joined the Catholic Church induced others to join the church because of the network externalities associated with the business and social contacts found in the rulers' church. It was good for both social and business interactions to be in the rulers' church.
- Hardin develops an economic theory of knowledge to explain religious belief as a form of knowledge.[39] He shows how such knowledge causes/maintains religious belief and how the religious belief of an individual is heavily influenced by the beliefs of the individual's community. Although the church had no such modern theory, it had a brilliant marketing scheme for recruiting, training, and educating its members, starting with infant baptism. In the process, parents and the community were responsible for educating children to be 'good' Catholics. In short, church teachings were inculcated and reinforced for

Catholics throughout their lives by lay members, not just churchmen.

- The church had many famous writers who produced many texts, including the texts of the New Testament, to establish the church's credibility and defend it against critics. Of course, the Gospels and other books of the New Testament are especially important. But there were many other writers who include Irenaeus of Lyons, Origen, Justin Martyr, Tertullian, Clement of Alexandria, Apollonius, and Eusebius of Caesarea.

- Monks and monasteries were seen by their religious customers as powerhouses of prayer and intercession with God.

- Saints, missionaries, and the stories of their lives provided powerful testimonies to the power of the religion and the product credibility of the church.

- From the early years, the church always had some ascetics who renounced worldly pleasures for a life devoted to prayer and reflection. They provided powerful 'proof' of the validity of their religion.

- Miracles and miracle stories were effectively used by the church to 'prove' its power to intercede with God.

- Most priests had little formal schooling and training in religion before the twelfth-thirteenth centuries, but the church always had a cadre of powerful preachers and bishops who could eloquently explain why the church's religious practices and beliefs represented the 'truth'.

- Catholic Church leaders often took vows of poverty or celibacy. Although many did not live up to their promises, the vows signaled that churchmen were apart from secular society and, for many church customers, increased the credibility of churchmen as 'honest' intermediaries with God.

- The church's elaborate worship spaces and expensive ornamentation attracted some customers by showing that the church was successfull in dealing with past and current religious customers.

- Economists and other social scientists have investigated rituals and found that repeating the same ones increases the trust in credence goods, including religion. Iannaccone has applied those ideas in an interesting model that emphasizes that religion can provide more than just a promise of salvation.[40] A church can increase a member's religious human capital through familiarity with repeated rituals, dogma, and other factors. Consequently, membership in a particular religion can be somewhat addictive over time, reducing the likelihood of religious switching and increasing the likelihood of passing that faith on to following generations. Consistent with these modern ideas, the Catholic mass ritual tended to be essentially the same for every mass in each church, even before more uniformity was imposed throughout the entire Roman Catholic domain during and after the twelfth and thirteenth centuries. Thus, the churches people normally attended repeated the same mass rituals every week.

- Life is full of other rituals that signal major changes, such as marriage, initiation, and funeral ceremonies. The Catholic Church successfully asserted its religious authority over these ceremonies as the only legitimate provider and thereby signaled its credibility in providing real services. It even turned the previously secular ceremony for knighting warriors into a religious one.

- The church hierarchy, especially the papacy, acted as the CEO of its multi-divisional firm that sought profits in a variety of ways that are discussed in following chapters. One way to effectively implement its policies was to act as a monopoly franchise licensor and establish diverse operations in its huge domain. As any business franchise holder would do, franchise licenses had to be purchased by the church's agents (e.g., charges for bishoprics and abbacies and a cut of the profits from their operations).

Basic Theology for Mining the Profits of Sin:
Only the Catholic Church can Offer Redemption from Sin[41]

This study obviously does not focus on theology. Yet the basic theology of sin—with redemption for eternal salvation only through the Catholic Church—is essential in explaining how the church could mine the profits of sin from its religious customers on its toll road to salvation. How that theology was used, how sin could be redeemed only through the church, and what happened to the alternative of love and forgiveness emphasized by Jesus are discussed in this section.

The idea of original sin has a long religious tradition that can be traced back to story of Adam and Eve in Genesis, the first book of the Jewish Torah (and the first book in the Old Testament of the Christian Bible). A theology of sin that condemned one to eternal damnation, with no chance of redemption, undoubtedly would attract very few religious customers. But the Catholic Church's theology also included redemption that could be obtained only through the church. (Much later, Protestant religions adopted a similar emphasis on Christian, rather than only Catholic, redemption). An interesting feature of 'salvation insurance' for redemption from sin is that the contract never can be fully specified or 'tested' and accurately reported on by a living witness who has cashed in on the insurance.[42] It is a pure credence good that is based on trust. The

Catholic Church was keenly aware of this issue, and it dealt with it in several ways. For example, these included: miraculous reports on salvation from witnesses in the next world that were relayed to those in this world; 'proof' in the form of widely reported miracles of how the saints could intervene with God to provide help to their customers; and ancient/repeated stories about the lives and heavenly experiences of the martyrs and saints.

Early Christian-Catholic Proponents of Catholic Redemption from Sin: St. Paul and St. Augustine[43]

St. Paul was a proponent of the Catholic version of original sin only a few years after the time of Jesus.[44] A main plank of Paul's position is in his Letter to the Romans (5:12, 6:12, 6:21, and 7:24) in which he argues that sin and death entered the world at the beginning of history and, without redemption, each human would suffer eternal death. Freeman summarizes the Roman Catholic Church's theology of sin as follows: "The scriptural backing for original sin was flimsy; only five texts from the whole of scripture can be claimed to support it, and it has been argued that three of those, including the crucial verse from Romans [5:12], rest on mistranslations into Latin from the original Greek. To accept original sin is to accept that . . . even a baby can be damned to eternal fire." [45] Clearly, Paul's influence was profound on the subsequent development of Christianity as a whole and the Roman Catholic Church in particular.

A little more than three centuries later, St. Augustine more fully developed the 'science of sin' for the Roman Catholic Church. He was able to convince church leaders to adopt his idea that original sin is a genetic trait of all humans. However, Augustine's idea of original sin—and an idea taken up in

Protestant religions more than one thousand years later—evidently is based on the inferior Latin translation of the original Greek texts of the Bible.[46] Because the books of the New Testament originally were written in Greek, Greek theologians knew that the meaning of the key Greek word is a 'cosmic' force that burdens all mankind, not a genetic trait passed on to each human through procreation. Small wonder the Greek Church never accepted Augustine's idea of original sin—Jesus never mentioned it in his Gospel teachings.[47]

Augustine dealt extensively with sin and guilt in the *City of God*, his masterpiece that so deeply influenced Roman Catholic thinking and theology. He represents moral failing as an attack on the Creator's work, and the degree of affront to God varies with the seriousness of each sin. The Catholic distinction between 'mortal' and 'venial' sins—along with the idea that punishments would be proportional to the gravity of the corresponding sins—evolved from such reasoning.[48] Augustine argued that mortal sins extinguish the right to enter heaven, and such sins can be remitted only by the church.[49] His arguments were one of the factors that paved the way for the church to use price discrimination in assessing penalties for particular sins (different sin prices for the same sins for different people, depending on their willingness and ability to pay).

Early Dissents against Original Sin

What cannot be known is how the violence, chaos, and murder rampant in the empire when Augustine was developing his influential views on sin affected both his views and those of other churchmen who embraced them. But it seems reasonable to wonder whether his grim theology could have taken hold in a world with more harmony and less violence. In any case, Augustine's harshest critic was Julian, future bishop of Eclanum, and the personal duel between the two lasted until Augustine's death in the fifth century. Augustine's biographer, Brown, explains how Julian criticized Augustine's theology:

"The God of Augustine was a God Who had imposed a collective punishment for the sin of one man. . . . 'Tell me then,' Julian will ask Augustine, 'tell me: who is this person who inflicts punishment on innocent creatures. . . . You answer: God. God, you say. . . . sends tiny babies to eternal flames. . . . It would be right and proper to treat you as beneath . . . mere common sense . . . . A God that was not just, therefore, was so far beyond natural reason that He could not exist . . . .' Julian represents one peak of Roman civilization."[50]

St. Thomas Aquinas and Other Masters of Sin After St. Augustine[51]

Following Augustine, other 'masters of sin' amplified the theory, but the ultimate masters of sin in terms of their impacts on the Roman Catholic Church probably were Saints Paul (d. ca. 67), Augustine (d. 430), and Thomas Aquinas (d. 1274). As the master theologian of the medieval church, Aquinas approvingly cited Augustine's definition and then expanded it by including sins of omission.[52] Adding sins of omission further expanded the number of sins for which the church's customers could be charged.

Mining the Profits of Sin

Obviously, the sin-guilt-redemption combination was a powerful one in manipulating obedience and providing fertile ground for collecting from church's sinful customers. The Roman

Catholic Church's entire scheme for selling eternal salvation in exchange for penances is undoubtedly one of the most brilliant marketing plans in the history of the world. And as Hopkins explains:

> "Since sin could not be eradicated, it might as well be exploited. . . . Over time, the Church gradually elaborated an effective list of sin prices. To put it crudely, the Church marketed sin, and expanded into guilt. Sin was not just a matter of behavior; it could occur in the desires of thought and in the unconscious fantasy of dreams. Christian clerics were determined to make the faithful pay for their dreams, as though they could salve their conscience by generosity to the poor and to the church. . . . Guilt, sin, laxity, repentance, penance, and the readmission of the fallen, to say nothing of alms and legacies, used in combination, were all important forces in the church's drive for worldly success. St. Jerome, himself an avid netter of rich virgins devoted to chastity, caustically remarked that while 'the scriptures were being decorated with purple and gold . . . Jesus lay abandoned outside, naked and dying.' "[53]

What Happened to Love?[54]

Jesus tells us in the Gospels that love of God and love of our neighbors are the two greatest commandments. In many Gospel passages, Jesus portrays God as the Good Father who is full of compassion and wants only the best for his children. These passages include the parable of the prodigal son who returns home in Luke, the good Samaritan in Luke, and the Beatitudes in Luke and Matthew. And there were other voices in the early church for love rather than sin, notably including Origen (c. 185-254). But those voices of love were castigated and condemned by the church's hierarchy.[55] Modern scholars, including Pagels, also have discovered that numerous other heretical texts (referred to as the Gnostic Gospels) from early Christianity promoted the idea of a loving God and love for God's creation.[56] Further, the emphasis on love was taken up by many heretics as well as churchmen through the centuries, as exemplified by St. Francis in the thirteenth century. But a theology of love never replaced the theology of sin that predominated during the period covered here and even beyond.[57]

The emphasis on sin rather than love laid the basis for a western society based on sin, guilt, and fear.[58] Lay literature also emphasized sin and guilt. For example, the supreme literary achievement of the Middle Ages—Dante's *The Divine Comedy*—was entirely about sin, especially in assigning different places in Purgatory's suffering realm (the 'place' or state of suffering for sinful souls after bodily death and before heaven) that depend on the gravity of one's sins.[59]

Some Economic Issues in Creating and Using the Catholic Church's Toll Road to Salvation

Sin, guilt, and redemption provided the foundation for the church's toll road to salvation, but the church still faced several economic issues in operating as a profitable business enterprise. The ones discussed in this section include: how to deal with team production and customer shirking issues; priests as the church's direct links to its religious customers; paying priests for holy services and incentive pay; the competition for religious business between mendicant friars and local priests; profits from a new preaching approach for urban audiences; and the thirteenth-century preaching 'revolution'.

Dealing with Team Production and Customer Shirking Issues

Religious services involve team production, as discussed in Chapter 1. Because of that, religious shirkers detract from the overall religious experience. Consequently, most religious organizations, including the Catholic Church, create rules and customs to increase religious participation and reduce shirking. Because the church was a monopoly producer with vast secular holdings and because of the social and economic benefits of belonging to the religion, the shirking potential was especially great for Catholics, many of whom presumably joined the church for non-spiritual benefits. The church responded by imposing numerous requirements (e.g., confirmation, mass attendance, confession, marriage/divorce regulations, and tithing) to weed out shirkers or at least reduce their shirking. Recalcitrant religious customers could be excommunicated or condemned as heretics who 'deserved' various forms of 'holy' violence. The penalties also included economic sanctions that removed opponents from any commerce or support from the Catholic community, not just the loss of the salvation the church was selling. In other words, the church invented effective sanctions to force reluctant or doubtful religious customers to remain in the church for economic and social reasons, not just for religious ones.

Priests as the Church's Direct Links to
Its Religious Customers

Evidently, the emperor Constantine was the first to bestow the Latin title *papa* on the popes. Later, the church adopted that same title for its male priests, who were the direct links to the church's customers for most religious services. The church presumably adopted the title for its priests to connote their loving and powerful care for their 'family' of religious customers—even though there were some female priests and deaconesses in some areas as late as the twelfth century. The church may have adopted the title for marketing its religious credibility, but Jesus says in the Gospels that God alone is the only Holy Father.

Before the Roman Catholic Counter-Reformation that responded to the rise of Protestantism in the sixteenth century, there were no diocesan seminaries.[60] But like any other business, the church had to train its workers, so priests learned their craft as on-the-job apprentices under an experienced master. This typically led to contracts that specified the duties of the priests and their apprentices. In standard fashion, that often involved a five-year apprenticeship (usually specified in specific contractual terms) under an experienced priest.[61] Because the priest provided food, lodging, and instruction, the contracts typically had a guarantor who was responsible for a surety bond that the apprentice would complete his five years as agreed.

Preaching on moral issues was the main responsibility of the bishops (who typically were more educated and eloquent than ordinary priests) for most of the period covered in this book, and priests of local churches only became much more involved during the preaching 'revolution' of the thirteenth century. Until then, ordinary priests conducted mainly routine masses without deliberately designed preaching on moral issues, although there were some exceptions. Training to have educated priests who could forcefully preach on moral issues did not have much impetus until the thirteenth century. But as Christianity spread far and wide, many Catholics attended bishops' churches and cathedrals only for special occasions. Thus, ordinary priests took on more preaching responsibilities, regardless of their training and preparation. And many influences converged to put pressure on ordinary priests to increase the effectiveness of their preaching in order to compete for donations. In particular, the effective preaching of the Dominican and Franciscan mendicants that started in the thirteenth century put intense pressure on local priests and bishops to compete for donations.

Paying Priests for Holy Services and Incentive Pay

Priests might have worked for God, but somehow they had to be paid by man. In about the sixth century, the practice of clergy living with bishops, who supported them out of their church revenue, began to change; the clergy began to form their own church communities in the countryside.[62] By the eighth century, there were many priests living alone in scattered churches, and they had to be maintained. At one point, that involved secular work for many priests, such as working their own plots. But that reduced their commitment to holy services, and some priests on fixed salaries also did not work as diligently for the church as their superiors wanted.

The church attempted to increase collections from parish priests by establishing defined sources of revenue for them (called benefices). The benefices provided priests with a set of revenue opportunities, including a portion of the earnings from the altar and other 'holy' services. However, the total depended on priestly efforts, especially in satisfying their religious customers. Thus, it also was a pay scheme designed to encourage more effort than a straight salary that did not vary with the priest's effort.[63] Because the bishops and papacy took their cuts, the hierarchy could monitor the work of their priests, based on the earnings they generated.[64] Of course, there were reporting problems, as with any profit-sharing scheme such as this, where the principals (bishops/popes in this case) cannot perfectly monitor their agents (priests in this case). Further, as with any incentive scheme such as this, priests had an incentive to overcharge. Consequently, customer complaints eventually led to attempted reforms to reduce blatant sales of holy services (the reforms are discussed in Chapter 9).

Mendicant Friars Compete for Business With Local Priests

The first few years of the 1200s saw the emergence of both the Franciscan and Dominican Orders, and both mendicant orders reported to the pope, thus cutting out bishops as middlemen. The heretical challenge to the church's product credibility, wealth, and power undoubtedly was one basis for Pope Innocent III's approval of the new Dominican Order, whose men were trained specifically to take on the heretics in preaching and a little later as the first inquisitors.[65] The pope also approved the Franciscans as examples of evangelizing poverty for the laity. The new mendicant orders of Franciscans and Dominicans also went on to fulfill the church's preaching mission throughout the wider world with their missionary work in many 'heathen' lands outside of Europe. Innocent III's concern for effective preaching also led to legislation at Lateran IV (1215) that required bishops to recruit persons who would be 'mighty in word and work' and thus fulfill the 'duty of holy preaching' effectively.

The mendicant orders were part of major changes in Catholicism that included its aggressive attempts to eliminate its religious competitors and regulate all aspects of the lives of its religious customers. Further, many in both mendicant orders eventually based their evangelization on an ideology of guilt, so numerous Dominicans and Franciscans were preachers-confessors, inquisitors, or both at once, and their targets were sin and heresy. Because the laity often saw their local priests as lacking in 'holiness', they would seek out a monk or a mendicant friar of the Franciscans or Dominicans as a father-confessor. This threatened the livelihoods of local priests, who were accustomed to receiving donations as part of confession and their absolution of sins for their customers. Consequently, the local bishops and priests viewed the mendicants as interlopers and unfair competitors in the business of sin.

Profits from New Preaching Approach
For Urban Audiences

Starting in the early 1200s, the mendicant friars of the Dominican and Franciscan Orders preached to urban audiences that had many members who simply did not fit into the old conception of feudal society.[66] Their new audiences included merchants, bankers, schoolmasters, notaries, traders, moneylenders, and those who used oral arguments in their daily business. Thus, effective oral preaching was a natural medium for reaching them, and that is exactly what the friars used to convey their message. The friars entered the scene talking or, some would say, shouting on the street corners. With their lively sermons, the mendicant preachers appealed to the leaders of the new commercial economy on their own terms. In the earlier church, preachers focused on pagan conversion, heretical opponents, and recruitment, but the new market for the mendicant preachers also featured penance for the sins of Catholics.[67] There is no Biblical basis for monetary payments to redeem sins. Yet, the Franciscan and Dominican preachers (as well as local priests and bishops) marketed penances for sins and successfully solicited donations, including those to supposedly reduce the time in purgatory for their religious customers and their customers' relatives. Their success in soliciting donations and payments also meant that many local bishops and priests fiercely opposed the friars entering their territories because of their loss of revenue and prestige. But local opposition was countered by papal authorization for the preaching of the friars throughout the papacy's domain (and the papacy shared in the sin payments collected by the friars).

Thirteenth-Century Preaching 'Revolution' [68]

A revolution in preaching occurred during the thirteenth century, both because of the mendicant preachers' effectiveness and the new policy of having parish priests preach regularly about moral issues in their masses. Jacques de Vitry (d. 1240) was a great preacher, and his powerful sermons were gathered together, copied, and categorized for specific audiences, such as merchants, widows, virgins, peasants, soldiers, and others. His sermons then were used by many other priests, and they deserve their place at the head of the preaching revolution among secular clergy.

The preaching revolution of the thirteenth century also reflects the influence of Pope Innocent III (1198-1216). He was a pope who had unprecedented emphasis on the spiritual welfare of the laity, and he believed that welfare could be promoted and improved through good preaching. Further, good preachers could counter the rising dangers of effective preaching by the heretics during the twelfth and thirteenth centuries. For example, the powerful preaching of the Cathars and Waldensians castigated the corruption of the Roman popes and their hierarchies. These heretics had begun to compete effectively for the hearts and minds of the church's religious customers, so their preaching had to be countered.

Conclusion

There were many varieties of early Christianity, and the rapid growth of the new religion provided an initial customer base that could be exploited for wealth and power. The variety of Christianity that won in terms of wealth and power was the Catholic Church, but its initial success was possible only because of the relatively large number of Christians in the Roman Empire, especially by the time of Constantine. In winning the battle as the main and eventually the (legal) monopoly provider of Christianity, the Catholic Church had to devise many strategies—including collaboration with secular rulers—to defeat its competitors.

Success as a religious organization that could extract wealth from its religious customers at every stop along the church's long toll road to salvation that is discussed in Chapters 3-7 required a compelling foundation for the faith. The church accomplished that by using a theology of sin in which salvation could be won only through the assistance of the church. That assistance had to be purchased with time and money. But constructing and using that toll road to mine the profits of sin involved several economic issues, some of which were discussed in this chapter as background for the following chapters. For example, priests had to be recruited and trained as the church's direct links to its religious customers, but that led to principal-agent problems for the hierarchy in encouraging their priests to work hard and pass on a 'fair' share of the profits from sin on up the hierarchy. Despite these and other issues, the church hierarchy ultimately was strategically successful in making themselves and their church fabulously wealthy and powerful.

3

Strategies to Attract and Retain Religious Customers on Church's Toll Road to Salvation

The church had to establish and defend its product credibility as a religious institution to attract and retain religious customers, both before and after it was firmly established as the (legal) monopoly provider of Christianity in the Roman Empire. It also had to be agile enough to deal with the collapse of the Roman Empire late in the fifth century by negotiating new agreements with a long line of rulers. The expanding wealth and power of the church through the centuries testifies to the strategic brilliance of the church in creating the necessary policies to successfully deal with its religious customers and a long line of secular rulers. But it took more than strategic alliances with many rulers to develop the church's immense wealth and power. Among the many strategic maneuvers of the church, the following ways it used to attract and retain its religious customers are discussed in this chapter:

- Co-opting pagan customs and shrines.
- Using the 'holiness' of monks and monasteries.
- Using missionaries to spread the reach of the church.
- Using great cathedrals as a sign of success in its operations.
- Satisfying diverse religious tastes.

Co-opting Pagan Customs and Shrines

There is a strong case for believing that much of what early church writers described as paganism actually came from unorthodox versions of Christianity or blends of some pagan practices with Catholicism.[69] In other cases, the claims of extensive paganism surrounding Christian borders are probably sheer propaganda. It also is known that otherwise orthodox believers often continued to observe some customs from pagan practices, especially health cures and customs to ensure good crops, for example. Further, it is very difficult to know the actual religious practices of many cults, and church accounts often are highly fictional in negatively representing those practices. Also, many pagan customs were practiced privately within homes rather than openly in public gatherings. In any case, one reason for the success in spreading Catholicism, especially to rural areas, was to incorporate pagan customs into Catholic practices.

The pagan custom that probably stirred the most controversy within the church was Catholic reverencing of icons and images. Religious images and icons clearly were banned by

Jewish Scriptures, which the church had adopted as its Old Testament. However, once Constantine chose the church to provide a religious sanction for his rule, he and other rulers, as well as wealthy converts, were anxious to show the power of imperial Rome's new religion by donating to create elaborate churches and icons. Thus, the pressure for religious icons and images in the Catholic Church came from its secular collaborators and religious customers, not church leaders, many of whom remained uncomfortable with what amounted to pagan practices in Catholic churches and homes. However, because of the practice's popularity, church leaders eventually incorporated it into the Catholic faith and developed justifications for it.[70]

Other economic motives also surfaced in the 'iconoclast controversy' that arose over reverencing images and icons.[71] Some bishops set out to ban the veneration of icons and relics, but that provoked strong reactions from monks, who saw it as an attack on a key portion of the income they generated, especially from pilgrims attracted by their powerful relics and elaborate icons. Thus, after bargaining and negotiation among the competing parties, the 754 Council of Hiereia certified the veneration of images as an acceptable Catholic practice.[72]

The church also adapted some pagan dates and other customs. For example, some pagan holiday dates were used for Catholic feasts, such as December 25 for Christmas. The church and Catholic emperors also converted many pagan shrines and buildings into Christian ones. Another example of a pagan practice directly incorporated into medieval Catholicism is the *barbatoria*, the first shaving of a youth to mark his transition to manhood.[73] The Catholic prayers created for the *barbatoria* asked for a long and successful life for the young man.[74] Individual Catholics also practiced some pagan customs not sanctioned by the church, including the use of amulets and charms to ward off evil and provide protection and health.[75]

Monks and Monasteries

Monks and their monasteries were viewed as powerful and credible providers of religious services. Monks were widely considered conduits between heaven and earth in two main ways: they were advocates who could effectively seek divine help for their clients; and they transmitted the voice of God with their prophetic predictions and insights.[76] Even some bishops made donations to monasteries to secure their powerful prayers for their own salvation. The religious power of select monasteries made them important for the church's product credibility, but it also gave those monasteries political and socioeconomic power in addition to tremendous wealth. Although monks were restricted to their monasteries by ninth-century reforms, their perceived holiness meant they still interacted with the world because of a constant stream of visitors and pilgrims. Such visitors provided a significant flow of donations to the monasteries. In short, *sacrum commercium* flourished throughout the 600-1100 period.

Monasteries Enter Competition for Mass Donations[77]

Because many older monasteries were lay foundations, they could not benefit from the new practice of altar donations that blossomed in the early Middle Ages. Undoubtedly, this helps explain why they began to change into religious institutions that had priests who could celebrate masses. Historical evidence also shows that masses at monasteries were especially popular with donors. Thus, gifts received for conducting masses and saying prayers for particular persons was a booming business line in the monasteries. The celebration of such special masses also provided the priests with private incomes for celebrating them. For example, the *Rheinau Sacramentary* of about 800 specified the following prices for masses: twelve masses and eighteen hundred psalms cost 240 denarii or 20 solidus; six masses and nine hundred psalms cost 120 denarii or 10 solidus; and two masses and one hundred psalms cost 12 denarii or 1 solidus. But that was only the beginning, for some donors wanted those masses continued perpetually, and that cost substantial endowments. The main mass type perpetuated by such endowments was the requiem mass that was celebrated in vast numbers to atone for the sins of both the living and the dead. Legal agreements stipulated in detail how the 'gift' by the donor would result in masses and prayers for the donor's family, and a legally binding record was drawn up and presented at the high altar of the abbey church. In short, this was salvation for sale in contractually binding agreements to honor the donors' requests.

Wealth of Monasteries

Many monasteries were fabulously wealthy.[78] For example, a twelfth-century register of the great Monte Cassino monastery lists six hundred twenty-one charters for properties as of the early seventh century. And thirty-six panels in the bronze doors of the monastery still have the names of many of the estates it claimed by the early twelfth century. Monte Cassino and other monasteries trumpeted their vast holdings, as they were a main basis of their socioeconomic status, power, and wealth.

One other example will suffice to illustrate the immense wealth of some of the church's medieval monasteries. The great monastery of Cluny was founded in 910, and it soon was fabulously wealthy. For example, Cluny established its control over vast areas during the last half of the eleventh century, and it had collected around five thousand property deeds by 1120.[79] It had multifunctional deaneries that served as agricultural centers, places of commerce and business, hermitages, and pilgrimage churches. Cluny's enterprises generated huge wealth and power for the order, and it had eleventh-century immunities granted for its operations by both the papacy and secular powers. Of course, Cluny paid for its immunities. The magnitude of the payments for it and other monasteries depended on the bargaining power of the monasteries, relative to that of the bishops, popes, and secular powers.

The wealth and power of the monasteries arose from their product credibility for the church's religious customers. But that also meant powerful monasteries alarmed both the church hierarchy and secular rulers because they could challenge the wealth and power of rulers and other church leaders. Thus, starting early in church history and continuing through much of the timeline for this book, the rulers and bishops initiated a series of monastic reforms to control the monks and their socioeconomic and political influence, and some of those are discussed in Chapter 9.

Children and Monasteries

An interesting feature of the medieval Roman Catholic world is how closely some of its practices approached those of ancient pagan religions.[80] The ancients brought gifts and sacrifices to their gods and asked for help from natural forces, such as trees, rocks, and streams. The new Catholic God evidently was thought to demand sacrifice and gifts. The rich offered land, money, and valuable objects to honor God and his direct representatives on earth, the church and its churchmen. Sacrifice was a Catholic tradition taken from pagan and Jewish practices, but a new Catholic twist in the Middle Ages was to sacrifice one's children to monasteries at about the age of seven. Although the poor had little money or land to give, they could give their own children as religious sacrifices for training as monks. The sacrifices of children for religious lives were perceived to be mutually beneficial exchanges that repaid families with monastic prayers and relieved them of the expenses of raising their donated children. The monasteries featured these child oblates as religious sacrifices for the glory of God.

However, these children also were used for less holy purposes, especially because there really was no concept of the rights of children for the period covered in this book.[81] The male monasteries emphasized the soft and effeminate nature of young trainees who apparently could be treated as sexual objects by mature monks.[82] Thus, it evidently was acceptable for young boys in training to perform oral sex on the monks and to be the recipients of anal sex, but the reverse was strictly prohibited. And once a young boy became a man, his mouth had to be ritually pure to chant the praises of God, so he was never again supposed to perform oral sex on another man or boy.

Missionaries

Catholicism spread widely between the fifth and eleventh centuries, partly through the efforts of many missionaries.[83] By the end of the eleventh century, almost all of Europe had been converted voluntarily by missionaries or forcibly by rulers. The first pope who was a great proponent of missionary work was Pope Gregory the Great (590-604), and many other popes strongly supported the efforts. However, Pope Nicholas I (858-867) probably was the most active of the early medieval popes in furthering the missionary efforts of the church. The efforts of missionaries often were aided by: traveling merchants; Catholic rulers who invaded pagan areas and forcibly converted the people; and pagan rulers who converted and then mandated the conversion of their people. Of course, some of these conversions likely were only skin deep.

Some Well-Known Missionary Efforts

Although the efforts of a huge number of unknown and unnamed monks and priests contributed mightily to the spread of the faith, the known missionary work is largely based on what often are literary rather than historical accounts of missionary saints.[84] Be that as it may, many missionaries who later were made saints are known to have traveled widely and either converted non-believers or evangelized to spread the faith to more persons in already Christianized areas. A few examples are:

- The famous missionary work of St. Patrick in Ireland during the fifth century.
- The conversion of Gaul (basically, modern France) in the early sixth century after the conversion of King Clovis I.
- The conversion of England in the early seventh century, largely due to St. Augustine of Canterbury's missionary work under the direction of Pope Gregory the Great.
- Starting in the thirteenth century, the new Franciscan Order provided many missionaries who went to lands never before Christianized. For example, St. Francis was famous for his missionary and evangelizing efforts, including his attempt to convert the Muslim Sultan during the crusades.[85]

Other Missionary Strategies Used for Increasing
Church's Customer Base

The church honed its strategies for gaining more converts through the centuries.[86] Some of the more interesting strategic innovations used by the church to increase its customer base include the following:

- Pope Gregory the Great (590-604) and others may have been motivated by religious motives, but Pope Gregory used shrewd practices to spread the faith. By 595, he instructed his rector to buy English boys at slave markets to train as monks, who then could be sent home. The pope explained that native-born missionaries would be more effective than foreign-born ones.[87]

- Pope Gregory the Great also emphasized the importance of miracles to encourage non-believers to convert. He emphasized that miracles could play an important role in destroying idols and strengthening the faith of new converts, but he also noted that miracles were less important in assuring believers who had well established faith. After the pope's emphasis on miracles, his appointed missionary to England, St. Augustine of Canterbury, was soon reporting on a proliferation of miracles there.[88]

- In the early seventh century, Gregory the Great again showed his brilliant strategic thinking. He instructed his English missionary, Mellitus, to destroy pagan idols but not their structures/temples, which instead should be converted to Christian ones by sprinkling holy water on them.[89] The idea was that it would be easier to convert pagans by using their customary worshiping spaces for the Catholic religion. That approach provided substantial flexibility for local missionaries and clergy to adapt to the customs of their areas for much of the period from 600 to about 1100. But that also meant, despite repeated church prohibitions against magic and folk rituals, these and other pagan customs survived in modified forms among Catholics.

• Alciun of York was a well-known churchman working in the Frankish kingdom during the eighth century. In reflecting on the difficulty of converting Saxony, he wrote to a missionary and repeated the advice to King Charlemagne; he cautioned that trying to impose tithes on new converts was a mistake that had contributed to the extremely prolonged military campaigns of Charlemagne before he could impose Catholic conversion in Saxony. Displaying the acumen of a good game theorist, Alciun advised that, "It was necessary first to preach, then to baptise, and only once a man was of firm faith to submit him to the imposition of the tithe."[90]

• During the ninth century, St. Anskar and Archbishop Ebo of Rheims were put in charge of missionary work to the Danes, Swedes, and Slavs. An interesting aspect of Anskar's missionary efforts is that he followed Pope Gregory the Great's innovation of buying up slave boys, who were trained as clergy for missionary work in their home countries.

• In most of the German-speaking church for the 600-1100 period, the kings were viewed as divinely selected, so they had the power to decide on the religion for their entire people.[91] Thus, missionaries in those countries typically targeted Germanic kings as the highest priority for conversion because that also would result in the conversion of the king's subjects.

Great Cathedrals [92]

The great era of constructing the massive cathedrals in Europe began around the mid-eleventh century and then accelerated during the twelfth and thirteenth centuries. Thereafter, massive expenditures continued in the following centuries. In most cases, completing a cathedral took many decades, often well over a century. It may seem contradictory that such massive churches were built when society's resources were relatively limited, most people lived at bare subsistence levels, and the church was engaged in its expensive 'holy' violence of the crusades. Nonetheless, the church managed to extract the donations from its religious customers that were required to build the cathedrals. Regardless of the financing mechanism for the cathedrals, they were symbols of community and church success—and increased the product credibility, wealth, and power of the church.

Building and Using Cathedrals

Elaborate cathedrals included ones at the following fourteen cities (with starting dates in parentheses): Strasbourg (1015), Chartres (rebuilt c. 1020), Saint-Denis (1130s), Noyon (1150), Senlis (1153), Rouen (1155), Poitiers (1162), Laon (c. 1160), Lyon (1160), Paris (1163-64), Soissons (c. 1170), Toulouse (c. 1200), Amiens (1220), and York (1220).[93] Thus, the church's building endeavor was not a centralized and cooperative effort of the whole church to display the majesty of God and the Roman Catholic Church in one or only a few monumental structures. Instead, it was more like a strategic race to the top in creating sites that trumpeted the importance of competing cities, churches, and saints. In a society that valued display and majesty, a good way to signal importance was such a structure. Further, the cathedrals were used by the community for non-religious gatherings, shopping, and entertainment.

An important use of the Cathedrals was to signal the power of the local saints who presided over them, for powerful saints attracted many pilgrims and boosted tourism, as Geary has extensively documented.[94] In effect, the cathedrals were similar to the modern competition among cities to spend huge amounts in building sports venues for professional teams. Thus, there was never-ending competition for the best cathedral for economic reasons. In fact, merchants and worker communes/guilds aggressively marketed their cathedrals. They emphasized the spiritual power of their saints and the protections they could provide for particular industries and trades. Now, whether cities spent substantial sums on competing cathedrals without actually gaining any economic advantage over their rivals is a possibility, but the data are not available to know with any certainty. However, Ekelund Jr., Hébert, and Tollison find, on the basis of admittedly limited data, no evidence that, ". . . massive investments in cathedrals had much of an effect on city growth during or even after the Middle Ages."[95]

Costs and Financing of Cathedrals

It is impossible to estimate the total costs of cathedrals and the proportion of total output devoted to building them, but the costs in terms of the human and physical resources required for their construction clearly were substantial. Those resources instead could have been invested in infrastructure and education, for example, to boost the overall productivity of the economy.[96] However, Geary provides some interesting cost estimates, and Gimpel, who is a medieval architectural historian, believes that more stone was cut in France alone between 1050 and 1350 than during the entire history of Egypt.[97]

It appears that a significant portion of the costs for these structures was paid by the rising class of merchants and bankers, who were joining landowners as the wealthy elite. Because the new class was viewed with suspicion by most churchmen all the way into the thirteenth century and beyond, it was important for them to establish their own religious credibility within the church through large donations. Of course, there were clear economic benefits to the commercial men who contributed to these endeavors in this mutually beneficial religious and economic transaction of merits—notoriety for cathedral contributions was good for business.[98] However, some of the church's religious customers did not view the payments to the church as necessary for either economic reasons or salvation, as shown by periodic, local revolts (especially by workers) against the taxes and tithes imposed by the church.

Satisfying Diverse Religious Tastes

God is beyond full human comprehension, so we should expect diversity in the attempts to 'explain' and worship God. It would be essentially impossible for a single religious approach to satisfy all persons. People cannot even agree on the best novel or movie, let alone the best politician, so it is no surprise they cannot agree on the best 'explanation' of God and how to worship God. Even where state faith monopolies have existed, as for the Catholic Church, there always have been schisms, sects, and disagreements because one doctrine cannot satisfy the whole range of religious preferences.[99] Recognizing the importance of offering diversity in its religious offerings, the church quite successfully attempted to maintain and increase its market share by offering many different approaches to religious practices—but within the context of doctrinal unity on questions considered key to defining the one 'true' faith, as determined by the hierarchy. However, virtually all attempts to diversify the church's religious practices and opportunities involved dangers of criticisms and splits. In short and as with any economic choice, there were costs as well as benefits to product diversity.

Offering Religious Diversity

There clearly was substantial diversity among different areas, and many pagan practices that were important to local people also were incorporated into local Catholic religious practices, as noted above. In fact, there were so many variations among areas that the hierarchy and teachers viewed some versions as heretical or bordering on heresy. Eventually, more uniform religious practices were imposed throughout the Roman Catholic domain during and after the twelfth and thirteenth centuries.

Diversity also was available within a given area through many religious orders that had quite different approaches to the Catholic religion. A large number of different religious orders were approved through the centuries to satisfy these diverse approaches within the one Roman Catholic Church. And especially starting in the thirteenth century, 'third orders' of lay members in some religious orders also offered a more religious life but without requiring vows of poverty for persons who continued to live a secular life but wanted to increase their participation in religious activities. These third orders for lay persons in the Franciscan and Dominican Orders were extremely popular, and other religious orders responded by also adding them.

There were other forms of product diversity offered to the wealthy, who had many more options than the poor did to pay the church for their salvation.[100] For example, the monasteries offered the wealthy a way to atone for their sins by either donating to the monks or sometimes entering the monasteries by providing handsome entry 'gifts' as their death approached. Those with substantial wealth could endow their own monasteries to ensure a continuing stream of holy prayers for their souls and those of their relatives. In short, monasteries offered a religious product that was especially attractive to some wealthy customers. But wealthy monasteries also attracted lay powers interested in administering and controlling them as abbots who had little interest in spiritual matters.[101]

Confraternities and Guilds

Network externalities (i.e., beneficial social and economic relationships that tend to increase with the number of other members) accompanied membership in the Catholic Church. But those externalities created incentives to join for non-religious benefits rather than any belief in the faith. By 1300 many persons were involved in church confraternities and guilds that were organized around particular interests and industries; they also offered members some protection against charges of heresy (by participating in church-approved organizations that provided witnesses for their Catholic character).[102]

However, members who joined the church primarily for external rather than religious benefits typically would like to free-ride on the genuine religious efforts of others, and that can diminish the value of the experience for believers, as Iannaccone has explained.[103] Thus, Catholic Church membership required time and monetary costs in terms of required rituals, such as mass attendance, confession, and penance. Those costs tended to discourage membership for some persons interested solely in the non-religious benefits of the church.

Conclusion

The church devised several clever strategies for attracting and retaining its religious customers. For example, it used some techniques for certifying its claims as the pathway to eternal salvation, such as featuring miracles by heavenly saints. In a bow to the fact that pagan beliefs were strong in many parts of the empire, the church also co-opted pagan customs, shrines, and dates. Monks were viewed as especially holy, so they provided credibility for their monasteries and the church as a whole. Missionaries were extremely active in converting millions of persons to the Catholic Church. Great cathedrals were another way in which the church attracted and retained religious customers. Finally and in recognition of the fact that persons have diverse tastes for religion, the church offered a variety of religious offerings for its customers. All in all, the fabulous wealth of the church and the top of its hierarchy attest to its power in attracting and retaining customers who paid handsomely for the eternal salvation on sale by the church.

4

PAYING FOR RELIGIOUS SERVICES
DURING LIFE'S JOURNEY ON
CHURCH'S TOLL ROAD TO
SALVATION

Life's journey on the church's toll road to salvation was a long one that had payment booths all along the way. And each of these stops allowed the church to mine the profits of sin. This chapter looks at:[104]

- Birth and baptism.
- Masses and Holy Eucharist.
- Requiring confessions of sins.
- Paying for sins and crimes with penances.
- Wealth and alms for the poor and the Catholic Church.

- The market for healing.
- Church tithes and taxes.
- Selling miscellaneous holy services.
- Profitable business lines make the church wealthy.
- Charging for salvation contradicts the life and teachings of Jesus and threatens the church's religious credibility.

Birth and Baptism

The church's marketing plan started early in life with birth and baptism. Because the importance of baptism for new-born infants was stressed, the Roman Catholic Church had parents preparing the way for their new customers before they were born. Then, the church's process emphasized the importance of training them for a lifetime of payments on the toll road to salvation.

Baptism was so fundamentally important, because it was the foundation for the entire faith and the first sacrament that made one a Christian. But early believers often wanted to wait as long as possible before receiving the absolution of all sins that accompanied baptism (e.g., the first Christian emperor, Constantine, was not baptized until he was on his death bed). This propensity to postpone baptism by adults led to strong church teachings against its postponement by Augustine, Chrysostom, Ambrose, and others during the fourth and fifth centuries.[105] Without the saving grace of the church's sacrament of baptism, unbaptized babies would suffer eternally but 'most lightly' in Augustine's version of the theology.

Once parents accepted the idea that their unbaptized babies could be condemned to eternal suffering, they dared not delay the baptism of their children. Thus, infant baptism was the norm by about 600. Although churchmen had no formal models that 'proved' the worth of inculcating the faith in children from birth, that would have been obvious from their experience. Once the church started emphasizing new-born rather than adult baptism, it had a system set up for recruiting and training potential customers before the age of reason. By the age of reason, the church often had faithful and lifetime customers, who would have many opportunities to pay for salvation during their lives. It was a remarkable formula for recruiting and training religious customers, who were ready to repeatedly pay the church for its services. Moreover, many of the church's religious customers were willing, even eager, to voluntarily recruit and train others to do the same— and at no cost to the church.

This approach to recruiting, educating, and training new customers obviously reduced challenges to church teaching and policies because children were raised to accept the 'fact' that the church had the answers for all religious issues, especially including how to earn eternal salvation. It was a clever way to create a larger customer base for future financial extractions.

Masses and Holy Eucharist

In early Christianity, the bread and wine were simply laid out with no particular ritual or liturgy involved, but everyone had to bring gifts to the mass, especially for the poor.[106] But in the Middle Ages, the mass was centered around sacrifice, consistent with ancient pagan and Jewish practices, and 'pure' hands were needed to offer the spiritual sacrifice of the Eucharist. In this case, purity included no contact with anything sexual, and that was an idea that led directly to more pressure for celibacy. The quest for pure hands at the altar, as especially emphasized by the Catholic ruler Louis the Pious in 816-19 Achen legislation, led to church policies that the laity no longer could handle bread and wine at the altar. That sacred role was reserved for priests with 'pure' hands.[107]

Early church leaders promoted the idea that the path to salvation ran only through the church and its officially ordained priests. By the early fifth century, many churchmen had made the theological case for the church's special powers. Augustine (d. 430) was the preeminent theologian of the early church up to Thomas Aquinas eight centuries later, and Augustine argued that the church's sacraments were channels through which God's grace flowed to individuals from the *church* as the official edifice of grace directly from Christ.[108] Ultimately, masses at which the Holy Eucharist was 'sacrificed' became the central religious service of the church. Besides 'required' attendance at every Sunday mass, churches commonly offered daily masses. There were many other masses for special occasions, especially including holy days of obligation. Of course, the church plate was passed at these religious services. Further, larger offerings were expected on special occasions, especially including Christmas, Lent (a period of forty days before Easter), Easter, and Pentecost, which celebrates the descent of the Holy Ghost upon the Apostles of Jesus.

Holy Days Enhance Religious Credibility and Donations

Holy days for the universal church are established by the church's authority, especially by the pope after Rome's centralized power was solidified.[109] The main holy days included masses for Good Friday, Easter, Pentecost, and Christmas. But there were many other holy days, referred to as feast days below. These feast days were added for the apostles, martyrs, and saints, such as St. Mary.

After the church became the favored religion of imperial Rome in the early fourth century, the number of days of theoretically required mass attendance grew, especially as bishops were empowered to add feast days for local saints in their dioceses.[110] For example, the following number of holy days and feast days are referred to by church authorities: nineteen by St. Boniface (fourth century), forty-one by Gratian (twelfth century), and forty-five by Pope Gregory IX (thirteenth century). During and after the thirteenth century, some dioceses had more than one hundred days of no work required for Sundays, holy days, and feast days. Obviously, many of the church's religious customers did not attend that many masses, regardless of requirements.

What was it that stimulated such an expansion of the days on which the faithful were supposed to attend mass? Economic motives were front and center, as Resl explains:
"In order to increase revenue-generating opportunities or enhance the appeal of a specific place, individual institutions introduced additional feasts or acquired new relics. The festival of Corpus Christi [a feast day for the Eucharist itself] is an example of a highly successful liturgical innovation which spread quickly across Europe in the late thirteenth and particularly the early fourteenth century and was received enthusiastically by clergy and laity. It also created substantial revenues for the institutions which adopted it."[111]

Sacramental Prestige of Holy Eucharist Increases[112]

A change in sacramental prestige between baptism and the Eucharist slowly emerged during the early medieval period. Originally, baptism was considered the more prestigious sacrament, because it gave new lives to sinners. But churchmen began putting more emphasis on the Eucharist as they realized they were intervening with God on behalf of their communities every time they offered the Eucharist, whereas baptism occurred only once for each person. Throughout the early medieval period the reverence associated with the Eucharist grew.

By the mid-eleventh century, two disparate influences collided to challenge the holiness of the church's priests, especially in performing mass rituals at the holy altar. On the one hand, the increase in the sacramental prestige of the Eucharist was notable, and the new supremacy of the Eucharist was central and defining for both liturgy and theology. But the other influence was the attack on the institutional church from many critics who emphasized the corruption of the church and its priests. That threatened the product credibility of the religion, especially including its masses that were conducted by allegedly corrupt priests.

The church responded to the above changes in many ways. One response was to implement a series of eleventh-thirteenth century reforms (discussed in Chapter 9) in an attempt to 'purify' the church and its priests. A second response was church teaching that the individual holiness of the priest performing its sacraments had nothing to do with the power of the sacraments. The church teaching was that its sacraments depended on God, not the priest performing them. Thus, if the priest were properly ordained and followed church procedures, the sacraments were fully effective. But even internal critics continued to challenge the idea of impure priests conducting masses.

A third response was the formal declaration of the theology specifying that priests of the Roman Catholic Church have the unique power to turn ordinary bread and wine into the real body and blood of Jesus at the altar. This theory, which is referred to as transubstantiation, did not come under serious discussion until about the ninth century. But it was fully developed by the thirteenth century, when it was made a requirement of faith by the Fourth Lateran Council (1215). Thus, excommunication was the penalty for denying that Roman Catholic priests could perform the miraculous transformation involved in transubstantiation. Regardless of whether this theology was based on purely religious considerations, it surely had the effect of increasing the prestige and power of the church's priests.

Saints Present at Masses and Religious Services

The cults of saints/relics and the celebration of their feast days were strongly promoted by church leaders. In the beliefs of the times, the saints were present for the people at their masses and religious services—and they helped increase the power of those services to the extent of actually residing inside church altars. Virtually every church eventually had at least one, and often more, saints who were honored with additional Masses that generated extra donations from the church's religious customers.

Paying for Mass Intentions and 'Holy' Sanctions of Violence

The church's customers could pay for special prayers that were referred to as intentions at masses, such as special intentions for their souls and those of their departed relatives. But you also could buy 'holy' sanctions for violence. In a startling contrast to Jesus' teachings of nonviolence, it was possible to pay for prayers to supposedly ensure victory in military battles. In fact, offerings to churches and especially monasteries to ensure victory in battles were the norm throughout the Middle Ages.[113] For example, the ruler Louis the Pious ordered the abbey of Fulda to celebrate one thousand masses for a campaign in Bulgaria. Of course, the masses and monastic prayers had to be repaid by the king. He and other rulers made some fabulous gifts to monasteries for their victories.

Requiring Confessions of Sins

Teaching and preaching strongly emphasized guilt and sin from early in church history. And the mendicant preachers of the Dominican and Franciscan Orders, who began preaching early in the thirteenth century, were even more powerful exponents of sin than most local preachers.[114] They and local preachers relentlessly emphasized various categories of sin and guilt in homilies and confessionals. Thus, the Roman Catholic conception of God came to emphasize a fearsome God, who is a harsh judge and extracts divine justice for revenge.[115]

The sacrament of confession was an ideal tool for extracting payments from the church's sinful religious customers— and for determining their willingness/ability to pay for their sins, as discussed in Chapter 1. And that determination allowed the church to practice price discrimination in assessing different penalties for the same sins for different persons. Using confession for generating revenue and abusing religious customers was long ago discussed by Adam Smith in his famous book, *The Wealth of Nations* (1776). Smith explained how oral confession is both oppressive and ineffective in enforcing the Roman Catholic Church's impossibly detailed attempts to regulate moral behavior.[116] He also discussed confession's agency costs (the costs of a third party attempting to extract private information from a religious customer). More recently, economists have developed those original ideas of Smith by showing that confession is simply a rent-extraction device for nonproductively transferring wealth from the church's customers to the church and its churchmen.[117] That is, confession and penance were economically inefficient from society's viewpoint because they imposed costs without increasing society's output.[118]

Paying for Sins and Crimes with Penances[119]

There was a parish structure in existence in most of Europe by 1100, and there were a huge number of texts on confession and penance.[120] That set the stage for regular confession to one's parish priest, and that practice was mandated as a requirement for all Roman Catholics at Lateran IV (1215). As part of its role in administering civil law for a price, penance also was a commonly used device for punishing many civil crimes. Thus, penitential manuals dealt with many public sins that were unacceptable according to social norms. Despite any public-good benefit of enforcing social norms with penances, the direct economic benefits to the church are obvious in terms of the power conferred by such a role and because the church's imposed penances could be bought off with donations to the poor or the church.

Although many local priests were embarrassed and even frightened about their confession responsibilities, confessors' manuals of varying degrees of sophistication, including very simple ones, were produced by specialists.[121] Famous church penitentials evolved from the sixth century onward to guide priests-confessors in assigning penances as tariffs for a whole menu of sins. The father-confessor would grant absolution upon completion of what he considered a genuine confession, contingent on the sinner fulfilling the assigned penance or paying for its commutation.

Further, because local priests usually had a good idea of their religious customers' financial situation, those who embraced their new responsibilities could effectively practice price discrimination by assigning different penances for the same sins, based on their customers' willingness and ability to pay, as noted above.[122]

Irish Penitential System Spreads throughout Europe[123]

Sin in clan societies, such as Ireland, where the famous penitential manuals originated, was conceived of as a personal affront in taking away someone's honor, and that person must be repaid in some way to restore face.[124] Until that honor is restored, no punishment is too severe. This is the background under which the Irish penitentials viewed sin as an affront to God, who had to be repaid. Under this system, detailed guidelines were developed, based on the severity of each sin and the corresponding punishment required to repay God for the affront.

This new system of penance that originated in Irish monasteries had repeated penance, with private confession and penalties assessed according to the severity of the sin. In contrast, penance previously had been both harsh and public.[125] After the sixth century, the Irish pattern first spread among monasteries throughout western Europe, and then it also became the common one for the laity.[126] An early handbook probably composed in the eighth century is organized around the principal vices that were contrary to human salvation, and this idea evolved into organizing the handbooks around the seven deadly sins.[127] Interestingly, the church hierarchy and learned churchmen were extremely scornful of the penitentials when they first began appearing. There also were many attempts by church councils and authorities to banish the penitential handbooks from use.[128] Nonetheless, it is clear that the penitentials did not vanish from use.[129] In particular, lower clergy and the monks continued to find them indispensable.

Some penitentials and local church synods recommended extremely punitive and coercive punishments. For example, the Eleventh Council of Toledo (675) had to condemn the practice of putting sinners to death. More than four hundred years later, the Synod of Gran, Hungary (about 1114) decreed that bishops should build two jail houses in each city to coerce penitents into confessions. Eventually, the bishops had to resign themselves to the continued use of penitentials, so they attempted to improve the manuals and their consistency. After 906, material previously contained in older penitentials was incorporated into canonical collections of official church sources, rather than continuing as stand-alone handbooks for priests and confessors.[130] Either those collections or a new form of literature on sin (*summae confessorum*) provided the church's confessors with detailed guidance for rooting out the sins of their religious customers. But around the turn of the thirteenth century, Alan of Lilie, Thomas Chobham, and Robert of Flamborough wrote that the older penitentials simply were too harsh for anyone to follow in their contemporary world, even if earlier generations could endure such difficult remedies for sin.

Summae Confessorum and Other Literature of Sin[131]

Peter the Chanter was a master theologian of the late twelfth century, and he and his students had a lot to say about sin.[132] It probably was one of his students who composed a metric checklist for confessors in *Poeniteas cito peccator*, which remained popular for centuries. Given the rarity and expense of books during that era, the large output of these handbooks shows the popularity of instructing priests in the art of examining the guilty consciences of their flocks and extracting confessions from their religious customers. In addition to enhancing the power and prestige of priests, the confession obligation imposed by the Fourth Lateran Council in 1215 stimulated even more literature about sin, including detailed handbooks for confessors.

After Peter the Chanter and his students, the new Franciscan and Dominican Orders of the thirteenth century rose to prominence in creating penitential handbooks or *summae confessorum*, especially those that focused on merchants in the rapidly developing commercial economy.[133] Langholm's exhaustive study of handbooks that treat merchants' sins examines eighty-nine of them, including forty for the period from about 1200 to 1350. About half of these works were written by Dominican and Franciscan authors. The most famous of the early Dominican handbooks is St. Raymond of Penafort's *Summa de poenitentia*, first composed probably around 1224-26 and revised around 1240.[134] This masterpiece about sin, penance, and the remission of sins was distributed in condensed forms from the thirteenth century onward, and it even was adapted into verse by various poets during the sixteenth century. This and other handbooks provided detailed guidelines for interrogating sinners and overcoming their shame in order to extract full confessions and assign appropriate penances.[135]

Although the Dominicans began writing systematic treatises of sin and penance before the Franciscans, the Franciscans joined them as the main purveyors of sin and penance shortly after the death of St. Francis in 1226.[136] Thereafter, both mendicant orders were main players in the theory and practice of sacramental confession and penances.[137] One handbook listed one hundred and fifty-three sins of thought, word, deed, and omission.[138] That many possibilities for sin definitely made the confession-penance business a profitable one for the church's confessors. Once handbooks became commonly used by confessors, the examination of conscience concerned the Seven Deadly Sins, the Ten Commandments, the five senses, occasionally the twelve articles of the church's Creed, and more besides.[139] The second edition of a later and famous handbook enumerated seven hundred and eighty-three ways to fall prey to the seven deadly sins.[140]

Despite the extremely detailed way sin was preached and interrogated, Baun, argues that it probably is wrong to think of medieval society as terrified of the terrible punishments dreamed up by churchmen.[141] His rationale is that penances also provided consolation, not just holy dread, by confirming that humanity lived in a moral universe in which justice would prevail, sins would be punished, and virtue would be rewarded.[142] Nonetheless, regardless of the social value or uses of the penance system, it was a large revenue generator on the church's toll road to salvation.

Probing the Sickness of Sin Like a Doctor[143]

Public confession was a widespread practice of early Christianity by the second century. Private confession began to spread by the sixth or seventh centuries and was mandated by the Fourth Lateran Council in 1215. It was the belief that, with the possible exception of honest lapses in memory, what was not confessed was not absolved.[144] And the idea developed that the confessor was to use a formal list of questions to probe the recesses of a penitent's conscience to root out all the sickness of sin, much as a doctor would carry out a careful diagnosis of a patient's illness. The classic list used was who, what, where, by whose help, how often, how, and when?[145] Even if the exact lists were not the same, a similar approach had been used for centuries. Some of the masters of sin were concerned that their religious customers were reluctant to confess spiritual sins, such as envy, avarice, pride, and sloth, so they paid extra attention to ways of extracting confessions for such sins.

The writers did not agree on how extensive the questioning of their sinful patients should be. Some had almost impossibly detailed lists of questions, but others had more modest lists of general questions. Partly, this distinction reflected differences in opinion on whether penitents should be grilled in detail like criminals or questioned more gently to elicit voluntary, not coerced confessions.[146] Nonetheless, many leading churchmen of the thirteenth century continued to emphasize a juridical process of cross examination.

Probably the most famous example of extreme questioning is the *Angelica*. The *Angelica* had 975 possible questions for confessors—not counting additional sub-questions and references to yet more questions in other sources. Much later, Luther called the *Angelica* the *Diabolica* and burned it in his protest of Roman Catholic confession practices.[147]

Using Confession to Impose and Enforce Penances[148]

The spread of the new Irish penitential system from the sixth century onward meant that the practice of confession gave priests a substantial tool in applying pressure, supposedly just for divinely spiritual purposes. Some sins had such long penances as to be essentially inapplicable, but they could be bought off by various equivalences that included the possibility of cash payments for penitential masses or ransoms at a certain price. In fact, it was not uncommon to sell penance reductions, as the Archbishop of Canterbury did. He began a campaign for construction of a church to honor St. Thomas, and those who contributed annually received a one-third reduction in all of their penances.[149] The strategy evidently was successful because, from 1198 to 1206, records indicate that about one-fourth of Canterbury's total income could be attributed to St. Thomas.

It was one thing to specify penalties for various sins, but it was another to effectively assess and enforce them. Confession was not necessarily a regular part of the religious life of the laity, and there was a reluctance of many laity to subject themselves to the penitential discipline of churchmen, many of whom were widely considered to be corrupt. Once again, the church illustrated its strategic savvy with the demand of the Fourth Lateran Council in 1215 that one must confess to his own priest at least once a year in order to remain a member of the Catholic community (some later church councils increased the minimum number of annual confessions to three). Although the obligation of confession was not adopted by the Greek Church, the Roman Catholic Church claimed it was a divine institution and confirmed the claim at its Council of Trent in the 1500s. The Roman Catholic confession requirement enormously increased the power and jurisdiction of the confessor. The priest acquired the power to represent the church as a 'man of God', a father-confessor with substantial power in deciding on penances.[150]

The demand of the Roman Catholic Church's Fourth Lateran Council was that all sins must be confessed, but that strict idea was relaxed about two hundred years later, when the Council of Florence (1438-45) modified it to include just 'all the sins one remembers'. The confession requirement had socioeconomic bite because the importance of being in the Catholic community was not just religious. It also allowed one to enjoy the social and economic benefits of being part of that community from which heretics, Jews, and other 'undesirables' were excluded.

Wealth and Alms for the Poor *and* the Catholic Church

The Roman Catholic Church's toll road to salvation transferred vast wealth and property to the church and its leaders, monasteries, and religious orders.[151] How was such wealth justified in light of the church's own sacred Scripture in both the Old and New Testaments? The Jewish understanding of property in the Old Testament is that all property is on loan from God, so the rights of the needy to receive support always had to be recognized by those who currently had the most on loan from God. In contrast, the pagan Greek philosopher Aristotle's view of distributive justice was not one of equality but one of distribution proportional to merit, a view that has a long history in Catholic thought as well. This aristocratic view of wealth held that those in higher classes were entitled to more because it was necessary for maintaining their deserved status. However, what Jesus saw was a rich and a poor class, based not on merit but on exploitation by rich land owners, rulers, and greedy Jewish Temple authorities. Some of Jesus' parables feature two classes, epitomized by the rich land owner and the poor peasant.

How Was Wealth Viewed and How Much Was Enough?[152]

That the church, many churchmen, and the church's wealthy patrons had too much wealth was a long-running criticism by outsiders, who usually were labeled as heretics. But insiders (especially ascetics) also were critical of the wealth and extravagance of many churchmen. Such criticism always was hard to answer, especially in light of many Gospel teachings. The early writers often emphasized that attitude mattered more than actual possessions. For example, Bishop Irenaeus of Lyons (d. about 200) was one of the many who addressed the questions by arguing that sufficiency for one might be too much or too little for another—it depended on what was fitting for one's social rank and obligations. In this line of thinking, the key was to win the internal battle against the desire for wealth, to retain wealth but despise it! And it had to be used properly. In short, the early condemnations of greed actually contained justifications for wealth.

Although some voices in the church continued to advocate a life of evangelizing poverty, the dominant church position from around the beginning of the third century onward was that wealth was justified if: there was no avarice/desire for it; it was necessary for one's social status and obligations; and it was properly used, interpreted to mean the church expected a generous percentage from the bounty of its wealthy religious customers. What about Jesus' Gospel advice for the rich young man to sell all that he had and give it to the poor? The churchmen solved that one easily by asserting that Jesus' advice was not intended for most but only for those who wished to achieve spiritual perfection.

In the thirteenth century, St. Thomas Aquinas reiterated the earlier argument that the amount necessary for a person's maintenance depended on one's station in society, not on the bare minimum needed for subsistence. Abandonment of earthly riches was only for those seeking a state of spiritual perfection. The church's scholars provided the theoretical justification for this approach by emphasizing good works as a key to salvation and as a recompense for large profits. They even argued that rich persons were necessary for the stability of cities because they could step in and provide relief during economic or military emergencies. In this line of reasoning, the wealthy also served another purpose by providing substantial resources for the church's magnificent buildings. Consistent with the fact that many theologians were from rich families, they managed to develop an argument that avarice was a sin even for the poor. Because avarice was defined relative to one's station in life, the poor could and likely did commit the sin of avarice. They did this by desiring some of the wealthy's riches, rather than going about their assigned roles as poor persons barely surviving as workers or humbly carrying out their duties as objects of charity for the rich.

Wealthy Must Give Alms to the Poor

Because the early church soon came to be dominated by society's elite, who held most of the powerful bishoprics, it is not surprising that they developed theological rationales to justify wealth and inequality, despite the teachings of Jesus.[153] Although church leaders managed to justify wealth and inequality, most were adamant that the wealthy had an absolute obligation to provide alms for the poor—and alms meant substantial support, not just loose change. Some church fathers, including the Cappadocians Basil of Caesarea, his brother Gregory of Nyssa, and their friend Gregory of Nazianzus, even went so far as to assert that need in the world was due to the unwillingness of the rich to share their bounty with the poor, because the rich were seduced by the devil to think they needed all sorts of useless things.

Many other church fathers joined in admonishing the rich to share with the poor.[154] One of the strongest advocates of alms for the poor was Bishop Chrysostom, who preached that what the rich have is on loan from God, and their responsibility is to manage it properly by using only what they need and distributing the rest to the poor. Otherwise, they are guilty of embezzlement. Chrysostom argued that God's purpose for humans is their unity and solidarity—the physical welfare of the poor and the salvation of the rich are at stake in this mutually beneficial arrangement. Chrysostom emphasized that alms should be given to the poor because they are needy, not because they are virtuous, so the rich should make no judgments.

In the mid-third century, Bishop Cyprian was a wealthy convert who strongly advocated almsgiving in his work (*On Works and Alms*) for four basic reasons:[155]

- It was a means to atone for sins committed since baptism.
- It increased the power of prayer and fasting.
- Those who gave would not suffer any physical want, and he even implied that their wealth may increase.
- It was commanded by Christ as a way of storing up treasure in heaven.

How did the church and its leaders directly benefit from alms for the poor? Interestingly, churchmen managed to steer many of those donations to the church rather than directly to the poor, as churchmen would know better how to allocate those alms than the wealthy. The basic advice was that the best form of salvation insurance in this instance was to give alms that could be administered by the church. It probably is safe to assume that not all of the donations actually benefited the poor. The lavish lifestyles of powerful bishops and monasteries indicate that a significant share of what was given to the church by its religious customers ended up for the glory of churchmen rather than the glory of God.

The Market for Healing

During the early Middle Ages, a range of curative options were available for health problems.[156] They included the use of local herbs, medical assistance from someone with experience and a good reputation, or visits to a saint's shrine or church to ask for a miracle. In fact, pilgrimages were big business for the church, as pilgrims sought out cures and advice, based on the commonly accepted assumption that physical and spiritual health were closely connected. And these beliefs went back to very early Christianity in which public exorcisms invoked Christ's name to drive out devils or demons. In fact, exorcisms were so popular for many centuries that specific church positions in large churches were filled by exorcists.

Catholic authorities reinterpreted pagan gods as a conspiracy of demons, just as they reinterpreted Jewish history as an allegory leading up to Jesus as the Christ.[157] In this way, the emerging Christian beliefs had three realms: the entirely good who had angels and righteous souls dwelling with God; the entirely evil in whom the devil lived; and this world where good and evil intermixed. In this classification, spiritual creatures were either good or evil, and there were demons who attacked humans. Thus, any possession by a demon meant possession by evil, and that possession would be indicated by wild contortions, screams, incoherent speech, or other obvious symptoms. Anyone might be possessed by a demon, so the church's exorcists had their work cut out for them.[158]

The saints and martyrs also participated in the healing market.[159] Furthermore, stories of the lives of the saints that recounted their miracles proliferated in the Middle Ages, along with shrines where the saints' miracles and healing were reported.

Clearly, these shrines participated in the market for healing that thrived throughout most of the Middle Ages. But there were other healers as well, and they relied on magic for their 'remedies', whereas the departed saints relied on healing power conferred by God. The surviving stories, which are mainly from church sources, expound the virtues and power of the saints and demean their competitors in the informal market for magic that had its roots in pagan practices.

Another portion of the healing market was for medical doctors, a discipline that reemerged quite strongly in the West in the eleventh century as Latin translations of the long-lost works of pagan Greek philosophy and medicine became available.[160] Still, the main basis of calling oneself a doctor was reputation based on results, not formal medical training and certification. Interestingly, Christianity always had been a healing religion, so it was natural that medieval medicine often was practiced by Catholic priests and monks.[161] In fact, medical analogies were frequent in Jewish and Christian literature, and Catholic preaching also referred to healing. Most large monasteries had large infirmaries, so the sick could be treated both spiritually and physically. Women also participated in medical practices but usually as part-time nurses, caregivers, and healers who had lower status than males.

The Roman Catholic position on bodily health emphasized that sin causes bodily illnesses and even death. The Fourth Lateran Council (1215) stated that there could be no physical healing unless the soul first had been healed.[162] Thus, the main 'medicine' administered by the church was in the sacraments of the church itself, as Horden explains, "Indeed the church's one, great, truly essential means of promoting good health was baptism. Baptism was the equivalent of early inoculation: the means to forgiveness of original sin and an exorcism, a rebirth into health. It was not the only sacrament relevant here. We have already sampled the therapy of penance. . . the potentially therapeutic effects of the Eucharist were also recognized. From the earlier fathers on, the Eucharistic liturgy was a *pharmakon* (drug or medicine), and the prayers for the healing of the sick incorporated into its text were unambiguous."[163]

The church's emphasis on curing sin as the basis for bodily health is shown strongly in a fourteenth-century treatise (*Liber mensalis*) by the Dominican Philip of Ferrara, who died around 1350.[164] The treatise was designed to prepare his Dominican brothers for encounters with laity and the religious practices they could promote on such occasions. Because sin caused illnesses, the treatise advised the Dominicans to convince sick persons and those with them to repent and confess. But the friars also should take such opportunities to recruit new members for the Dominicans. And they were instructed to encourage people to donate now when they were alive, rather than leaving it to others after they departed, because the others might not pay to save the souls of the departed. And he included short and entertaining examples that could be used for persuasion of different types of persons.

Church Tithes and Taxes [165]

The church had many ways to generate revenue, as discussed in this and other chapters, and its thirst for money was unquenchable. In its scramble for more revenue to fund its expensive operations, the church made some strategic moves to establish more stable and secure revenue sources. The church had long preached the moral obligation for providing it with the first fruits from harvests, and ten percent of agricultural produce and livestock also was supposed to be given to the church as a tithe. The church started trying to impose formerly customary tithing practices as a requirement on all during the sixth century, but effectively collecting them from many persons was only possible with the support of Catholic rulers. The tithe was reinforced as a mandatory duty by both the Bavarian and Frankish rulers at about the same time in the eighth century. The emperor Charlemagne (768-814) evidently was the first to place the tithe requirement into civil law.

The Roman Catholic Church reaped a bumper crop of tithe payments because it probably was the largest landholder in the entire western world for much of the period covered in this book. Thus, it could closely monitor workers on its lands to be sure it received its full tithe. Given the tithes from its own lands and from lands owned by others, they were a substantial revenue source for the papacy, bishops, churches, and monasteries that had large land holdings. The tithe was such an attractive revenue source that many churchmen even sold its rights to laymen.

The church justified its additional tithe extractions from the people—above and beyond its many other charges for holy services discussed in this and other chapters—as essential for serving the purposes of God. And since the church was God's direct representative on earth, churchmen knew what God wanted. Churchmen even cited passages from the Old and New Testaments to assert that tithing was a divine mandate. Needless to say, there were many protests about these tithes and their supposedly divine uses.

The people looked for ways to get around paying the tithe, and one technique was to have some party who was exempt from the tithe to nominally hold the land for the actual owner/worker.

Many exemptions had been granted through the years, for example, because of customary land uses or as personal privileges for rulers and clergy. In response, the Fourth Lateran Council (1215) decreed that: tithes took precedence over any other tax payments and were to be paid on total output, not net output, once other tax and rent payments were paid; and entrusting lands to parties exempt from tithes, which was a common practice, no longer would be tolerated. As one mechanism of enforcement, the church had to play its card of eternal salvation. Churchmen asserted that any arrears in tithes had to be paid at death in order to hope for eternal salvation.

However, the agricultural tithe/tax was not the end of the story for the church's taxing powers. As an amazing display of its own secular power, the church extended its demands to a tax on all economic activity as market transactions became more important after the tenth century. But that still was not enough for the papacy's expensive operations, especially after its warfare and crusading began at the end of the eleventh century. Thus, the papacy added an income tax on its churchmen and others, theoretically to pay for its holy violence against its enemies. But scholars question whether the income tax actually was for the crusades or other expenses, and it was more difficult to collect because it had less support from secular rulers.

The church ultimately succeeded in creating the West's first universal tax system since the Roman Empire's disintegration in the fifth century. Interestingly, its assessment and collection system was so effective and comprehensive that it later served as a model for nation-states to create their tax collections systems. Once rulers developed enough centralized power in their realms to impose taxes on all of their subjects, they modeled their tax and collection systems on the one created by the Roman Catholic Church.

Selling Miscellaneous Holy Services

The church's sacraments, mass attendance, confession, penance, healing, tithes and taxes, death and burial, and other profitable business lines discussed above or in later chapters were the church's basic revenue generators. However, its priests also had many other, usually smaller, earning opportunities from providing a variety of miscellaneous services. In other words, the church was able to leverage its basic business lines into many other opportunities for extracting payments for the ordinary rituals of life.[166] As early as the second century, Tertullian had used the Roman legal term *sacramentum* (oath) to describe religious loyalty or commitment to the church. Churchmen took advantage of the loyalty and commitment of their religious customers to generate specific kinds of donations, some of which ended up in their pockets, despite ninth-century legislation specifically prohibiting charges for holy services. These include the following:[167]

- Payments for wax, candles, oil, lamps, cloths, chalices, and other items for religious worship.
- Prayers during their lifetimes for donors and their families.
- Blessings for a pilgrim's pack, well, or newly planted fruit tree.
- Regular or seasonal feasts/fasts and commemorative feasts.
- Vows by individuals for various purposes.

Profitable Business Lines Make the Church Wealthy[168]

The many ways the Roman Catholic Church charged its customers on the toll road to salvation discussed in this and other chapters made the church wealthy. Pastoral revenues for churches and bishoprics built up through the centuries. Despite many official prohibitions of charges for the sacraments and other holy services, people were willing to pay to get the clerical services they wanted and the clergy definitely solicited and accepted their payments. Because the total sum of offerings and tithes could be substantial for a church, it became easier to treat them, especially tithes, as negotiable bits of revenue that were bought, sold, and traded.

A major consequence of the accumulation of both wealth and a steady flow of income for many churches was that, by the early Middle Ages, churches were attractive investment opportunities for those interested in them as economic rather than religious entities. The investors included bishops, many religious orders, and many lay powers. That led to what is referred to as the proprietary church controlled by individuals rather than the institutional church. Wood's detailed study of the proprietary church explains the extent of the proprietary church, including the taxing system established by the church and enforced by secular rulers:

> "By the later sixth century in the Western Church, regular offerings included wax for candles, oil for lamps, candles and lamps themselves, eggs, cheeses, and other produce for the clergy, sometimes money. . . . Perhaps most important was care for the dead, especially ancestors, by making offerings to have their bodies buried in hallowed ground and to help their souls out of purgatory. But besides these particular purposes or occasions, Christians were morally obliged to give part of their wealth to the Church . . . an obligation defined in biblical terms as firstfruits. . . . Firstfruits (*primitiae*) were not sharply different from other

offerings, and might loosely correspond to pagan autumnal offerings for next year's harvest. But the tithe, a much weightier burden, was owed rather than offered; it was quantitatively defined, unlike firstfruits; . . . It was this above all that had to be enjoined by preachers and councils, and that came to have the ruler's backing in eighth-century Francia. Exactly how and in what sense the tithe became 'compulsory' is still obscure. . ."[169]

In short, churches and monasteries became extremely valuable economic commodities, based on the business lines discussed in this and other chapters. And that obviously led to many abuses, as both churchmen and lay powers competed for their ownership. The business of the church was so profitable that individual institutions often were treated as exactly that—business operations disguised as religious institutions.

Many individual churches were profitable economic commodities, but the most notable profit centers in the church's multi-divisional firm were in the richer religious orders, the richer bishoprics, and the papacy.[170] During the Middle Ages, the papacy had an entire bureaucracy set up to collect its revenues, including its taxes and tithes. The papacy's vast resources were centralized for control and management in the office of the *camera* from the latter part of the twelfth century to the end of the Middle Ages. The *camera* was the papal treasury under authority of the pope, curia, and cardinals. The *camera* managed the papacy's cartel enterprises with general enforcement, judicial, and auditing functions. Regional and local fiscal agents were responsible for collecting rents and serving as cartel sub-managers.

The church's unquenchable thirst for revenue provoked many protests. For example, Matthew of Paris' monumental

Chronica Maiora in the mid-thirteenth century frequently notes that only the Pope and his agents were greedier than the English King.[171] In rural areas, there were frequent complaints of greedy royal and papal agents who were always snooping around for their share.

The papacy had to set up such an elaborate enforcement and monitoring system for collecting its share of profits from sin because there were nearly irresistible temptations for the papacy's local agents (priests and bishops) to reduce the papacy's share.[172] As in many other instances when the hierarchy had to adapt, it strategically dealt with this malfeasance by instituting new policies. First, the papacy increased its enforcement apparatus to gain a larger share of local revenue. Second, the papacy created an entirely new business line—the sale of indulgences that supposedly absolved punishments for some or even all of a customer's sins. And the papacy made sure it cashed in on indulgences in two ways. The Dominican and Franciscan Orders reported directly to the papacy rather than to local bishops, and this gave the papacy a better return on the indulgences sold by the mendicants, who specialized in marketing them. And the papacy also invented indulgences that only it could grant, so there were no middle men involved. The sale of indulgences was a universal practice by the fourteenth century.

Charging for Salvation Threatens Church's Religious Credibility

The ironic aspect of the church's emphasis on guilt, sin, and judging others is that this emphasis contradicts the teachings of Jesus. Jesus instead preached love and free forgiveness—based on faith in God, not in the church—and he warned against judging others in Matt 7:1-2 and Luke 6:37-38. Moreover, Jesus never even hints that salvation could be bought and sold in the Gospels. To the contrary, Jesus observes that the poor widow's tiny contribution is greater than large donations from the wealthy, because hers was from all that she had and theirs was from their surplus (Mark 12:41-44 and Luke 21:1-4). Further, his first apostles strongly warned against buying the gifts of God. For example, St. Peter was outraged that Simon Magus thought he could buy the power to confer the Holy Spirit on others, as recounted in Acts 8:18-22. (This passage about Simon's attempt to buy holy gifts is the basis for the church's labeling the sale and purchase of holy services as simony.)

Charging for holy services also threatened the church's product credibility and opened it up to severe criticisms from within the church and, more dangerously, from heretical critics who claimed to offer purer religious alternatives.[173] For example, the Master General of the Dominicans, Humbert of Romans (d. 1277), and others argued the sacraments lacked in justice because they favored the rich.

The church responded to criticisms in two main ways. First, it labeled and attacked its critics outside of the church as heretics who should be eliminated. Second, reforms had to be announced because the criticisms against the corruption of the church and its churchmen reached new highs in the eleventh and twelfth centuries, threatening the church's product credibility and the revenue from its toll road to salvation. In response to both internal and external criticism, the church initiated a major set of reforms during the Middle Ages that are discussed in Chapter 9.

Conclusion

During life's journey on the toll road to salvation, the church developed a remarkable ability to make its religious customers pay for their sins, hopes, and desires. Further, the historical evidence shows how effective the church was in accumulating wealth for itself and its churchmen from religious customers who sought to buy the eternal salvation sold by the church. And from the church's point of view, its insurance product was an ideal one that never could be convincingly tested—no living person could actually know whether they would collect on the salvation insurance sold by the church.

The church's focus on sin rather than love had many consequences for society as a whole and for the church's ability to reap profits from various business lines that depended on sin for their justification. Love was banished to the margins of a mainstream theology that was used to create wealth and power for the church and its churchmen along its toll road to salvation. The church's focus on wealth and power rather than on free mercy and love explain stark contrasts between the church and Jesus. *Jesus forgave sins because of faith*, but church leaders:

- Mercilessly judged others rather than emphasizing the free forgiveness taught by Jesus and his first apostles.
- Created and nurtured an entire culture of fear, guilt, and sin that could be exploited for wealth and power.
- Sold spiritual benefits on the church's toll road to salvation throughout life, at death, and even beyond with the invention of Purgatory.

5

Paying for Sexual Behavior, Marriage, and Divorce on Church's Toll Road to Salvation

Starting at least from the second century, churchmen had intense interest in regulating the sexual behavior, dreams, and thoughts of other churchmen and lay persons.[174] In the early church, some of this concern clearly was religiously based, especially the calls of celibacy for churchmen and virginity for women, and that attitude also was common among the pagan religions of Rome at the time early Christianity was emerging. However, certifying marriage and divorce had become and remained secular matters, until the church made a successful strategic move to assert its religious authority over them during about the ninth to eleventh centuries. Although religious motives also may have been involved in the church take-over of marriage, divorce, and sexual matters, economic motives clearly are shown by the additional collection booths the church established for them on its toll road to salvation. Entering the minds and beds of Christians to regulate sexual thoughts, dreams, and behavior through confession and penances that could be bought off for a price opened up an extremely profitable business line for the church. And marriage, annulment, and divorce regulations also proved to be profitable business lines for the church.

Regulating Sexual Dreams, Thoughts, and Behavior

Virtually everyone could run afoul of the minutely detailed regulations invented and used by the church in scrutinizing the sexual lives of their customers. Around the turn of the fifth century, the era's master theologian, St. Augustine, explained that the fundamental principle of Catholic sexual behavior was simple—intercourse was permissible only between a legitimately married man and woman and only for procreation. Anything else was a serious sin. Consistent with Augustine's focus on original sin, however, he also opined that marital intercourse would have been so much better, had Adam and Eve not succumbed to the 'Fall'. Perhaps St. Augustine's own sexual behavior helps explain his concern for the sexual conduct of others. Before his conversion:[175]

- He fathered a son by one concubine.
- Then, to prepare for marriage to a more suitable (i.e., wealthy) mate favored by his mother, he sent his first concubine and son

back to North Africa from Europe where he was living at the time.

- When the planned marriage was cancelled, he worried about being promiscuous, so he took on a new concubine in Europe to satisfy his sexual urges with only one woman rather than a variety of them.

Council of Elvira (c. 306 AD)[176]

The Council of Elvira was the first one recognized as an official church council by most scholars, and it dealt extensively with disciplinary issues on matters such as marriage, adultery by women, and other sexual matters. A few of the council's canons on sexual behavior include the following:

"7. If a Christian completes penance for a sexual offense and then again commits fornication, he or she may not receive communion even when death approaches. . . .

9. A baptized woman who leaves an adulterous husband who has been baptized, for another man, may not marry him. If she does, she may not receive communion until her former husband dies, unless she is seriously ill. . . . 13. Virgins who have been consecrated to God shall not commune even as death approaches if they have broken the vow of virginity and do not repent. . . . 35. Women are not to remain in a cemetery during the night. Some engage in wickedness rather than prayer. . ."[177]

Other Early Church Views

The bishops of the early church also emphasized the danger of sexual transgressions, and they attempted to regulate the sexual lives of their congregations with detailed regulations.[178] Further,

Constantine, the first Christian emperor of Rome, made it clear that sexual transgressions by female virgins were especially serious. As Pomeroy reports, "Constantine was explicit about the guilt of the victim. In his decision on raped virgins, he distinguished between girls who were willing and those who were forced against their will. If the girl had been willing, her penalty was to be burned to death. If she had been unwilling, she still was punished because she should have screamed and brought neighbors to her assistance, but the punishment was lighter. Constantine also specified capital punishment for a free woman who had intercourse with a slave, and burning for the slave himself. This penalty was the outcome of a perpetual concern that free women would take the same liberties with slaves as men did [to fulfill their sexual desires]."[179]

Medieval Church Views

Even with the collapse of Rome during the fifth century and the church's many strategic moves required to survive and thrive as an institutional entity during the turmoil of the next several centuries, the fascination of churchmen with sexual issues nonetheless continued and even increased. Church writers created a large number of penitential manuals designed to educate confessors on how to interrogate their religious customers in excruciating detail about their sexual transgressions.[180]

What sexual sins were of such concern to church writers from the sixth to twelfth centuries? Virtually every type of sexual dream, thought, and behavior imaginable—with the exception of intercourse between a married man and woman for the sole purpose of procreation—was included. Moreover, these detailed codes of sexual behavior included equally detailed price schedules for assigning penances. A small sampling of the issues in these manuals dated from 550 to 1150 illustrates their preoccupation with sexual issues:[181]

- There was only one proper form of intercourse between married partners (what today would be referred to as the 'missionary position').
- Egbert's penitential allowed a payment in lieu of penance for violating sexual abstinence during the Lent before Easter.
- For clerics, the longest penances were for relations with a religious woman and the shortest were for a simple cleric who had sex with a young girl.
- Up to the early ninth century, the penitentials dealt extensively with various aspects of homosexuality.
- Women were seen as temptresses in many penitentials, so clerical celibacy had to be safeguarded against the attempts of women to seduce 'innocent' clerics.
- Seminal emissions, including unintentional ones during the night, were covered extensively.
- Sexual abstinence was considered important for married couples, based partly on various reasons in the Old Testament. But some manuals extended abstinence for many more days, including the three Lents (the periods before Christmas and Easter and after Pentecost).

Delumeau explains the church's position on sexual matters and marriage from the 1300s into the 1500s:

"One of the chief characteristics of this period's intensive Christianization consists in the mass diffusion of a rule of life conceived by ascetics. . . this Draconian ethic incorporates marriage only with reluctance. . . Chiavaro writes that 'a rapid estimate of these days in the medieval calendar leads to the conclusion that for nearly half the year one had to abstain from amorous marital relations. If to this calculation are added the periods of menstruation and full pregnancy . . . for the greater part of the year, sex between spouses was forbidden.' "[182]

All in all, as Delumeau has suggested, no other civilization has ever been subjected to such a detailed investigation of sexual activity, especially within the confines of marriage.

Economic Dimensions of Sexual Regulations: Confession and Penance[183]

The church mined the profits from sexual sins as an integral part of confession and penance. To do this, churchmen wrote and used detailed manuals that specified numerous sexual sins and the penalties that should be assigned for them. Regulating sexual behavior in such detail was a profitable business line on the church's toll road to salvation from at least the sixth to eighteenth centuries, and the potential profits surely increased with the requirement of confession to remain in the Catholic community that was imposed by the Fourth Lateran Council in 1215. The profits arose because penances for sexual sins could be bought off with payments to commute the imposed penance, and some penitents gave their alms for the poor to the church to administer and distribute.

The penitential handbooks and other manuals were used from the sixth-seventh centuries into the thirteenth century, and they played a central role in developing the sexual ethos that guided priests-confessors in assigning penalties. The most common penance was a fast of a given number of days that was extremely long for serious sins. But such penances commonly could be bought off by donations to the church or the poor, with the latter preferably paid to and administered by the church. Even though the penances in the handbooks were not always imposed or served, the perceived gravity of various sexual sins is shown by the relative magnitudes of the proscribed penances.[184]

Beginning in the tenth century, regulations on sexual behavior were incorporated into canonical collections (official church sources), instead of just stand-alone sources for the church's priests.[185] Many of the sexual issues from the earlier penitentials were included in Buchard of Worm's *Decretum* that was widely used in the eleventh century and in Gratian's famous twelfth-century *Decretum*. A new form of literature also emerged during the twelfth century—*summae confessorum* that provided detailed guidance for dealing with sexual transgressions.[186] The many branches of lust were even expanded to include men as adulterers, if they were too desirous of their own wives (by Penafort, among others). This was a good way to extract payments from Catholic men who loved their wives 'too much'. In short, the penitentials, canonical collections, and *summae confessorum* had sexually related issues as a major concern and provided priests detailed guidance for interrogating their religious customers and assigning the appropriate penalties for the sexual sins committed.

The penitentials examined by Payer focus on a large variety of sexual sins and the associated penances that could be bought off, including the following for married persons:[187]

- Adultery was understood as sexual relations between two persons, at least one of whom was married. The penances usually were fairly short, but penances were much more severe for offenders who held higher ecclesiastical offices.
- Sexual abstinence was promoted.

- The only 'proper' position for intercourse was what today would be referred to as the 'missionary position'. Other positions were punishable.

The penitentials examined by Payer also focus on a variety of other sexual sins and associated penances that could be bought off, including:[188]

- There was much more emphasis on homosexuality than on heterosexual relations between unmarried persons. Oral sex was strictly prohibited.
- Bede's manual refers to some kind of instrument, perhaps an artificial phallus, used by nuns in homosexual relationships.
- Bestiality was prohibited, but many of the penances were quite light, compared to many other sexual transgressions, perhaps reflecting the rural nature of a society in which bestiality was quite common. However, bestiality would climb up the ladder of sexual sinfulness to the top or near the top in later centuries as the West developed a stronger market economy.
- There were a substantial number of canons for monks and clergy. However, there was little concern for the sexual acts of clergy with unmarried as opposed to married women.
- Seminal emissions were covered extensively in the canons, and some proscribed that a priest could not preside at mass after an unintentional nocturnal emission.

Seriousness of Various Sexual Transgressions [189]

There are different ways to convey the relative seriousness of sexual sins, based on church sources. Delumeuau summarizes the various sexual sins included in the penitentials as follows:

"The sixteen categories of sin were arranged in the following order: (1) the immodest kiss; (2) the immodest touch; (3) fornication; (4) debauchery, often understood as the seduction of a virgin; (5) simple adultery (when one partner was married); (6) double adultery (when both were married); (7) willful sacrilege (when one of the partners had taken religious vows); (8) the abduction and rape of a virgin; (9) the abduction and rape of a married woman (a more serious sin than the previous, being compounded with adultery); (10) the abduction and rape of a nun; (11) incest; (12) masturbation, first of the sins against nature; (13) improper sexual positions, even between married couples; (14) unnatural sexual relations; (15) sodomy; and (16) bestiality."[190]

Another way to see the relative gravity of various sexual sins is to compare penances within the same penitentials. Penances usually were graded by length of time, so that is a measure of perceived gravity, especially within the same penitential. And it always was more expensive to buy off the longer penances than the shorter ones. In order to indicate how relatively harsh sexual penances were, some comparisons of penances for adultery and killing are provided for two well-known medieval penitentials in Table 5-1.[191]

Note that the penalties for adultery in Table 5-1 are far longer for women than for men, consistent with the church's view of original sin that alleges the main problem for sexual transgressions is women who are temptresses for otherwise 'innocent' men. For example, in each source, an adulteress receives a penance of seven years, whereas the longest penance for a man who commits adultery is three years in *Cummean* (for begetting a child with a vowed virgin) and four years in *Theodore U* (for adultery with a married woman). Also, in *Cummean*, the penalty

Table 5-1
Penances from Two Medieval Penitentials for Adultery and Killing*

Cummean: Adultery for Laity

>Neighbor's wife or virgin daughter: 1 year

>With Female slave: 1 year, sell the slave

>With vowed virgin: 1.5 year

>Beget child with vowed virgin: 3 years

>Adulteress: 7 years

Cummean: Killing

>Unintentionally, by accident: 1 year

>In anger: 3 years

>Premeditation: life, live for God dead to world

Theodore U: Adultery

>With female slave: 6 months

>With vowed virgin or neighbor's wife: 3 years

>With married woman: 4 years

>Adulteress: 7 years

Theodore U: Killing

>On command of secular lord: 40 days

>In public war: 40 days

>By accident: 1 year

>In anger or revenge: 3 years

>With premeditation: 7 years

>Killing a monk or a cleric: 7 years

>In quarrel or homicide: 10 years

*Payer, *Sex and the Penitentials, 550-1150,* 1984, appendix c.

for a father's sex with his virgin daughter is a penance of only one year.

Adultery is more serious than some forms of murder, according to the severity of the penances in Table 5-1. For example, killing in anger merits a penance of only three years in both *Cummean* and *Theodore U*. However, killing a monk or a cleric rises to the level of being an adulteress in *Theodore U* (seven years). Although an adulteress was assigned a penance of seven years in *Theodore U*, killing someone on the command of a secular lord merited a penance of only forty days.

Minority View: Sexual Leniency for Married Partners [192]

Against the general tendency to see many sexual sins, including those between marriage partners, a more reasonable position was advocated by some. For example, Albertus Magnus's thirteenth-century *Summa Theologica* asserts that there is 'no sin in conjugal rapports'. Aquinas also approved of conjugal coitus and pleasure in marriage but, just as Augustine did centuries earlier, he opined that sex would have been even better had Adam and Eve not committed Original Sin.[193]

Regulating Marriage and Divorce

Because of its emphasis on the importance of asceticism and celibacy, early Christian and Catholic teaching was fractured over the value of marriage.[194] For example, some who challenged the idea that marriage was somehow an inferior state argued that otherwise the Creator's work would be impugned. But they received stinging rebukes from St. Jerome, one of the early Catholic Church's most notable thinkers and theologians. St. Augustine, the leading theologian of the early church, was more subtle in his analysis of marriage, but he still argued that celibacy was at the top of the spiritual hierarchy.

Catholic Marriage Regulations

Although marriage was a civil institution until well into the Middle Ages, Christians nonetheless received clear messages about the rules of marriage from St. Paul's New Testament Letters, as Osiek notes, "Through these passages, believers in Jesus must have gotten the same message as was communicated in civic politics and official [pagan] religion: the well-run household is the foundation of society, and well-run means maintaining the hierarchical structure that had always been the philosophical and political ideal. . . . Marriage remains ideally the hierarchical relationship of benevolent monarch to his loving and submissive wife."[195]

The early Catholic Church had clear positions on the rules for secular marriage, but converting marriage to a church sacrament and collecting payments for exceptions to its regulations was a long process.[196] Fully incorporating marriage within the church was delayed for at least three reasons. First, the early church fathers and higher clergy generally took a dim view of marriage—celibacy for men and virginity for women were considered far higher states. Second, the collapse of Rome in the fifth century occurred before marriage and divorce had been taken over by the church, and the resulting turmoil occupied the church in defending and sustaining itself as a powerful institution. Finally and largely as a reflection of the above issues, the possibility of using marriage and divorce for collections on the church's toll road to salvation evidently did not become abundantly clear to churchmen until the ninth-twelfth centuries. Then, policies on marriage and divorce were taken up as part of overall church reform that increased the power of the church and its ability to extract payments from its religious customers.

During the turmoil in the West after Rome's collapse, the Roman Catholic Church's rulers in the Frankish Kingdom were fervent supporters of the church; they emphasized church regulations of marriage, along with clerical celibacy, ritual purity, and monastic reform.[197] Thus, church councils began tightening definitions of a 'legitimate' marriage, especially during the Carolingian era from about 750 to 900, but there is doubt about the practical effect of such restrictions, except in a few high-profile cases.

However, the higher ranks of the clergy and avowedly celibate monks basically saw marriage as licensed sex in the period leading up to the eleventh century.[198] Thus, prior to the second half of the eleventh century, it was not clear that marriage ever would become a sacrament. Much of the impetus for marital reform and sexual purity came from the clerical confraternities and medieval monasteries that fostered all-male atmospheres. They emphasized male camaraderie, privilege, and low opinions of women, partly because they focused on original sin and ritual impurity. Interestingly, however, some of these same 'pure' males used young boys, concubines, or prostitutes for sexual services and gratification, despite many official calls for celibacy. But the supposedly celibate clergy nonetheless saw themselves as moralists who should regulate the sexual relations and marriages of the laity.[199]

Church reformers in the second half of the eleventh century started to push for a more sacral and public marriage arrangement that also precluded marriages to close kin, a practice that was commonly used to keep property within the family unit;

for those with wealth, marriage was a legalized way to transfer property to future generations.[200] The move of the church to regulate marriage was seen by many as interference in something that private parties could handle themselves. Nonetheless, starting from late in the eleventh century, the church developed liturgies to sanctify marriage and regulations to define legitimate marriages.

Economic Dimensions of Church's Marriage Regulations

Before the church intervened in the marriage market, marriage was used as an important economic and political tool by families with wealth, as noted above. Thus, secular law, which was controlled by the elite, had strong protections for inheritance, partly by allowing marriage between close relatives. And churchmen assisted in protecting inheritances by administering sacred oaths. But once the church took over the marriage market, secular marriages were almost exclusively for those outside the church (heretics, Jews, Muslims, and pagans). Whereas secular marriages easily could be terminated without cause, the church prohibited divorce, thus effectively increasing the potential costs of marriage because any dissolution of a marriage would be more costly. However, church marriage could be avoided by believers only at the risk of their eternal salvation and excommunication. And removal from the Catholic community involved social and economic costs, not just religious ones. Thus, the church's strategic move to take over the marriage market was successfully executed.

The church laid down specific penalties for those living in sin to encourage church marriages, but many churchmen still wondered about licensing sex.[201] Despite theological debates over the status of marriage in the grand scheme of things, the church took control of the marriage market and linked compliance with its marriage laws to another collection booth on its toll road to salvation. But charges for marriages, annulments, and divorces were featured as donations because the sin of selling holy services had to be avoided by churchmen. Marriage sacraments instead involved what were described as offerings rather than fees. In reality, however, there was a schedule of charges that were called offerings for marriage sacraments and for other priestly actions. This was another area in which the priests could practice price discrimination, based on the willingness and ability of their religious customers to pay for marriages and especially for annulments and divorces. Thus, the wealthy paid much more than the poor for these services.

Church intervention in the marriage market also allowed it to reap some wealth by cracking down on the common practice of concubinage. Many laymen and priests had concubines who lived with them, did household duties, provided sex for them, and bore them children. Before the ninth century, concubines were considered part of households and their children were legitimate heirs. But by denying inheritances to the illegitimate children of concubines, the church was able to confiscate some inheritances intended for those children. Nonetheless, concubinage continued as a common practice among both churchmen and laymen, and it was not definitively banned by the church until Lateran V in 1514.

The successful efforts of the church to usurp the marriage market involved substantial costs for both the church (a sprawling bureaucracy) and lay society (through the transfer of wealth to the church via regulations, court cases, and property seizures).[202] This created inefficiencies, in this case because of extra regulations, enforcement efforts, court cases, and the transfers of wealth. These effects involved costs without any increase in society's wealth and, as discussed later in this chapter, lower marriage rates probably resulted from higher marriage costs.[203]

However, by altering its definition of a valid marriage and by varying marriage regulations, the church increased its revenue through payments and more cases before ecclesiastical courts, as well as some property seizures from those in illegal marriages or with illegal inheritances.[204] By linking its marriage sanction with eternal salvation, the church also was able to increase its extractions by charging its customers more to avoid or commute its sanctions. Because a valid marriage required the blessing of a priest, that also gave local priests more power and revenue. Interestingly, given the disadvantage of women in society's legal system, it may be that the church's regulation of marriage and divorce actually improved their positions in the marriage market, thereby increasing their allegiance to the church.

Marriages traditionally had been allowed between first cousins but not between closer relatives than first cousins.[205] However, once the church intervened in the marriage market, it first extended the marriage restriction to second cousins and then eventually to sixth cousins, before backing down to third cousins in the thirteenth century.[206] The various changes in marriage regulations created revenue opportunities for the church because it greatly increased the number of those seeking exceptions from the church to avoid 'sinful' marriages. Revenue also was created for the church's courts, because competing families and the church could claim that others were not legally married and thus not entitled to keep their holdings.

Selling Annulments and Divorces[207]

Prohibitions of divorce also opened up a revenue stream by granting exceptions that again could increase church revenue by using price discrimination to vary divorce prices, based on the willingness and ability of religious customers to pay for them. Before the twelfth century, the church did not require the dissolution of prior marriages, but that lenient practice was revoked at the 1166 Synod of Constantinople. Thereafter, all legal marriages and divorces had to conform to current church law, so many existing marriages and divorces became illegal when church regulations changed.

Paying for Exceptions by the Rich and Powerful

As usually was the case for church policies during the period, there were loopholes for the rich and powerful. Lunt has extensively studied various church fees and taxes for the period shortly after the time frame for this book.[208] The variation in marriage fees for various kinds of exceptions to the church's definition of a suitable relationship between marrying partners reveals how the church used price discrimination to reap profits from granting exceptions to its detailed rules.[209] For example, exemptions from these regulations were granted to nobility for sizable sums that varied with their ability to pay. Further, the medieval historian Duby and the economists Davidson and Ekelund Jr. document and analyze the exemptions given the rich and powerful to get around church restrictions on how closely spouses could be related.[210] They either paid handsome amounts for the exemptions or exchanged political favors with the papacy for them.

The church's marriage, annulment, and divorce laws (and changes in them) were especially profitable for royal marriages and divorces.[211] Kings often married against church law in their quest to extend and consolidate their power, so this opened up a lucrative market for papal exemptions to church laws on marriage, annulments, and divorce. For example, King Robert the Pious of France (996-1031) was caught up in a famous one of these cases. He was anathematized by a church council in 998 for his refusal to obey church marriage laws. Finally, the case was settled by the King giving secular control of 'his' monks at Cluny and Fleury to the church in exchange for its sanctioning of a divorce and third marriage. William the Conqueror also eventually agreed to great works for the church in order to have his excommunication for marrying a close relative rescinded.

In the mid-thirteenth century, England's King Henry III wanted a new wife to advance his economic and political interests. The problem for the king was that he was under the marriage/divorce jurisdiction of the pope. According to church policy, he and his wife had been married in a valid Roman Catholic ceremony, and divorce was prohibited by the church in most cases. Although some later kings rejected church regulation of their marriages and divorces, rulers in Henry III's era still allowed papal jurisdiction, except in cases when their benefits of refusing papal authority clearly outweighed the costs.

The biggest loophole for divorces until the thirteenth century was the church's prohibition of marriage between those who were too closely related and, through the centuries, the church varied which degree of relatives was prohibited. Until the church changed its rules in the thirteenth century, rich and powerful men almost always could 'prove' that a marriage they no longer desired involved a relative who was too closely related to them. Unfortunately for King Henry III, that loophole was largely closed before he sought his annulment. Although the economic and political reasons for his desired annulment were obvious to all, the papacy could not simply grant his wishes without appearing to violate its own rules. Consequently, the king and his agents worked hard in an elaborate and time-consuming process to gather together documents that could not be challenged in 'proving' his first marriage invalid and his second valid. Pope Innocent IV managed to accommodate the king by issuing a long and detailed bull to justify the annulment of the king's first marriage. This was one of the highest profile annulments granted by the papacy, but many other influential men also had the money and influence to secure them.

Unintended Consequences of Church Regulations

Before the church took over the marriage market, secular marriages could be dissolved easily.[212] Thus, those considering marriage after that change knew the costs of dissolving marriages had been increased substantially in terms of the time, energy, and money involved in dealing with church laws and courts. Consistent with the fact that this change clearly increased the expected costs of marriage, Ekelund Jr. et al. found that an unintended consequence of the church's increase in the cost of marriage evidently was a decline in marriage rates and increases in concubinage and prostitution, starting in the ninth century (early in the process of tightening church regulations). Even though the church opposed concubinage and prostitution, its tightening of marriage regulations and its expensive annulment and divorce process made concubinage and using prostitutes relatively more attractive propositions than marriage for some persons.

Conclusion

There clearly were some religious motives in the church's attempts to regulate the sexual behavior of its religious customers and its own churchmen, especially early in church history. Yet its detailed regulations for sexual matters, marriage, annulments, and divorce also provide clear signs of the economic motives that became so important for church policies in these areas. The historical record also contains compelling evidence on how the church used these policies and its courts' jurisdiction over such cases to enrich itself and its churchmen. In short, marriage, annulments, and divorce were another profitable stop for the church on its toll road to salvation. For example, the church could use price discrimination in varying its charges for escaping the penances for sexual sins, based on the willingness and ability of its customers to pay. And it could do the same in charging for exceptions to its marriage, annulment, and divorce regulations. It was able to enforce its various regulations by excommunicating and denying eternal salvation for those who refused to obey—an especially effective sanction for believers and even non-believers, because removal from the Catholic community involved economic and social costs, not just religious ones.

Few, if any, of the church's detailed regulations for sexual matters, marriage, and divorce can be traced to the teachings of Jesus. He never preached any detailed regulations for the bedroom behavior of his followers. He never taught that married couples were to avoid affection, except in the process of procreation. And the church was especially harsh in its treatment of women accused of adultery. By way of contrast, the following was Jesus' teaching in John 8:3-11 when he encountered a woman accused of adultery:

"And the scribes and Pharisees bring unto him a woman taken in adultery. . . and said to him . . . Now Moses in the law commanded us to stone such a one. But what do you say? . . . Jesus . . . said to them: He that is without sin among you, let him first cast a stone at her. . . . But they hearing this, went out one by one. . . . Then Jesus . . . said to her: Woman, where are they that accused you? Has no man condemned you? . . . No man, Lord. And Jesus said: Neither will I condemn you. Go, and now sin no more."[213]

6

PRODUCT CREDIBILITY AND PAYING FOR SAINTLY ASSISTANCE ON CHURCH'S TOLL ROAD TO SALVATION

The saints and their relics were used by the Catholic Church through the centuries as holy persons and objects for religious product credibility and to attract converts as well as wealth through bequests and other donations.[214] Medieval spirituality essentially made the departed saints 'living' beings through icons, shrines, relics, miracles, and stories.[215] From late antiquity, virtually every altar contained the relics of saints or martyrs as a connection to the divine—the saints' power was transmitted to whomever or whatever touched their relics, shrines, and altars. It is not surprising that Catholics reverenced their saints and saints' relics, because reverencing and even worshiping notable persons who had departed was common in ancient societies and the pagan religions that competed with evolving Christianity.[216] And adopting this practice made the Catholic Church more competitive in attracting pagan converts.

Because the power of the saints was so remarkable, they were asked to do many jobs in churches, shrines, monasteries, and communities. For example, they answered prayers, offered healing and advice, provided victories in battle, gave protection against plundering, improved the chances for salvation through choice burial spots near church altars or in revered monasteries, and increased commerce from pilgrims and tourists. In short, the church was able to cash in on the saints, who needed handsome compensation for their spectacular achievements.

A problem for the church in reverencing the saints and their relics was that a market shortage for powerful saints developed, and a booming market responded to the supply shortage through skyrocketing prices. Not surprisingly, relic merchants and holy monks also resorted to theft or fraudulent relics to secure notable saints.

The market for powerful saints and their relics, as well as the sale of stolen and fraudulent relics, finally subsided with the rise of St. Mary as the church's greatest saint. She was ubiquitous and largely replaced the jobs of many local saints. She and her powerful intercessions on behalf of her patrons could be everywhere (rather than in only one or few places) because, according to church teaching, she had gone straight to heaven, body and all.

Saints in the Catholic Church

Catholics presumably inherited the prohibition of religious icons and figures from Judaism and its scriptures.[217] Nonetheless, the veneration of saints, their relics, and icons began at least by the second century.[218] Despite concerns about reverencing saints and their relics, major theologians of the early church endorsed the practice. At the same time, those theologians and later ones denied that saints and their relics were or could be worshiped. The church's preeminent medieval theologian, St. Thomas Aquinas, also 'confirmed' that God performs miracles in the presence of saints' relics.[219]

Especially after Constantine's adoption of the Catholic Church in the early fourth century, any idea of banning religious icons ended quickly. Pilgrimage sites made and sold pilgrimage souvenirs and typically became sites of major markets and fairs. These sites were profitable ones for the church and its churchmen for hundreds of years, well beyond the timeline for this book.[220] Barro, McCleary, and McQuoid also have shown how sainthood can be viewed as a profit-maximizing economic decision of the Catholic Church.[221] Thus, even if there were some religious motivations, historical evidence and economic reasoning leave little doubt that product credibility and making money were major motives for the church's endorsement and promotion of the role of the saints and their relics in Catholic practices.

Most scholars attribute the start of the boom in saints and relics to the pilgrimage of Constantine's mother, during which she supposedly found remnants of the 'True Cross' in the early 300s, even though her 'discovery' was not added to the story of her pilgrimage until about thirty years after she completed the journey.[222] In any case, a heated race for relics by relic merchants and churchmen had begun by then.

Before the end of the fourth century, notable bishops were strongly promoting cults of martyrs and saints—after all, the saints worked hard for church donations. For example, a major theologian of the early church was St. Ambrose, Bishop of Milan (374-397); he mysteriously discovered local relics and led the procession of them through the city for a religious celebration to welcome them. Others ridiculed these dubious discoveries, but Ambrose had the remains buried in his new basilica within a day.[223]

Saints Compete with Pagan Beliefs

There are ancient roots from earlier religions for the church's economic use of saints and their relics, as Horden and Purcell explain.[224] The ancient religious institutions of Greek and Roman towns hosted fairs and festivals that featured commerce, and they were major landowners that often were wealthy. Just as later would be the case with the Catholic Church, the ancient religious institutions basically justified the economic positions of urban landowners, as their mutual interests overlapped.

It also is clear that the rise of saint cults was not due to any popular movement independent of church leadership, as noted above.[225] Rather, the bishops took control of what could have been considered private religion. And church leaders turned the reputed miracles into publicly shared testimony on the greatness of God working through the saints *and the church*. In this way, the stories could be used to advance the interests of the church. Further, it is clear the church received tremendous wealth to build shrines for saints and martyrs. In a world organized around sin and justice, saintly commerce provided a bonanza of wealth for the church on its toll road to salvation. The Bishops also could use the saints for calming city tensions and increasing their power, as Brown explains:

> "The saint was the good *patronus* . . . whose intercessions were successful, whose wealth was at the disposal of all, whose *potentia* was exercised without violence and to whom loyalty could be shown without constraint. The bishop could stand for him. . . . The Christian definition of the urban community was notably different from that of the classical city. It included two unaccustomed and potentially disruptive categories, the women and the poor. The cult of the saints offered a way of bringing precisely these two categories together, under the patronage of the bishop, in such a way as to offer a new basis for the solidarity of the late-antique town."[226]

After Constantine, the rapid growth of the church also was accompanied by the growth in superstition and the rise of the cults of the martyrs. Clearly, martyrs and saints could be used to compete against pagan practices, as Jones explains.[227] The saints and martyrs replaced the pagan gods, their shrines, their temples, and their old festivals. They also replaced the old gods as the good patrons of their communities. Sometimes the church celebrated Christian festivals on the same days as pagan festivals to compete with and hopefully replace the pagan ones. Although the cults of the saints were a popular movement, they clearly were encouraged by church leaders.

As another example of Catholic competition against the pagans, the shrine to Saints Cyrus and John probably was established by Cyril of Alexandria in the early fifth century, partly to counter pagan pilgrimages to a nearby healing sanctuary of Isis.[228] As Holman explains: "The legend of the shrine's foundation comes from the Vita of the saints . . . and is attributed to Cyril (ca. 427/428). Seeking relics for his campaign against Isis, Cyril was divinely directed to the two sets of bones, buried together in the Church of St. Mark in Alexandia. He prayed, and their identity was revealed."[229]

Saints, especially martyrs, also became important in individual devotional practices and pilgrimages because it was believed that being in touch with their relics conveyed some saving grace to the individual, as Davies explains.[230] The creation of the saints' shrines and chapels was partly a strategic move to displace the worship of pagan gods, but this also opened up the possibility of abuse by churchmen in selling fraudulent relics, even though church authorities tried to be sure relics were authentic. Further, popular saints and their worship competed with and threatened regular church worship, but that problem was strategically countered by moving the saints and their relics into the churches, starting in the fifth century.

Saints and Miracle Stories Enhance Church Product Credibility, Wealth, and Power

Product credibility is essential for the economic success of any organized religion and its leaders.[231] And the saints definitely were leaders of Catholicism, so their credibility had to be established. Miracles were a common element of pagan religions and, based on existing written sources, similar miracles started proliferating in Catholic areas around the middle of the fourth century. Mainly literary rather than historically accurate versions of saints' lives were a popular literary form, hagiography.[232]

Regardless of the historical accuracy of the accounts, these stories were important in establishing the credibility of departed saints as strong proponents of Catholicism and powerful intercessors with God. And frequent miracle occurrences obviously were good business for the churchmen who pedaled sacred objects or services at saints' shrines, as discussed later in this chapter.[233] The writers of these saints' lives also used them for other purposes besides just conveying their miraculous lives, especially for enhancing the authority of bishops and attacking their theological enemies.[234]

Information about saints sometimes was gathered as their relics were collected.[235] Consequently, competing stories about the same saints proliferated, and each was believed by its adherents, if not by their competitors and modern observers. The boom in saints' relics and their stories was stimulated by several factors that included: the need for heavenly intercessors in a world of difficulty and violence; their importance in displaying socioeconomic and political power; documentation of their 'authenticity', so their patrons knew they had healing powers; and enhancing the economic and political power of the churchmen who had them.[236]

Jobs of the Saints [237]

Saints and their relics had many jobs besides the missionary work discussed in an earlier chapter. For example, they answered prayers, healed illnesses, provided protection, stimulated commerce, made altars and churches holy, contributed to military victories, and performed miracles. And they did not work for free, because significant bequests and other contributions were expected in return for their marvelous accomplishments.

Using Saints for Political Authority and Commerce

The discovery of saintly relics was not confined to just a few places and bishops.[238] Brown convincingly argues that a most distinctive feature of the rise of Christianity in western Europe was the ability of churchmen, especially the bishops, to promote the idea of the invisible *potentia* of the saints and their visible earthly representatives, the bishops. By the end of the sixth century, the shrines of the saints had become the centers of ecclesiastical life in most cities of the former western empire. They were believed to be present at their shrines, many of which still were outside of the city walls during the fourth century. But by the end of the sixth century, the boundary between the living and the dead was breached by the relics of many saints, who had entered the cities and Catholic basilicas under the supervision of the bishops. In fact, a very good case can be made that the bishops of the great cities of the former western empire rose to power and wealth in large part because they controlled the tombs of the saints outside their city walls and eventually brought their relics into the cities.[239] This strategic move clearly was good for bishops in mining the profits of sin from their religious customers.

The rise to power and wealth by western bishops on the basis of the saints was not duplicated in other areas of the empire.[240] But wherever western Catholicism went in the Middle Ages, it went with the 'presence' of the saints. In some ways, what saints' cults did was return polytheism to a practical possibility. And this should not be understood simply as popular religion for the masses, as sometimes has been claimed. Indeed, in many ways, the rise of the saints was led by the elite of the church, the bishops. The veneration of body parts, clothing, and other relics of saints became a major devotional practice during the papacy of Pope Gregory the Great (590-604).

From early in church history, Rome distributed relics throughout the West, whereas Constantinople in the East hoarded them.[241] In the seventh century, Constantinople acquired a treasure trove of relics and artifacts—reportedly including over 3,600 items that represented 476 saints. This vast treasure gave Constantinople its sought-after title as the New Jerusalem, a powerful card that was strategically used by the Byzantine emperors for authority and in negotiations. Constantinople's treasury of relics also attracted substantial tourism from pilgrims and travelers. Westerners who visited the city could not comprehend the amazing collections they saw.

At the beginning of the thirteenth century, many of Constantinople's important and valuable treasures became part of the Fourth Crusade's booty after the Roman Catholic Church's (Western) crusaders slaughtered the Christians of Constantinople and looted their city.[242] And many of those relics were turned over to Pope Innocent III, who invoked divine will to justify their theft and movement. In short order, the relics and other valuable treasures resumed their careers by conferring political power and attracting pilgrims in the West, especially Rome.

The fragmentation of saints' relics greatly multiplied their presence throughout the West, and this created commercial opportunities around the centers of pilgrimage sites and saints' shrines.[243] It also became necessary for great churches to have relics in and around their premises to maintain their prestige and revenues. They had to attempt to outdo other places to maintain their prestige and wealth from the donations of their own members and tourists, especially pilgrims.

Catholic rulers also participated in the veneration and use of the saints and their relics for their own purposes.[244] Under the pagan religions of Rome, the rulers had no need for saintly relics because they themselves were considered divinities. Although church teaching was that Catholic rulers were divinely appointed, they certainly were not divinities. Thus, Catholic rulers needed saintly help in ruling their subjects and conducting their military campaigns.[245]

The rise of the cults of the saints in the West also was one of the motives for cashing in on the private ownership of churches and shrines.[246] Aristocrats could 'seal' their status with a saint's shrine on their own property. In addition, the importance of saints in generating donations gave wealthy individuals another reason to enter the market for buying and selling Catholic churches and their revenues.

Saintly Commerce and Profits from Shrines and Pilgrimages

An interesting development for shrines was the restoration of ancient practices from Egypt in which petitioners submitted oracle 'tickets' with two answers to the saint's clerical assistants. Frankfurter explains:

"But from about the fifth century on, pilgrims bringing their demands for clairvoyance and mediation to the holy martyrs at their shrines enjoyed a new means of communication with holy beings: the issuing of oracle 'tickets'. This was a millennia-old Egyptian ritual technique by which one would deliver a question to the god in two alternative written answers. The god, or now saint, would return the correct ticket, which would thereby assume the form of a protective amulet for the recipient. The procedure was aided by scribes and shrine attendants. . . . The requests would be formulated as appeals to God himself, suggesting an ecclesiastical hand insinuating a Christian orthodoxy into this altogether Egyptian ritual practice. . . . But if an earlier age of historians saw this kind of syncretism as tantamount to the smothering of Christianity under heathen ritual, we can now regard such practices as giving sanction and definition to Christianity in the landscape."[247]

Prior to about the eighth century, only a few places and shrines attracted large numbers of pilgrims; for example, the Holy Sepulcher in Jerusalem was the most prestigious one, but it also was remote for most Christians.[248] Pilgrimages became especially popular after the First Crusade (1095-99), and Rome became popular partly because only the pope supposedly could absolve certain, grave sins. Rome and Jerusalem were considered the main attractions, but holy shrines in many other places attracted large crowds, and sacred sites sprouted up along popular pilgrimage routes. Bishops added an array of saints' relics to their churches to attract large crowds and the money that came with them. Incentives to visit certain saints were added by Pope Urban II (1088-1099), when he offered indulgences that supposedly reduced the punishments for the sins of those who would visit certain shrines. Of course, commerce flourished at pilgrimage sites.

Pilgrimages were big business for churches, communities, and shrines by 1300.[249] Part of the popularity was due to the fact that pilgrimages could be used to pay off penances that typically were stated in days. (Penances also could be bought off with payments to the church.) Typically, pilgrims earned 'indulgences' to pay off penances in 40-day packages.

Popular demand for something tangible made pilgrim badges and other souvenirs hot sellers.[250] And it was believed that, if they had been pressed against the shrine, such items had the healing power of the saints themselves. The badges also provided entry into local guilds back home that were dedicated to particular saints, and such guilds provided their members with the economic benefits of access to relationships and business with other guild members. Further, it became fashionable, especially after the Inquisition began in the thirteenth century, to be seen as participating in orthodox religious practices, such as pilgrimages, to refute potential charges of heresy.

The Church did not have a monopoly on saintly commerce because of independent peddlers, so it tried to ensure that the booming business at shrines was directed to churchmen, not others.[251] For example, as pilgrimage practices developed during the course of the twelfth century, it became a requirement to purchase an official church badge from a shrine in order to prove that the pilgrimage had been completed. What this did was create a market for official badges and penances associated with pilgrimages. The market was so lucrative that local bishops entered it, and this heated up the competition for the most effective shrines and relics. All in all, there was fierce competition among sites, because they rose and fell based on the revenue they generated.

By 1300 there were hundreds of pilgrimage sites available rather than just a few special ones.[252] Donations were made directly to saints at great pilgrimage sites, and the church's religious customers could choose donation sizes from as little as paying for candles up to very large endowments—churchmen sold saintly items for purses of any size. Of course, clergy had to assist the saints in collecting and managing those donations as well as the payments for oracle tickets. Consequently, being a shrine manager or attendant could be a highly lucrative occupation.

An interesting and perhaps unintended consequence of the changing commercial practices associated with saints was that many churches suffered serious economic problems because of the decline in pilgrimages to visit and confer with their saints, especially in Jerusalem, southern Gaul, and Spain.[253] The reason was that more pilgrimage opportunities and saintly contacts were available in most local areas because: the bishops had moved saints into their towns, cities, churches, and shrines; monasteries featured and promoted their saints; and the proliferation of shrines on roads that carried enough traffic to support them or by powerful ones who could draw crowds on their own. Thus, many long-distance pilgrimage sites and shrines that previously did a brisk business found that the revenue generated by their saints fell substantially.

Saints' Jobs in Catholic Masses

The saints were present in altars throughout the Catholic domain, so they participated in the masses.[254] Because saints' relics were in the altars, they could directly assist in carrying intentions, prayers, and the sacrifice of the Eucharist to God. And another way to boost the prominence and revenue potential of the saints was to add masses to the annual calendar to honor particular ones.[255] Rome's prominence was increased by emphasizing St. Paul in worship and church teachings, as well as from a large basilica built over his grave during the reign of Pope Damasus (366-84). Later, Pope Leo I (440-61) glorified Saints Peter and Paul as the true patrons of Rome and as replacements for Rome's pagan heroes, Romulus and Remus. Because Saints Peter and Paul were so important in church history, they provided especially powerful help for Rome, its churches, and its popes.

Another aspect of church worship is that feast days commonly were celebrated in churches that had large collections of relics.[256] And such feast days generated additional contributions for the church, as Resl explains, "In order to increase revenue-generating opportunities or enhance the appeal of a specific place, individual institutions introduced additional feasts or acquired new relics. . . . pilgrims were accustomed to leave gifts while attending services at the places they visited. The attraction of such pilgrim traffic was therefore highly desirable; so much so, that relics and claims were forged or fabricated."[257]

Saints' Jobs in Catholic Burial Business for the Wealthy
The holiness of saints and their ability to directly intervene with God on behalf of their petitioners made burial near the tomb of a saint a prized spot. Of course, these beliefs paved the way for a booming business in selling choice burial spots. Thus, by the fourth century and continuing well beyond the Middle Ages, there were strong wishes by Catholics to be buried near a saint, but only the wealthy could afford such important burial spots.

Saints' Jobs for Monasteries
Saints' relics were extremely important for monasteries because they provided protection that was hard to come by with the violence and fragmentation of secular power from the fifth into

at least the eleventh century. The way the protection worked is the belief that attacking a monastery was equivalent to attacking its saint, because the saint would provide due retribution in the next world, if not in this one. In this world, that could include bad crops and natural disasters, and those possibilities led to popular support for protection of the monasteries. It appears that this strategy actually worked fairly well for hundreds of years, especially given the alternatives. And the saints provided other valuable services by inspiring generosity by donors for burial, paid entries into monasteries late in life, insurance against the terrors of purgatory, and other holy services. Strong saints were essential to the economic viability, even survival, of many monasteries for centuries.

Saints Work to Decrease Violence

The medieval world was an extremely violent place. Of course, the violence reduced the productivity and economic value of all resources, including the church's massive holdings of land and those of its wealthy religious customers, so churchmen had an economic motive for less violence within their domains. And Saints could decrease violence simply by their presence. For example, in 989, a synod at the abbey of Charroux was convened that evidently led to what later was referred to as the 'Peace of God' movement. At this and later synods of this movement, the bishops attempted to gather large groups of the laity together to witness the proceedings. The purpose was to prevent violence during specific periods and to secure oaths from the warriors that they would comply.[258] The saints helped too by increasing the solemnity and sacredness of peace meetings with their presence.[259]

These gatherings and the nonviolence oaths did help to reduce the violence that was devastating lives and economic resources.

When Saints Fell Down on the Job

The saints obviously could not always perform the jobs they were given or fulfill every petition they received from their religious customers. What happened when saintly intervention failed to produce the results desired for good health, better crops, victory in battle, or other petitions? The saints' helpers, managers, priests, monks, and bishops had a ready answer. Any failure was because the saint did not wish to help, perhaps for reasons that could not be understood by mere humans, or such intervention was not divinely ordained, because no saint could overcome the will of God. In any case, it was not because the saints had lost their power. Nonetheless, repeated job failures would lead to the search for a new saint, when it appeared that the old one was tired of helping.

Market for Saints' Relics[260]

The many jobs saints could do generated huge demand for them and their services by bishops, priests, monks, and merchants. But there was only a very limited supply of authentic relics from the early saints of Christianity, especially including martyrs, the apostles, and the early evangelists who wrote the books included in the New Testament. In response to the market shortage and rapidly rising prices, relic merchants and thieves stepped in to supply authentic, stolen, and fraudulent relics.

Saints' Relics: Demand and Supply [261]

The demand for relics was fueled by several factors, including the many jobs performed by saints discussed above. And the top leaders of the church definitely contributed to the demand for the saints and their relics. For example, the popes saw the saints as essential for missionary work and in providing sanctity in established and new churches. And some medieval church councils also mandated their use in churches and their altars.[262] In addition, the competition of religious leaders and communities to have the 'best' relics kept the demand for genuine and fraudulent relics booming. There even were some armed battles among different religious groups that were after the same relics.

The supply of especially good relics could not keep up with the demand, because there were only so many apostles, martyrs, and luminaries from the early church. Further, the supply of new saints was curtailed by the Synod of Frankfurt in 794 that tried to bring the invention of fraudulent relics under control by requiring that new saints could be invoked only with the approval of the ecclesiastical hierarchy.

Given booming demand and limited supply, there was a market shortage of good relics, and there were limited ways to satisfy that shortage besides rising prices that would limit the quantity of saints demanded. The main options for acquiring new relics were: the redistribution or new discoveries of saints already located in a place (a rare possibility in medieval times); obtaining permission to acquire 'surplus' relics in ancient places, especially the catacombs in Rome; going to the few places that had an abundance of saints; going to the very few places that had relics of new martyrs; buying them in the market for saints in which

Roman martyrs were especially valuable; and obtaining authentic or fraudulent relics from relic merchants and thieves.

The sellers in the relic market included both churchmen and professional merchants, who were high-class fences or simply grave robbers of authentic or fraudulent saints' relics.[263] Smuggling relics was easy because the whole body of a departed saint could fit in a small bag. Selling Roman relics to buyers from Frankish and English areas was an especially lucrative business. And when distant places were involved, the same saint could be sold more than once. Even though the church repeatedly denounced relic sales, the commerce continued, probably because many churchmen had no interest in actually enforcing the prohibitions and some of them might need new relics. Even the popes benefitted from gifts or thefts of relics from the catacombs because that meant the influence and prestige of Rome and its saints were spreading to more places. Rome also gave up little when saints departed, because they might reappear again when needed.[264] In any case, claims of having the same relics usually were completely discounted or explained away by each of the rivals who claimed them.

Market Shortage Motivates Relic Thefts and Fraudulent Relics[265]

A problem with the product credibility, power, and profits associated with saints was that questionable and clearly fraudulent relics began to explode in many sites throughout the church's domain.[266] Thus, with very limited success, the church sometimes attempted to ensure that only genuine relics were used and venerated. But the prestige and profits of having their own saints—legitimate or not—were simply too great for all churchmen to follow papal decrees, and the papacy was too weak to enforce its decrees. And the historical record makes it clear that the theft and sale of fraudulent relics continued for centuries. Thefts were especially common during the ninth through eleventh centuries.

Relic thefts for the West often were conducted by laymen seeking powerful patrons for their towns, and the victims usually were eastern Catholics, especially the Greeks.[267] The interest in powerful saints by laymen was not just a religious matter, because good saints could create a competitive advantage over other cities for pilgrimage business and tourism. Venice's successful theft of the evangelist Mark's relics from Alexandria in 827 is one famous example. This theft and its elaborate justification to 'prove' that St. Mark wanted to move to his new home in Venice allowed the emerging city-state to successfully: reject the jurisdiction of both Rome and Constantinople and remain independent; deploy Mark's symbol (a lion) as a trademark for its extremely successful mercantile exploits and exports; and use its new saint to boost Venice's tourism and pilgrimage business. Another extremely successful theft for commercial purposes was by Bari, which managed to beat out Venice to claim the relics of St. Nicolas. St. Nicolas stimulated a huge pilgrimage boom up to and through the twelfth century. Merchant communities throughout Europe envied the success of the *Societas Sancti Nicolai*.

But the most monumental thefts of relics by western Catholics were carried out by the Roman Catholic Church's crusaders during the 1204 sack of Constantinople. Vast stockpiles of relics were carried off by the crusaders and taken to the West, especially Rome. And these relics stimulated a large increase in pilgrimages and tourism, especially for Rome.

The theft and movement of relics was not considered morally wrong by the participants and often others, especially when the thefts were by holy monks.[268] And the monks could cite Old Testament passages where trickery, lying, and stealing were used to accomplish divine purposes. But probably the major defense was that relics could not be moved without the saints' permission, so the movement alone justified the saints' new homes.

Good Stories Enhance Value of Stolen Relics

Although there was no universal agreement about the rights and wrongs of the thefts, there had to be justifications because the saintly relics were believed to be living saints who became intimately involved in their new communities.[269] The stories of relic thefts and translations from one place to another were primarily literary rather than historical ones. Although the accounts differed, many have the following elements which, with appropriate modifications, also mostly characterize gifts of relics that were permitted by the original home of the saint:

• A monk or cleric is on pilgrimage and stops somewhere where there are stories of an impressive saint, and he is inspired to steal it in the dead of night.

• He enters the church or shrine, prays, implores the saint to come with him, breaks open the tomb, steals the relics, and returns home. Saints only willingly traveled if they wanted a new home.

• An exciting and eventful trip follows, usually involving a distant place.

• The new saint is greeted by a throng of the faithful in his new home, and the saint starts performing miracles in short order.

- An account of the theft and translation of the saint that included miracles provided credence for the whole process. The accounts portrayed the thefts and translations as ritual kidnappings, because saints were perceived as living saints who willingly journeyed to their new homes.

Although prestigious gifts usually were seen as the best way to acquire relics, it also seems that the justifications eventually placed stolen relics in a higher category than ones simply purchased in the relic market. The stolen ones were more easily justified than the purchased ones and had better stories attached to them. Geary provides a bibliography that contains over fifty separate accounts of relic thefts for the years between 800 and 1000, and he notes that hundreds more were stolen and translated.[270]

Criticisms of Church's Use of the Saints

There were critics of the veneration of saints and their relics both within and outside of the church, as already noted. Frankfurter explains some of the criticism within the church:

"In the fourth century Bishop Athanasius depicted (caustically) the reverence Egyptian Christians held for corpses even if their saintly identities were unclear. The urgency to find ever more saints to sanctify towns inspired, he felt, preposterous relic inventions. Still in the fifth century, the severe abbot Shenoute railed against the continuing popular enthusiasm for finding relics and visiting martyr-shrines. Yet it is at this time that the church embraced the cult of saints in all its fullness: promoting relic inventions and translations; developing liturgies through which people might comprehend their landscape as a veritable network of heavenly patrons; and sponsoring the composition of martyrologies to be read aloud at saints' festivals."[271]

Early in his career as Bishop of Hippo, St. Augustine (d. 430), the early church's leading theologian, also was scathing in his criticism of his 'heretical' Donatist opponents, partly because they 'worshiped' relics from the Holy Land.[272] Around 400, he dismissed the practices of early Christians in recording and preaching the miracles of the saints and martyrs as something that was appropriate for an immature faith but unnecessary for the more mature faith of Catholics. And in 390, he actually wrote that the miracles of the early church were no longer allowed to take place. Interestingly, however, he decided a few years later to use such relics and their miracles in his own sermons to stir the zeal of the faithful, after obviously deciding that miracles still were allowed. In fact, he started to record healing miracles that supposedly occurred in the presence of holy relics and shrines, so the stories could be 'verified' and used by him and other preachers. And there was no shortage of miracles to record—St. Augustine himself recorded seventy in Hippo in less than two years. Part of this change in Augustine's position is explained by his belief that miracles were necessary to 'bend' the 'shocking hardness' of non-believers, as discussed in the last book of his *City of God*.

At about the same time Augustine changed his position on miracles, one of the church's greatest critics of the cult of relics spoke out. But he was rebuked by the more prestigious churchman, St. Jerome, as Rapp explains: "One of the great critics of the validity of the cult of relics was Vigilantius, a priest in Gaul (c. 406). 'Why do you adore and kiss a bit of powder wrapped up in cloth?' he asked, insinuating that this kind of veneration reeked of pagan idolatry. Jerome rebuked him in no uncertain terms: 'If apostles and martyrs while they are still in the body can pray for others, when they should be concerned for themselves, how much more [can they do this] when they have achieved their crowns . . .' "[273]

The booming business in saints and relics also had many other critics through the years, both inside and outside of the church. Vauchez comments as follows on one of its later critics: "Around 1120, for example, the monk Guibert of Nogent . . . vehemently denounced the abuses of certain ecclesiastics who were prepared to exploit popular credulity in order to increase the prestige and revenues of their sanctuary by exhibiting false relics; he expressed his amazement that three different churches in France should claim to have the head of St John Baptist."[274]

In addition to the possibility of abuse in the church's new economy of saints and relics, there also were persistent concerns about the dangers of Catholics reverting to other pagan practices.[275] For example, the synod of Laodicea during the last half of the fourth century prohibited bishops and ordinary clergy from creating and selling amulets with syncretistic inscriptions that blended Christian messages with closely related pagan beliefs. This synod also prohibited bishops and ordinary clerics from being magicians, sorcerers, or astrologers.[276]

Defending Product Credibility of Saints and Relics[277]

The proliferation of saints and holy shrines was of concern to some in the ecclesiastical establishment, and those concerns increased as saints proliferated and criticisms mounted. Thus, churchmen and rulers responded by trying to assure the faithful that the relics of church-controlled shrines were authentic. As a result, Carolingian legislation vested in local bishops the right to authorize cults of saints in their dioceses. However, the legislation's impact varied, depending on the power of local bishops.[278]

The papacy did not take more complete control of the canonization process that leads to sainthood for hundreds of years. In fact, the 993 canonization of Ulrich of Augsburg is often thought to be the first by the papacy. Previously, local saints had been recognized by local bishops, who were interested in having a bevy of saints under their jurisdictions to attract the faithful and increase their own power and wealth. Interestingly, it was the eleventh century before the popes (beginning with Benedict VIII and Leo IX) began regularly and actively participating in the creation of the cults of the saints. Papal participation at that time, however, was an adjunct to established practice, not a replacement for it. And the process of declaring someone a saint was heavily politicized before and after the involvement of the popes.

As the popes were able to exercise more power, the determination of sainthood became another tool of control for them during the eleventh to thirteenth centuries. The papacy took control of the canonization process sometime after Pope Alexander III's twelfth-century decretal asserted that only the pope could permit the veneration of anyone as a saint.[279] The rising prominence of saints from Italian cities after the twelfth century is partly explained by the papacy's sponsorship of the Franciscans and Dominicans who were active in these urban settings as preachers, confessors, inquisitors, and representatives of the papacy's interests. After such service, many were declared to be saints by the papacy.

As part of the Gregorian Reforms, the papacy again tried to bring the abuse of the saints-relics under control. Pope Innocent

III tried to bring the recognition of new saints under papal authority by asserting in the canonization of St. Homobonus of Cremona (d. 1197) that the papacy would approve new saints only after detailed scrutiny. This more rigorous process evidently was first used in about 1185, but its full form was not in place until around 1230. In 1234, Pope Gregory IX relied on an 1172 decree by Alexander III to prohibit the celebration of the cult of a new saint without papal approval. Nonetheless, the practical effect of insisting on papal approval of new saints was limited for hundreds of years, as bishops still instituted new feasts for local saints within their own dioceses until the sixteenth century.

It appears that part of the reluctance of the papacy to more forcefully take control of the canonization of new saints and verification of saints proclaimed by popular opinion is explained simply by the practical realities of religion on the ground. First, it would have been very expensive and probably impossible to verify the validity of relics. Second, demoting local saints who long had been revered by the people undoubtedly would have stirred up a hornet's nest of discontent and anger among the church's religious customers.[280]

Rise of St. Mary as Greatest Saint

The jobs of local saints often were largely replaced during the eleventh-thirteenth centuries by the rising popularity of St. Mary, the church's universal saint.[281] St. Mary had no relics and could live everywhere rather than in only one or a few locations because, according to church teaching, her body had been taken directly to Heaven. The devotion to Mary first was centered in the monasteries, but it spread widely among Catholics. In many cases, prayers were directed to Mary rather than to God, and that naturally raised theological questions that were difficult to answer.[282] But the church's official position was that one could pray to Mary and the saints for intercession with God without worshiping them. Nonetheless, as part of the Protestant Reformation, Luther charged that the pope and his monks had turned the Virgin Mary into a god, who was worshiped. In addition to the much more important role of St. Mary, the increasing veneration of Christ and the Eucharist began diminishing the importance of the departed saints.

Although her cult developed much later than many saints, Mary became the most celebrated saint of all Biblical characters.[283] The church's teaching that she was the Mother of God set her apart from all other saints. She was so supercharged with holiness that she could be localized everywhere, unlike other saints. And once her cult began growing in many places, she acquired even more power.

Conclusion

The Roman Catholic Church promoted and supported the cults of the saints and their relics as one of its many stops on the toll road to salvation. The power of the saints was remarkable, and they received huge bequests and other donations for the many jobs they performed—those jobs included adding holiness to masses, healing, advice, miracles, victories in battles, and many others. But, as with any profitable opportunity, competition heated up among churchmen and communities to have good relics that attracted substantial saintly commerce. That led to a booming market for good relics and a market shortage. Besides skyrocketing prices, problematic responses were relic thefts and fraudulent relics sold by relic merchants. Despite church attempts to control those problems, it was not until the rise of St. Mary as the church's greatest saint that the market for authentic and fraudulent relics subsided. And St. Mary's ubiquitous presence substantially reduced the importance of many local saints.

7

PAYING AT DEATH AND FOR PURGATORY ON CHURCH'S TOLL ROAD TO SALVATION

From early in church history, death bequests and endowments probably were a profitable stop for mining the profits of sin on the church's toll road to salvation. The reason was that, in order to achieve eternal salvation, a final settlement had to be made for all the sins that had not been paid for before death. And later the church invented the concept of Purgatory—that 'place' or state of suffering because of sins before ascending to heaven—to reach beyond the grave for payments. Since sinners who had not fully paid for their transgressions were condemned to suffer in Purgatory, the church allowed for a reduction of that suffering in exchange for payments before or even after death.

Altogether, contributions at death and to relieve suffering in Purgatory undoubtedly accounted for substantial revenue on the church's toll road to salvation. Further, the church had a range of prices that varied with the degree of various sins, and it was able to practice price discrimination to vary those prices according to the ability and willingness of its customers to pay. In short, the church was able to establish policies for death and Purgatory with the aim of maximizing its profits from the sins of its religious customers.

Death and Burial[284]

Last rites and burial were valuable religious services in the Roman Empire long before the Catholic Church began to extract donations from its religious customers.[285] As Hopkins reports, pagan wills had many similarities to later bequests to the Roman Catholic Church and its churchmen, such as: sacrifices or libations at the tombs of the departed; remembrance in a good light by freeing slaves and contributions for public feasts; and giving back some of what had been extracted from the poor.[286] Interestingly, the attempts of Roman pagans to preserve their memories indefinitely by death bequests eventually were doomed by skyrocketing inflation that eroded their value, by the diversion of bequests from their intended purposes by churchmen, and by tomb robbers.[287] These problems were precursors of similar problems later in the Roman Catholic Church.

Catholic Practices for Death and Burial

In pagan Rome, the living and the dead were separated by the walls of the cities—with the dead buried outside of the city walls because of possible contamination of the living.[288] But in the Christian world, the rise of the cults of the saints was most responsible for breaking down the ancient barriers between the living and the tombs of the dead. After all, if departed saints and their relics could reside in cities and churches, why couldn't ordinary humans do the same after death? Once burial customs starting changing in the fourth century, the process of moving the dead into the cities and churches accelerated. By the seventh century, it was very common for bishops to be buried in their cathedral churches. Once this began, burial places corresponded to a perceived moral scale, with the holiest of the dead at the center of the church, often under or near the altar, and others radiating out around them in their order of holiness. The normal order was saints, bishops, abbots, monks, and pious and wealthy lay men and women. Of course, the laity had to make handsome donations for choice places inside of churches. Further, the medieval economy of death replicated the social hierarchy of the living. Thus, poor Catholics in good standing only qualified for burials in modest graveyards.[289]

Funeral practices from early Christianity were fully incorporated as major Catholic ceremonies and sacraments during the early Middle Ages.[290] And those practices often heavily reflected hybrids that combined some pagan and local customs with Catholic norms. Catholics generally shared the belief that the living could and should provide 'refreshment' for the dead and lessen their pains in the afterlife through alms, psalms, prayers, and masses in their names. The wealthiest families could endow their own foundations for burial with the aim of ensuring that a community would be devoted to prayers for their eternal salvation. Full Catholic funeral services generally were reserved for monks, clergy, and rich/powerful laity until about the mid-ninth century.[291]

Mining the Profits of Sin from Death

Much of the church's vast wealth came from death bequests, sometimes in the form of endowments for church institutions, including monasteries that were considered especially holy by lay persons. However, no one knows the exact proportion of its wealth that came from the business of death because the church always has guarded its finances from scrutiny. But the historical evidence indicates burial rights probably were one of the most valuable religious products for sale, because the deceased and their families were concerned to pay up to ensure better chances for salvation. The focus on the moment of death elevated the importance of the last rites (the sacrament of extreme unction), for that was the decisive moment when one would either conquer death or be forever condemned.[292] The church's central hierarchy did attempt, at least in its stated policies, to uphold free choice and no charge for burial in response to complaints from the church's religious customers over simony (charging for religious services, including last rites). However, the papacy ultimately recognized the importance of charging for burial rights as part of the economic viability of its local agents, the bishops and priests. By the twelfth century, the papacy maintained Catholics' rights to choose their burial spots that still depended on their wealth, but it also protected the rights of the burial churches to receive compensation.[293]

The medieval economy of salvation from death bequests was exemplified at the fabulously wealthy monastery of Cluny.[294] It evidently received the largest number of gifts from donors (and buried and commemorated the most monks and laity of any church in the Catholic world). Cluny was especially aggressive in these matters under Abbot Odilo (994-1049), who also first established the feast of All Souls that extended Cluny's salvation assistance to all Catholics everywhere. By the end of the eleventh century, Cluny's monks were almost continuously engaged in services for the dead and prayers for its many thousands of donors. Although many within the church had already started to question the church's economy of salvation, any who did so too stridently and publicly were considered heretics.

Problems with Death Bequests[295]

Problems with death bequests arose for both donors and the church. First, many donors were concerned about whether the instructions in their death bequests would be followed. These donor concerns partly arose because both pagan and Catholic religious officials sometimes ignored the instructions they received in death bequests left for their administration. To counter that problem, many bequests contained very specific legal requirements that had to be followed or they would revert to the donors' then-surviving heirs, perhaps even generations later.[296]

Second, the church sometimes encountered problems in keeping or defending the death bequests it received. The biggest problem was that heirs sometimes legally contested death bequests and endowments contained in the wills of their relatives. But the church usually had a competitive advantage in winning these cases because of its control of the court system. The church also responded to this threat to its donations in another way by encouraging donations by the living. It did this by emphasizing that donations by the living were more valuable for one's soul than death bequests. Nonetheless, it seems that death bequests continued to be the more popular way to buy salvation insurance for the final reckoning.

Competition for Death Bequests

As with most opportunities for profits, the bounty of donations and endowments from providing the last rites set up a fierce competition among churchmen. Bishops and local priests were the first beneficiaries of the generosity of their dying religious customers. However, three new competing groups later vied with them in selling salvation insurance to those approaching death. First, the monasteries emerged as strong competitors, because many of the church's religious customers viewed the monks as holier than ordinary priests. Further, the monasteries had another competitive advantage for death bequests and donations because they could offer a new kind of salvation insurance not available from churches by offering entries into their religious orders to be with the holy monks late in life as death approached. Consequently, powerful monasteries with good reputations had a booming business in selling entries to lay persons as death approached, as Paxton explains:

> "Between 760 and 762, a group of churchmen at the Carolingian royal villa of Attigny . . . . began to allow lay men and women to take vows at the end of life, so as to die in the monastic infirmary and be buried in the community's cemetery, and to record the names of all the participants in books, which grew to include as many as 40,000 entries by the twelfth century. When alms for the poor were added to the psalms and masses sung for the dead, the final piece was in place in the early medieval economy of salvation. . . . They accepted gifts to the poor (among whom they included themselves) in exchange for prayers for the souls of the givers and their dead relatives,

who had been spiritually accepted into the monastic or ecclesiastical *familia.*"[297]

Heretics were the second group competing to serve religious customers as death approached, especially the Cathars and the Waldensians during the eleventh-thirteenth centuries. Many persons viewed them as better bets for eternal salvation, because the considered their clergy as holier than those in the Roman Catholic Church. But the church eventually crushed any serious competition from these heretical movements.

Third, the church approved new orders of mendicant friars, who based their religion on a 'purer' model.[298] Within no more than thirty-forty years of their founding in the early 1200s and not long after the deaths of their founders, the Franciscan and Dominican Orders emerged as strong competitors for death bequests and other donations. Ironically, St. Francis had been especially forceful in his rejection of any worldly wealth, but his order soon benefitted from donations of wealthy persons, despite his teachings. In any case, deathbed sacraments for wealthy persons became a hotly contested battle within the church itself, especially among regular priests, monks, and the friars. In contrast, the poor found it difficult to receive deathbed services in many places.

Evidence from Wills

The ancient wills examined by Murphy are mostly beyond the approximate ending point of 1350 for this book.[299] Nonetheless, they provide some interesting insights into death bequests and donations to the Roman Catholic Church:[300]

• The religious ceremonies for death and your burial place were believed to directly influence your salvation chances. And the requests for burials inside of churches, especially in prominent places (e. g., by the high altar), increased after 1350, particularly in the wills of merchants. Of course, the money left for special burials had to be larger to justify such places of prominence. Poorer testators simply asked for burial in a church cemetery.

- Bequests that provided valuable items for church services were common, as that would guarantee continued prayers for the souls of the departed. For example, a chalice for the blood of Christ was especially valued.

- Good lighting for a funeral and the following days was considered essential for salvation. That required money for wax and candles, sometimes for long periods, according to donor requests and payments. However, the funds did not always serve their intended purposes, as churchmen sometimes pocketed the donations.

- The celebration of thirty masses in quick succession (trentals) was popular in the wills of those with enough money to buy such elaborate remembrances.

- The wealthy sometimes left money for masses and prayers to be held in their memory, supposedly in perpetuity.

- The prayers of hermits and recluses were considered especially effective, so some testators left sums for them to pray for their departed souls, sometimes supposedly in perpetuity.[301]

- Wealthy founders sometimes funded cathedral chapels or altars that were built for their memories and prayers.

- Another type of donation was for 'no-strings-attached' purposes of the church and its charitable work, and such donations were especially favored by churchmen. The mendicant orders often benefitted from these grants intended to secure 'spiritual credit'.

- The friars and Catholic hospitals were prominent among the bequests that did not go to churches and monasteries.

Different Views of Death

The questions at death included how many sins had been committed, how serious they were, and how many still had not been paid for prior to one's last days.[302] One extreme of the church's views of death was provided by many Roman Catholic writers, including monks and the future Pope Innocent III (1198-1216). They went back to scripture to find macabre scenes that detail the gruesomeness of death to the body and promoted the wildly popular view of death, the *danse macabre*. The *danse* caught on throughout all of Catholic Europe during the fourteenth century, and its popularity continued into the fifteenth and sixteenth centuries.[303] The church's grim view of death encouraged larger profits from sin by emphasizing the importance of paying up for sins that had not been redeemed before death.

The opposite view of death was definitely a minority position within the church, but it attracted strong, popular support. That view of death was emphasized by St. Francis of Assisi.[304] On his death bed in 1226, St. Francis may have composed the final verse of his Canticle of the Creatures, and that verse was about the beauty of death that should not be feared because it was part of God's Creation. This view was not popular with most churchmen, perhaps partly because the lack of fear would translate into less leverage in extracting donations from religious customers anxious to pay up for their misdeeds at death. And within only a few years of St. Francis' death in 1226, many of his own followers contradicted his optimistic view of death in their quest to mine the profits of guilt, sin, and death. Despite St. Francis' optimistic views of death, the Franciscans along with the Dominicans were fervent promoters of the *danse macabre* in their mendicant preaching.

Purgatory

Around the start of the eleventh century, the medieval world changed and what could be called a feudal system evolved.[305] The system increased injustices and inequalities for the peasants in many ways, but that was their cost of gaining the protection of their lords from the relentless violence of the age. The church had to respond to these changes and was a part of the changes, for church lords ruled over and provided security to their peasants, just as lay lords did.

The church also reconfigured its interactions with its religious customers to emphasize its carrot and stick in the changing world. The church's stick was Satan, who began to play a greatly increased role in church teaching after 1000. According to church teaching, it was the only earthly power that could intervene with God to prevent eternal suffering. The church's carrot in this scheme was relief in Purgatory, which was fully and officially 'born' to provide some hope for sinners, who included virtually everyone. The new 'place' was a strategically brilliant move because it allowed the church to reach beyond the grave for donations. Those donations could relieve the terrible suffering in Purgatory by paying for sins that had not been absolved by the church at the time of death. Almost everyone needed help with Purgatory's harsh punishments, so it became one of the church's very profitable business lines.

Purgatory was such a booming business for the church because it was wildly popular among the church's religious customers, probably for three reasons. First, it was widely embraced by popular culture. Second, the idea that virtually everyone would have to make a trip there was widely accepted. Third, it represented the final accounting for all of your sins, because no more occurred after death. If one paid up to alleviate suffering in Purgatory, there would be no need to pay again.

Evolution of Roman Catholic Church's Conception of Purgatory

Once early Christians accepted the idea that the end of this world was not imminent, speculation arose about what happened to the departed in the meantime.[306] When it was recognized that the church really was a school for sinners rather than a society of saints, more attention was paid to how sinners could redeem themselves. Le Goff convincingly argues that the emergence of the intermediate place in the church's salvation plan depended upon certain Roman Catholic beliefs, some of which are beliefs of most Christians:[307]

- The dead will be judged.
- There is individual responsibility and free will.
- There could be an intermediate place between Heaven and Hell.
- There is the possibility that the soul could achieve redemption after punishment.
- There is a second chance at immortality for those sinners who could not otherwise make it to Heaven.
- The living are able to ease the burden of the dead through certain holy acts.
- There is immortality after eventual resurrection.

Although the Greeks contributed initial ideas about Purgatory,[308] the major figure in its pre-history is St. Augustine, simply because of his importance as the major theologian of the Roman Catholic Church before St. Thomas Aquinas some eight centuries later.[309] After some changes in Augustine's views, he gave the church the ultimate salvation card—only Catholics could be saved (heretics and schismatics were condemned). Importantly for the church's later use of Purgatory as a revenue-generating device, Augustine argued that the intercessions of a few pious men, especially churchmen, could be effective in helping souls in the hereafter. He also argued that it is better to devote too much rather than too little effort for the dead, another idea that eventually was used to generate profits from Purgatory.

Pope Gregory the Great (590-604) was the last major contributor to the ideas for Purgatory before its full development about six centuries later.[310] He closely followed most of St. Augustine's beliefs, including the following that were important for the profitability of the concept later in church history: salvation possibilities definitely extended beyond the earthly life; the intercessions of departed saints and the faithful on earth could help those awaiting the final judgment; and the church's holy masses were especially powerful in helping the departed who were not beyond salvation.

Purgatory effectively brought the dead into the world of the living in popular culture and as a new order in society.[311] At about the same time Purgatory emerged strongly among church thinkers, Roman Catholic theologians also settled on two categories of sin. They decided that major, deadly, or capital sins could not be redeemed in Purgatory, but minor or venial sins could be. Of course, since virtually everyone had some minor sins, Purgatory provided abundant opportunities for the church to charge its sinful religious customers.

The Logic of Purgatory

Enormous changes occurred in the West from the end of the eleventh to the middle of the thirteenth century.[312] Philosophy and knowledge exploded, the commercial revolution was under way, the church was attempting to reform itself, and European expansionism was in full bloom. In fact, R. I. Moore, a notable historian of the medieval era, has argued that the commercial revolution, which eventually replaced the gift economy with the market economy, was the most fundamental change in western Europe between the invention of agriculture and the industrial revolution.

Pope Innocent III (1198-1216) was a witness of and actor in these momentous changes, especially in reestablishing the power of the church over the new society.[313] The pope was strategically clever enough to do that by adapting to the new society, not opposing it, as church leaders previously had done. And in the process, he established that there would be the church of Purgatory in between Heaven and Hell, consistent with popular beliefs of the time. The theory of Purgatory held that the duration of one's penances depended on God's mercy, the merits accumulated in one's life and, importantly for its revenue potential, suffrages undertaken by the church at the behest of friends and relatives of the deceased.[314] Purgatory became the normal place or state to purify one's soul, and the way to relieve the suffering of that purification process was through the church.

As the thirteenth century progressed, the accountancy of Purgatory fully blossomed, incorporating the long held idea that one's punishment would be proportional to one's sins and merits.[315] For example, the Franciscan, Alexander of Hales, argued that purgatorial punishment had to be proportional to be just, and he confirmed that punishments in Purgatory must be harsher than those suffered on earth. Amazingly, in his complicated passage explaining proportionality, he relied on Euclid's mathematical-geometrical ideas in his *Elements* written in about 300 BC in Greece. In any case, these ideas firmly grounded the church teachings that the price of help for Purgatory's suffering varied directly with the degree of sin and that it was much better to pay for your sins on earth than in Purgatory.

The Scholastics and Friars as Master Doctors of Purgatory

The Franciscans and Dominicans were established early in the thirteenth century, and most of the great thirteenth-century doctors of Purgatory were from their orders.[316] They expanded on the concept in many ways. For example, they explained that purgation obviously was necessary because a very large number of souls burdened by lesser sins could not enter paradise without purification. They even cited earthly apparitions of souls who were serving sentences in Purgatory as proof of its existence.[317] Three thirteenth-century scholastics played major roles in refining the church's thinking about Purgatory--the Franciscan, Bonaventure, and the Dominicans, Albert Magnus and Thomas Aquinas. The major influence was from Aquinas because he was considered the preeminent medieval theologian (and his influence on church teachings continues to this day).

One of Aquinas' main ideas was that Purgatory could benefit most souls, and that meant big business for the church's Purgatory busters.[318] Aquinas also argued that only the pope could dispense suffrage by his own authority. This theory fully extended the power of the pope from this world into the next because, under prior theology, he could send saints straight to Heaven by canonization; and under the new theology, he could eliminate or reduce the punishments one had to endure in Purgatory. This theological framework provided a big boost to the papacy's financial extractions by giving it exclusive powers to reach beyond the grave on its own authority.

St. Thomas Aquinas provided some detailed responses to common questions about Purgatory.[319] And many of his ideas enhanced the revenue opportunities for the church and its churchmen. These ideas include the following:

1. One can offer suffrages, good works, and prayers for the benefit of souls in Purgatory.[320]

2. Suffrages can benefit the damned and the saved, not just those who need minor sins cleansed.

3. The three most effective suffrages are alms, prayer, and the mass through which the church can transmit its merits to the dead, as it does for the living. Further, the most effective masses for those in Purgatory are those that contain prayers for the dead.[321]

4. Good works performed by the living for the dead may contribute to merits for the living in achieving eternal salvation. This idea supported the controversial idea of the 'reversibility' of help between the living and the dead.

5. Burial near a saint can be beneficial to the dead; before and after Aquinas, monasteries and churches solicited payments from the wealthy for such burials.

6. An overabundance of suffrages for one soul may 'spill over' to benefit those who have too few suffrages. Thus, the church's customers need not worry about wasting their payments for those in Purgatory, as someone would benefit.

7. Consistent with the popular culture of Aquinas' time, God allows apparitions to report on their progress in Purgatory and warn the living.

8. Denying the existence of Purgatory or the Church's ability to mitigate Purgatory's punishments amounts to heresy that deserves punishment here on earth.

9. Although God controls Purgatory, the church enjoys a joint authority with God in this new territory.

Aquinas was the key theologian who promoted Purgatory, but Pope Innocent IV was the first pope to make it an official 'place' in Catholic teaching.[322] He did this shortly before his death in 1254 in a letter (*Sub catholicae professione*) he sent to the Greeks in his efforts to reconcile the two sides. This letter made repentance the determining factor in whether one could pay for venial sins in Purgatory or whether one would pay for them eternally. This letter opened up Purgatory as a doctrinally defined concept in Roman Catholic theology. He was careful to leave out some elements of Purgatory that were objectionable to the Greeks, but he asked them to accept his definition, which included a temporary fire that could purge slight and minor sins that had not been absolved by the church. The Greeks rejected this definition and were hostile to the entire notion of Purgatory. All the while, the Roman Catholic theologians of the time seemed to delight in making ever finer distinctions about various types of sins and their associated punishments.

The final result from thirteenth-century efforts was a slightly modified version of Purgatory that does not clarify whether only venial or all sins can be purified there; it appeared as an appendix to the Second Council of Lyons' Constitution *Cum sacrosancta* on November 1, 1274.[323] This 1274 statement is the first assertion of the belief in the purgatorial process, if not Purgatory itself, as an official dogma approved by a council of the Roman Catholic Church. Further, in that statement and the other two that firmly established Purgatory as a Roman Catholic dogma—the Council of Ferrara-Florence in 1438-39 and the Council of Trent in 1563—Purgatory is not defined as a specific place and its punishments are not defined specifically.[324] Nonetheless, there is ample evidence and abundant popular and theological literature that did define the place and the punishment as fire, and those elements fueled the imagination and the success of Purgatory.[325]

By the end of the thirteenth century, Purgatory was everywhere in popular and theological literature, wills, and art.[326] Then, the Jubilee of 1300 opened up indulgences for all of the church's religious customers, not just crusaders and exceptional cases. (Indulgences reduced the suffering one had to endure in purgatory for those sins that had not been paid for on earth. The papacy led the way in selling indulgences.) All of the action in developing the theory of Purgatory meant that manuals for preachers and confessors about Heaven, Hell, and Purgatory started to circulate in Latin around 1200, and vernacular versions started circulating around 1300 (printed versions started circulating after the invention of the printing press in the following century).

Although Purgatory won within the church as a policy, there were critics both inside and outside of the church.[327] The widespread use of indulgences was one reason the 'heretics' of the twelfth to fourteenth centuries criticized the Roman Catholic Church's invention and use of Purgatory. But there also were criticisms from free thinkers within the church. For example, mainstream churchmen were scathingly criticized by Francis Petrarch (d. 1374) for knowing how to define but not how to practice love. This criticism was part of a movement that challenged the idea that God could be so knowable to mere humans in how He would judge man. But the church hierarchy did not accept criticism that it could not affect salvation beyond this world. Thus, the widespread use of indulgences to reduce time in Purgatory continued for centuries.[328]

Mining the Profits of Sin from Purgatory[329]

When the church's monopoly power was eroding during the Middle Ages, Purgatory was another brilliant, strategic weapon for enhancing it. The church's 'power' to reach beyond the grave into Purgatory to aid the dead through its holy intercession was a clever strategy to increase the church's prestige and wealth. The papacy and the mendicant orders of the Dominicans and Franciscans especially profited from selling relief for purgatorial suffering.

The Church also gained a powerful weapon that could be adjusted to fit almost any sin.[330] The twelfth and thirteenth centuries ushered in a detailed 'accountancy of the hereafter' that endured for centuries. That, along with other church teachings about Purgatory, made it possible to charge anything from small to large amounts for relieving different types of sin, depending on the willingness and ability of different customers to pay. But it also provided the church with a good incentive for encouraging its religious customers to live a better life here and start paying up for sins while still on earth, because the punishments here are less severe than those in Purgatory.

The Dominicans and Franciscans were leading merchants of Purgatory during and after the thirteenth century. Their role was enhanced by a bull of Pope Gregory IX (1227-1241) that recommended using them as both preachers and confessors. And that allowed the mendicants to preach anywhere against sins and about suffering in Purgatory. Because they could preach and hear confessions anywhere, they substantially cut into the profits of sin reaped by local priests and bishops, who strongly protested against the invasions of the mendicants. But the mendicants were protected by the authority of the popes to whom they directly reported (rather than to any local bishop). Such authority benefitted the mendicant preachers but also the popes, who evidently received a higher cut of the profits of sin from the mendicants than from local bishops and priests.[331]

As the mendicant friars took on the job of preaching the realities of Purgatory for the church's religious customers, they used examples that called for the faithful to help out the souls in Purgatory.[332] A major purpose of their sermons was to frighten the faithful into recognizing the 'obligations' to their relatives in Purgatory. In fact, the friars had a near monopoly on preaching literature at that time, and they were its supreme practitioners. The Dominicans, Franciscans, and papacy clearly collected substantial revenues from the church's collection booth for Purgatory on its toll road to salvation, as LeGoff summarizes: "But what a gain for the Church in its hold over the faithful! At a time when its power was being challenged . . . the Church extended its power over the faithful into the other world. . . . It administered or supervised prayers, alms, masses, and offerings of all kinds made by the living on behalf of the dead and reaped the benefits thereof. Thanks to Purgatory the Church developed the system of indulgences, a source of great power and profit until it became a dangerous weapon that was ultimately turned back against the Church."[333]

Purgatory also was important in allowing entire groups, such as usurers and merchants, to escape from the 'sinfulness' associated with their occupations and buy a path to Heaven through penances and indulgences.[334] The friars used the lively language of the new marketplace to make their points. They willingly entered into negotiations with their audiences on the appropriate penances for various sins. In short, the papacy made a good strategic move in appointing the Dominicans and Franciscans as the leading merchants of indulgences. Little explains their merchandising approach as follows:

> "Another Dominican writer explained the system of indulgences, which came into more frequent use around 1230, as transactions with the church's Treasury of Merits. For a cash payment, the penitent person could get credit against his penitential debt from the store of supplemental merit and good works on deposit there from the lives of Christ, Mary, and the saints. . . . The friars would not have seen or described what they were doing as buying and selling and pleading and negotiating, but the point did not altogether elude their critics. . . . Matthew [of Paris] was at his sharpest when he likened the friars' traffic in indulgences to the sale of sheep on the wool market. . . . the Franciscans and Dominicans were correspondingly denounced for their avarice, their wealth, their merchandizing, their bargaining—in short, for their similarity to merchants."[335]

Schmidtchen and Mayer also have developed an interesting game-theory model of the Friars' sale of indulgences.[336] They show how the pope could earn greater profits by licensing the friars to sell indulgences in competition with local clergy. In their model, the papacy gains by diverting profits to itself from the local level and by regulating the number of indulgences sold by the friars.[337]

Full Marketing Scheme for Purgatory

Eventually, as the concept of Purgatory fully emerged, stricter accounting developed for the duration of punishments and how much particular indulgences and suffrages helped.[338] For example, the *Golden Legend*, written in about 1260, enjoyed popular success, and it includes Purgatory among its devotional themes. In laying out the principles of Purgatory, the *Golden Legend* provides details on how much one's sentence for various sins can be reduced by various suffrages.

The period just preceding death became extremely important because one had to be in a state of faith and repentance when entering Purgatory in order to benefit from suffrages.[339] The practice of paying to enter monasteries near the end of life to supposedly reach a state of grace became popular, especially among the wealthy who could offer handsome entry 'gifts'. Church authorities usually did not claim that such pious gifts would remit sins, just that the duration and harshness of the punishments in Purgatory would be reduced.

Pope Boniface VIII extended the indulgence mechanism to the entire church, when he announced indulgences for those who became pilgrims to Rome in the Jubilee year of 1300.[340] The Jubilee was a major event in enhancing the status and profitability of Purgatory for the papacy. The church's promoters of the Jubilee emphasized that it was for remission of sins and that it also marked the beginning of a new century. But this chance for penance was tightly controlled by the pope and the Church of Rome.[341] The pope granted pilgrims a 'plenary indulgence', a complete pardon for all punishments in the next world that otherwise would be suffered; previously such full pardons had been restricted to crusaders and exceptional cases. Importantly, this indulgence was extended to include the dead, that is, the souls in Purgatory. This thunderbolt came on Christmas day, and it 'established' the pope's authority to even free souls from suffering in Purgatory, definitely a money-maker for the papacy. The Jubilee indulgences generated an outpouring of money for the embattled papacy.[342]

A little more than a hundred years after its fairly complete conception, the church's merchandising of Purgatory benefitted from a stroke of luck when Dante composed his *Divina Commedia* between 1302 and his death in 1321.[343] Dante's *Divine Comedy* elegantly portrays the widespread belief in Purgatory and its graded punishments for various categories of sin. However, not all of Dante's ideas agreed with official church teaching. What Dante did was bring back Purgatory more as a place of hope that was closer to Heaven than Hell, more consistent with the theology of the twelfth century and away from the theology of infernal suffering during the thirteenth century. In his Purgatory, the mountain trembles in joy at the thunderclap that marks the entrance of each soul into Heaven after serving time in Purgatory.[344] Dante's Purgatory proved to be more popular with the church's religious customers than the official version, but his masterpiece nonetheless benefited the church's Purgatory busters because his version also had souls in Purgatory benefiting from church intervention.

Conclusion

From early in church history, the moment of death was a crucial one in the hope for salvation. Important questions were what sins had been committed, which ones had been forgiven by the church before death, and which ones still had to be paid for to achieve eternal salvation. Once the church had firmly established its position as the only earthly entity that could intervene with God to forgive sins, it was a short step to the idea that payments to the church—which varied with the degree of various sins—could redeem one's sins. Thus, death bequests and other donations became a huge source of revenue for the church.

Later in church history, churchmen invented the concept of Purgatory, which was a novel innovation that extended the church's reach beyond the grave to mine the profits of sin. Many churchmen were concerned about the idea because there really was no solid, Biblical foundation for it. Yet, during the Middle Ages, it came to be a wildly popular concept, both in the church and society as a whole. The church successfully established another collection booth on its toll road to salvation, and it was turned into one of its very profitable ones. The main beneficiaries through 1350 and beyond were the Dominicans, the Franciscans, the papacy, and monasteries that were able to market their prowess in helping both those approaching death and those already in Purgatory.

8

SUBORDINATING WOMEN FOR CHURCH'S WEALTH, POWER, AND DEFENSE OF ITS TOLL ROAD TO SALVATION

Some might argue the Roman Catholic Church's subordination of women is simply explained by historical circumstances, since nearly all ancient societies were patriarchal ones. Nonetheless, women played important roles in early versions of Christianity, and Christian teachings generally portrayed women in a much better light than did competing pagan religions. In fact, women were important in the remarkable growth in the number of early Christian followers. Jesus also had an important role for women in his ministry. And he broke the Jewish norm in his close, public association with some women and his defense of others, such as the woman about to be stoned for adultery. There also is substantial historical evidence of women serving as ordained deacons and even priests all the way into the twelfth century. Thus, the church might have developed with a different model of leadership that included women—especially if it stayed true to the teachings and life of Jesus, who was an outsider in imperial Rome and sought no earthly wealth and power.

However, the elite male church leaders who took over the winning version of Christianity clearly understood—based on their actions and the historical record—that using a religion for wealth and power eventually required the exclusion of women from leadership roles. Moreover, once the male hierarchy emphasized original sin as the basic element of Roman Catholic theology, churchmen claimed women were the genetic carriers of original sin. Such polluted persons surely could not join the 'pure' men in the church hierarchy.

In short, women had at least three strikes against them: ancient societies were patriarchal, the church's basic theology of original sin demeaned them, and the male leaders knew that their quest for wealth and power would be impeded in a church that had women in leadership positions. That is, the subordination of women by male church leaders was not simply an accident of history. Instead, it was a strategic decision to defend its wealth, power, and toll road to salvation.

Features of Christianity in Support of Women

The earliest Christian communities had no hierarchical structure like that of the later church.[345] Instead, early Christians usually met in homes, often those of wealthy members with larger homes in which women evidently were important leaders. And although the later (New Testament) letters of St. Paul often are cited to justify the inferiority of women in the church, those same letters reveal that women had special roles in the early church and were leaders of services in some early Christian communities. Women continued to play important roles in the Middle Ages as educators of children, abbesses, monastic founders, nuns, and canonesses, even though male clergy and monks were in charge of the economy of salvation.[346] Further, as discussed later in this chapter, there is convincing historical evidence that women were ordained ministers of the church all the way into the twelfth century. Thus, through the centuries, many bishops obviously saw women as worthy candidates for holy church service, even at the sacred altar, despite the more common view of the male hierarchy that their gender disqualified them from such service.

Despite its emphasis on the power and role of the father in the family, early Christianity also elevated the status of women in society.[347] Christian women could travel, donate their wealth to the church, found monasteries, and they had more freedom than pagan women in publicly moving about without male supervision. Families, marriage, and faithfulness in marriage were honored in Christianity. In contrast, pagan religions had no restrictions on male infidelity, but infidelity by a woman was a grave transgression in ancient Rome. As Alexandre explains: "Women enjoyed power as donors and founders. . . . The generosity of widows had long been an important source of wealth for the Church. . . . Most important of all, women's power from the inception to the final victory of Christianity lay in communicative character of their faith. . . . often women seem to have been in advance of men from the same family. Their influence at home encouraged others to convert, so that women played a crucial role in the transmission of the faith." [348]

The importance of St. Mary also increased during and especially after the fourth century.[349] Her elevated status signaled an important change for the image of women—Eve had been the cause of the Fall, but Mary was the Mother of Christ. For example, the Catholic Church was portrayed as the bride of Christ. Positive female attributes of beauty, tenderness, and constancy were used to describe female saints, especially Mary. Nonetheless, ordinary Catholic women still continued to be compared to Eve, and they were inferior to men in law, family authority, and the church.

Economic Motives and the Ultimate Subordination of Women

Despite the possibility that the institutional church might have included women in ordained ministries and other leadership positions, the dominant opinion of the male hierarchy about a century after the time of Jesus was that women should be subordinated. The basic issue quite clearly was that economic motives for wealth and power had risen in importance for church leaders, even though Jesus emphasized that wealth was in the next world, not this one. Although church leaders often preached Jesus' basic message, they constantly contradicted it in their actions and policies. If the church's leaders instead had been satisfied with the status of outsider—as Jesus was—then women easily could have been included in the leadership structure, as was the case in some heretical forms of Christianity.

The movement of the Catholic Church away from Jesus' position as an outsider in imperial Rome is not so surprising, because it originated and grew into a mighty force within Roman society. In that society, women were not included in public positions of power and authority.[350] And as Alexandre explains:

"An elaborate argument was developed to justify limiting the role of widows and deaconesses. The Apostolic Constitutions [written near the end of the fourth century] attributed the following to the Apostles themselves: 'We do not allow women to teach in the church. We allow them only to pray and listen to the masters. . . . For woman is the body of the man, extracted from his flank and made subject to him from whom she was separated for the purpose of producing children (Genesis 2:21-23). And it is written that he shall be her master (Genesis 3:16). . . . It was out of impious ignorance that the Greeks ordained priestesses . . . In Christ's law no such thing is possible . . . .' "[351]

Another reason for relegating women to less important roles in the Catholic Church was that women were prophets in early Christianity, and both female and male prophets posed dangers for the religious product credibility of the church and its hierarchy. As Catholicism was evolving to become the dominant form of Christianity, prophecy was considered a gift for the *people* of God. In the New Testament, there are references to *female* prophets in Paul's Corinthian Letters, Luke 2:36, and Acts 21:7-9. Female prophets also are reported in other early sources.[352] However, prophets of either gender could see things quite differently than the Catholic Church hierarchy. Prophets sometimes derided the church and its hierarchy for displaying wealth and splendor in this world rather than focusing on spiritual truth. Clearly, such dangerous criticisms had to be suppressed or, if possible, eliminated. Thus, prophecy was subsumed under the authority of male Catholic bishops in order to prevent its use against the church. And that move essentially suppressed female prophecy within the Roman Catholic Church, although rare exceptions continued, especially including some female saints who were prophetesses.

Another aspect of subordinating women was that wealthy widows often were viewed as economic commodities by men, who saw them as hot properties from early in church history.[353] Such cases were not rare because women typically married at much younger ages than men, early deaths were common, and young widows were not unusual. During the early Middle Ages, abductions, even from monasteries, of wealthy widows (referred to as ritual kidnappings) by men interested in their wealth also were not unusual. Although bishops routinely railed against such practices, some still were willing to declare a widow's subsequent marriage valid, if her parents consented and the man did penance for the abduction. Consequently, it was not difficult for the kidnappers to have such marriages declared valid by church authorities, regardless of the wishes of the women involved.

Subordinating Women in Christian/Catholic Literature

The way Christian literature evolved also helps explain the subordination of women in the church's official record. The written record of Christianity for at least the first one thousand years was produced by an elite few, mostly males. During those many centuries, only a tiny percentage of the population was literate, and literacy was restricted mainly to males. The elite male writers of Catholic Christianity made sophisticated arguments in favor of an institutional hierarchy of males who could control the church with absolute authority. For example, the earliest writings included in the New Testament are the first-century letters written by St. Paul or attributed to him.[354] They show how women were and still are portrayed in the church's own canon of sacred scripture:[355]

>I Corinthians 14:34-35: 34 Let women keep silence in the churches: for it is not permitted them to speak but to be subject, as also the law says. 35 But if they would learn anything, let them ask their husbands at home. For it is a shame for a woman to speak in the church.

>I Timothy 2:11-14: 11 Let the woman learn in silence with all subjection. 12 But I suffer not a woman to teach, nor to use authority over the man: but to be in silence. 13 For Adam was first formed; then Eve. 14 And Adam was not seduced; but the woman, being seduced, was in the transgression.

>I Corinthians 11:3-9: 3 But I would have you know that the head of every man is Christ: and the head of the woman is the man: and the head of Christ is God. 4 Every man praying or prophesying with his head covered disgraces his head. 5 But every woman praying or prophesying with her head not covered disgraces her head . . . . 7 The man indeed ought not to cover his head: because he is the image and glory of God. But the woman is the glory of the man. . . . 9 For the man was not created for the woman: but the woman for the man.

Early Christianities also had many voices besides the official ones in the New Testament. In particular, there were many stories of Jesus and his apostles by a group of writers collectively referred to as Gnostics, who were considered heretics by church leaders. Although Catholic Church leaders suppressed the Gnostic Gospels and destroyed the copies they found, some surviving copies were discovered during the twentieth century.[356] They have been translated into English and now are widely available. All Gnostic Gospels were excluded from the New Testament by church leaders, probably for at least two reasons. First, some of them suggested there was a path to God for individuals that did *not* run through the institutional church. Second, there is a much stronger feminine influence in the Gnostic Gospels than in the New Testament Gospels. For example, Bishop Irenaeus (d. 202) noted with dismay that heretical groups of Gnostics were especially attractive to women.

The reform movement of the mid-eleventh century onward also had a thriving literature of contempt for this world that demeaned women.[357] Of course, most of this literature was written by males, many of whom were in the monasteries, so it perhaps is not surprising that women fared especially poorly in it. The writers devoted lurid sections to the woes of marriage, women, child-rearing, and family life. For example, a famous eleventh-century church writer, Peter Damian (d. 1072), was especially harsh in his condemnation of women and their evil for churchmen—he referred to them as 'appetizing flesh of the devil, bitches, harlots, prostitutes, and witches'. But he was not alone. The effects also reached into broader society and included: popular anger against married priests and their wives, who sometimes were beaten or driven from town; and the flight of thousands of men and women from the 'impurity' of marriage to the 'purity' of a monastery.

St. Mary, Virginity, and Original Sin

During the fourth century, the importance of virginity as a holy trait for women increased and the Cult of St. Mary began, along with the Catholic dogma that she was ever virgin.[358] The Cult of St. Mary reached its height when she was declared to be the Mother of God and ever virgin at the Council of Ephesus in 431. Although that added a distinctly feminine presence to Catholicism, the idea that St. Mary is ever virgin and immaculately conceived (to avoid the stain of original sin) had other impacts that negatively affected the image of ordinary women, because they were compared to Eve rather than St. Mary. Eve and *all* other women are the bearers of original sin in that thinking. Such evildoers surely were not entitled to the wealth and power that came with positions of leadership in the church.[359]

The above ideas, combined with the church's basic theology (St. Paul's idea of original sin later developed in more detail by St. Augustine and further refined by St. Thomas Aquinas) precluded the possibility of women infiltrating the male hierarchy of the church. Once original sin served as the foundation of Roman Catholic theology and the male leadership's focus was on wealth and power, it was a short step to subordinating women, if not abhorring them. For example, the church's first council acknowledged as official occurred in Elvira in about 307, and it had several canons that reflected the inferiority of women.[360] The position of many churchmen was stated even earlier by Tertullian early in the third century, as explained by Alexandre: "In 'The Grooming of Women' Tertullian berates his female readers and reminds them of the third chapter of Genesis: 'You . . . are under your husband's spell, and he is your master. And do you not know that you are Eve? She still lives in this world, as God's judgment on your sex. . . . The devil is in you. . . . You were the one who deceived man . . . . For your wages you have death, which brought death even to the Son of God. . . .' "[361] In short, the church's conception of original sin led to the contempt for or hatred of women and girls.[362] However, it still was the case that powerful women exercised enough influence to infuriate churchmen. For example, John Chrysostom [d. 407] battled with Empress Eudocia and her group of powerful widows until he was exiled by the emperor.[363]

Other 'Defects' of Women

The discrimination against women began very early in church history, and it continues even up to today in some ways. As Rubin and Simons explain for the period of about 1100 to 1500, medical, theological, and legal thought all combined to develop, ". . . a robust and commonly held official wisdom about the inadequacy of women to think, to make moral judgements, to endure hardship, to exercise authority, to lead."[364] A gender hierarchy was pervasive in literature, homilies, and canon law during the 1000-1500 period. According to this thinking, women were inferior to men in significant ways that made them unsuitable for leadership positions.[365] For example, much like the male leaders of Judaism, many churchmen were especially concerned with the possibility that menstrual blood and childbirth could contaminate the sacred rituals and spaces.

By the twelfth century, even the rituals of death in many places required gender distinctions to denote the inferiority of women.[366] The custom of ringing the passing bell to denote the death of men and women distinguished between them by using three rings for men but only two for women. Since men supposedly resembled the Trinity, they needed three rings, but women only needed two rings because they represented the separation of God and humanity due to Eve's original sin that led to the fall of humanity from its original paradise into a world of misery. The distinction was justified as well because women had traits that were attributed to Jews and other heretics—they were feminine(!), soft, concubines, and prostitutes.

St. Thomas Aquinas was the church's master theologian of the Middle Ages, and his work came to dominate official Roman Catholic thinking at least up to the Reformation of the sixteenth century and, in many ways, up to today.[367] And he cemented the inferiority of women in official church thinking. Following the pagan Greek philosopher, Aristotle, he argued that women were deficient in reasoning and that their particular nature was defective and accidental (which was a reference to Aristotle's belief that women actually were misbegotten or deformed males). Of course, medieval scholars also used selected verses in St. Paul's New Testament writings to confirm the inferior status of women and the 'impossibility' that they could teach men or have any authority over them. In the process of subordinating women, they also had to dismiss the many references to Jewish prophetesses in the Old Testament as anomalies God had allowed before Jesus came as the new covenant to replace the imperfections allowed in the past.

It is interesting to note how the issue of subordinating women has played out after 1350. Even with immense changes in society and the status/roles of women during the first two thousand years after Jesus, Popes Paul VI (1963-1978) and Bendict XVI (2005-2013) still strongly repeated the argument against ordaining women that was made by their male forefathers from the medieval church.[368] In contrast, Pope Francis (2013-) appears open to increasing the role of women in providing sacred church services—in August, 2016, he created a commission of six men and six women to study the possibility of ordaining women as deacons in the Roman Catholic Church.[369] But there are no public recommendations from that commission as of May, 2017.

Women as Ordained Ministers
Actively Serving the Church[370] [371]

The fractured position of the church on women is perhaps most clearly illustrated by how the male hierarchy approached women as ordained ministers of the church—an issue that especially has been brought to light by Macy and others who have investigated many original documents and sources. Obviously, the inclusion of women as holy and ordained ministers shows they were valued members of official and sacred orders of the church. However, there always were tensions about their inclusion and roles.

In the early church, Christians adopted the concept of *ordo* from common usage, so ordination meant the appointment to a particular task or function in a particular community and not, as ordination came to mean during the twelfth century, an irrevocable spiritual power that could be exercised in any community.[372] Also, it clearly was *not* the case in the early church that only male priests could conduct liturgies. Women performed many of the functions reserved only to male priests and deacons after the twelfth century.

The ordination of nuns in the early Middle Ages included the same three key elements involved in the monastic vows of males—obedience to authority, a life of poverty, and a chaste life.[373] But for nuns, chastity involved an additional condition, for they were considered the 'brides' of Christ. In fact, chastity was considered so important for nuns that churchmen taught chastity was mandatory for their salvation, although chastity evidently was not required for the salvation of churchmen.[374]

All the way into the twelfth century, ordinations of women did occur under procedures used for the valid ordinations of *both* men and women at the time. However, since the twelfth century, official church history, theology, and canon law has wiped out historical traces of the ordination of women. The official position taken in rewriting the history of ordained women in the church is that *valid* ordinations of women never occurred, even though the ordinations discussed throughout this section were considered valid in their own historical context and certainly by contemporaries, including the male bishops who ordained women for holy service. The trick in denying that ordinations ever occurred or even could occur for women was that the church's definition of ordination was changed during the twelfth century. Based on the new definition, which churchmen claimed applied retroactively, the male hierarchy then excluded women from the ancient practice of ordaining them.[375] Thus, only men were blessed with valid ordinations.

Women Deacons

Despite the Roman Catholic Church's new definition of ordination that excluded women, dozens of references to women deacons into the twelfth century have been documented in several scholarly studies.[376] Women served as deacons until at least the eleventh century in the East and until at least the twelfth century in the West. In fact, until the change, ordination rites for men and women as deacons and deaconesses were essentially identical.[377] Despite any attempts to eliminate traces of women in ordained service, especially at the altar, there still is substantial evidence of women deacons in the Catholic Church that includes:

1. The earliest reference to women deacons is in the first-century Letter of Paul to the Romans (16:1-2), where he refers to Phoebe

as a deacon of the church at Cenchreae. He also states that 'women likewise are deacons' in I Timothy.

2. The most famous woman deacon in the West was Queen Radegund, the wife of King Clothar I (511-558). She left the king around 550 and demanded that the Bishop of Noyen ordain her as a deacon. The bishop ordained her, despite his fears of reprisal from the king.

3. Bishop Remigius of Reims left a testament in the early sixth century that granted part of a vineyard to his 'blessed daughter, Helaria the deaconess.'

4. Surviving memorials have been found for three deaconesses of the sixth century—Anna of Rome, Theodora of Gaul, and Ausonia of Dalmatia.

5. The Merovingian bishops of roughly ancient Gaul continuously tried for almost one hundred years to ban the order of women deacons in the West (the Morovingians ruled from about the middle of the fifth to the middle of the eighth centuries).

6. The emperor Justinian (527-565) was concerned about supporting the huge number of ordained clerics in Constantinople, so he declared that the staff should be set at the 'ancient number' of four hundred and eighty-five clerics and forty deaconesses.[378]

7. The seventh-century *Life of St. Sigolena* describes her consecration as a deaconess after the death of her husband, although some scholars believe this story is copied from Queen Radegund's.

8. In a charter from 636, Deacon Grimo of Trier refers to his sister Emengaud as a deaconess.

9. Pope Gregory II wrote three surviving letters to women deacons between 715 and 730.

10. When Pope Leo III returned to Rome in 799, he was greeted by a huge crowd that included the women deacons of Rome.

11. The eighth-century liturgical book of Bishop Egbert of York has written instructions for the ordination of women deaconesses.

12. The Gregorian sacramentary of the ninth century has the same prayer for ordaining a female deacon as that in Bishop Egbert of York's book from the prior century.

13. The Council of Rome (826) prohibited illegal marriages, including those to 'holy women and deaconesses'.

14. The decrees of the Council of Paris (829) decried the practice of women who were distributing communion and doing other things that would be 'shameful to mention'.

15. The church's ninth-century Pseudo-Isidorian decretals prohibited the marriage of deaconesses.

16. The tenth-century Romano-Germanic Pontifical has the complete liturgy for the ordination of a woman deacon, and the rite for women was conducted during the Mass. The ritual also includes a prayer that states the office of deaconess was instituted by the apostles for the instruction of young women. An almost identical liturgy is contained in the twelfth-century Roman Pontifical.

17. In 1018, Pope Benedict VIII gave the cardinal bishop of Porto the right to ordain women deacons. This privilege was again granted by Popes John XIX in 1025 and Leo IX in 1049.

18. In 1026, Pope John XIX gave the bishop the right to consecrate deaconesses for Leonine City, and Pope Benedict IX continued the privilege in 1037.

19. Women deacons existed in the diocese of Lucca, Italy at least up to the reign of Bishop Ottone (1139-1146).

20. Abbesses were considered deaconesses by many twelfth-century church writers, especially because they could read the Gospel during liturgies.

21. The famous twelfth-century theologian, Abelard, and his wife, Heloise, both referred to her as a deacon.

22. Gratian's famous *Decretum* was available in 1130 and revised in 1150. It became the standard for canon law and a key part of church law until at least the sixteenth century. Despite the changed definition of ordination during the twelfth century, five references to presbyterae and deaconesses managed to find their way into the *Decretum*, but they simply were ignored by churchmen.

Abbesses as Deaconesses

Abbesses also served the same roles as deacons in the West, as noted above. Several rites for the ordination of abbesses have survived and, as with deaconesses, their ordinations occurred during the Mass. Their ordinations included the laying on of hands by the bishop, and the new abbesses received the signs of their office from the bishop. During the ninth and tenth centuries, some church commentators on canon law explicitly referred to abbesses as female deacons. This is not surprising because abbesses taught young women and sometimes even young men, read the Gospel, and sometimes distributed communion. They also heard the confessions of their nuns, gave them penances, and reconciled them back into the community.[379]

Women Priests and Bishops

More surprising than the evidence of female deacons is the surviving evidence that women also served as *presbyterae* (women priests):

1. There are five known inscriptions to *presbyterae* dated from the fourth through sixth centuries (two from Italy, one from Potiers, and two from Croatia).

2. In 743, Pope Zachary prohibited anyone from physically joining himself to an abominable consort like a *presbytera* or deaconess.

3. Pope Leo VII (c. 937-939) repeated the 743 prohibition of Pope Zachary.

4. The male bishops at the Council of Paris in 829 were appalled that some provinces continued to flout divine law by having women serve at the altar and, worse yet, serve the sacred body and blood of the Lord to the community.

5. The tenth-century Romano-Germanic Pontifical has an interesting reference to the blessing of presbyterae.

6. Women continued to distribute communion into the eleventh or perhaps twelfth century, despite many church injunctions against women serving in that role.

Not only are there known references to women priests, there are references to *episcopa* or *episcopissa* (female bishop), as Macy explains:

> "There are only five known references to women bishops in Western Christianity. By far the most famous is the ninth-century mosaic of 'Theodora espiscopa' in the Chapel of St. Zeno in the Church of Santa Prassede in Rome. An inscription on a reliquary in the same church identifies Theodora as the mother of Pope Paschal I (817-824). . . . A

tomb dating sometime between the fourth and the sixth century is inscribed to the 'venerable woman, *episcopa* Q.' . . . Brigid of Ireland was described not only as a bishop but also as having successfully undergone ordination to the ranks of the episcopacy. . . . Hildeburga, the wife of Segenfrid, bishop of Le Mans form 963-996, was described as an *episcopissa* in the account of Segenfrid's death."[380]

Why Were Women Ever Ordained?

Why were women ever ordained in a church ruled by a male hierarchy that generally was suspicious of women, even overtly hostile to the idea that women could perform the sacred duties at the altar? First, there was very little centralized control of house churches in the first 50-100 years after the time of Jesus. Second, there was no all-powerful papacy that could enforce church doctrines and policies throughout the Roman Catholic Church until the twelfth-thirteenth centuries. For about the first one thousand years of church history, bishops had much more discretion over policies in their realms, so much more diversity existed in different areas than was the case thereafter. In particular, some bishops and even some popes clearly valued women as holy servants in ordained ministries. Finally, another reason is suggested in a fascinating letter by the tenth-century Bishop Atto of Vercelli—he acknowledged that ancient laws included women priests and deacons, but he asserted that their inclusion was only because of a shortage of males to serve their communities.[381]

Defining Women out of Ordination During Eleventh-Twelfth Centuries

At the Benevento synod called by Pope Urban II in 1091, the first canon asserts that: the sacred orders of the church are only for male deacons and priests; and those are the only sacred orders 'the early church is read to have had' and the only ones based on 'the commands of the apostles'.[382] This canon reflects the popular opinion among eleventh-century reformers that Jesus established only those two orders, which were only for men. This canon was included in Gratian's *Decretum*, which was first available around 1130 and revised in 1150.[383]

The exclusion of women from sacred service at the altar also reflects the fact that Jewish purity laws took full force in official church thinking during the twelfth century. Thus, the male hierarchy believed that women were unsuitable for sacred church work because of menstruation and childbirth—the association of blood with the sacred rituals of the altar is forbidden in this view.

The claim that women never were ordained even was extended to argue that St. Paul never intended to include women in any sacred ministry of the church, even though he refers to the deaconess Phoebe in his Letter to the Romans, and I Timothy also states that 'women likewise are deacons'.[384] The twelfth-century theologians argued that to read these Pauline texts to mean that women were ordained ministers of the church was heretical, because Paul did not actually mean what the texts plainly say.[385]

In about the middle of the twelfth century, the canonist Rufinus developed an argument that redefined ordination in a way that could be used to deny that women had ever been validly ordained in the church. He argued that a valid ordination was an ordination to the altar in *any* community, not a *particular* community. This new definition changed a thousand years of references to the ordination of women into the mere 'commissioning' of them for specific tasks in specific communities. In contrast, real ordination gave the priest or deacon the power of the altar in any community—it was a divine power that could be granted only to men. Rufinus' definition became the church's official definition of ordination and was retroactively applied to all prior church history, despite the historical evidence that ordination was not defined that way until the twelfth century. As Macy explains, "In one of the most successful propaganda efforts ever launched, a majority of Christians came to accept that ordination had always been limited to the priesthood and the diaconate and that women had never served in either ministry."[386] Churchmen went on to argue that, even if ordinations had occurred, they were not valid and would not 'take' because only men could be divinely empowered through ordination to the altar.

The new definition meant that women in church service were laicized. It was not in the interests of the male hierarchy to preserve a history of women that did not accord with the new view that women never had been validly ordained. Thus, the most interesting aspect of this attempt to rewrite church history is how much evidence of the ordination of women still survived in various forms.

The male church reformers triumphed in effectively removing any possibility of women continuing to serve at the altar—unless the church were to return to its ancient roots when women were ordained and served in liturgical roles thereafter reserved only for male priests and deacons. However, the evidence should not be romanticized, for there is no surviving record of any period in the early church (and clearly none after the second century) in which men and women served as equals in the church. Macy summarizes the final outcome of the exclusion of women from ordained service in the church:

> ". . . twelfth-century writers moved from conceding that women were once ordained, to teaching that women never were ordained, to teaching, finally, that women never could and never would be ordained. This final position is what canon lawyers and theologians would teach for the rest of the Middle Ages. . . Within roughly a century, women lost all standing as ordained clergy. . . . It was metaphysically impossible for them to be ordained, to have been ordained, or to ever be ordained."[387]

Why Remove Women from Ordained Status?

The previous discussion provides many reasons for excluding women from ordained service, and they were relied on by the male reformers of the eleventh-thirteenth centuries. Further, it is clear that the reformers were not only concerned about spiritual renewal and reform, because they were motivated partly, perhaps largely, by economic incentives to maintain/defend their wealth and power and that of the Roman Catholic Church in a society that had come to deride the church and churchmen for laxity and corruption.[388] In the process, the reformers strongly and successfully argued for a purer church and priesthood. That meant only celibate males were qualified to serve in ordained ministries, especially at the altar.

Related to the purity argument, the theology of transubstantiation that Catholic priests change ordinary bread and wine into the body and blood of Christ at the altar was strongly evolving among church authorities by the twelfth century and became an official dogma of the Roman Catholic Church at its Lateran IV Council in 1215. The male reformers could not envision how a woman could 'correctly' perform service at the altar, let alone participate in transubstantiation. This provided yet another reason for excluding allegedly impure women from altar service.[389] Macy summarizes the overall effect on women as follows:

". . . the attacks by the reformers on both women and [lay] lords could be seen as part of the larger struggle to define and defend an exclusive claim for sacred power. . . . The issue was power. Both women and [lay] lords had ancient claims to the ordained state, and the leaders of the reform movement denied both sets of claims. . . . All sacramental power was consolidated into the hands of the presbyterate, and the presbyterate defined itself to be exclusively male and celibate. Laity were . . . dependent on the priesthood for their salvation. . . . Ordination was redefined as sacral power, and women, even religious women, were no longer defined as capable of exercising such power. . . . The effects of this revolution on women were devastating. . . . [but] both men and women did escape the definition of women created by the clerical and intellectual elite. This was, after all, an intellectual construct and, in some ways, wish fulfillment on the part of a male elite. It never completely corresponded to reality."[390]

Conclusion

The standard explanation for the subordination of women in the Roman Catholic Church is that ancient societies and especially imperial Rome were patriarchal. Although that is part of the explanation, it alone would ignore the clear economic motives of male churchmen in subordinating women. Had the male leaders followed the example of Jesus, who was a notorious outsider in the Roman Empire, there would be no compelling reason to subordinate women—either in the early church or when women were finally defined out of ordained ministries by the male hierarchy during the twelfth century. However, a religion without product credibility among its religious customers can not generate wealth and power for its leaders. And the historical record shows that the male leaders of the church ferociously defended the product credibility of their religion for wealth, power, and defense of their toll road to salvation.

Once the twelfth-century male hierarchy developed its rationale for subordinating women, it could not be changed without calling into question the myth that church teachings and decisions are the truth. Of course, that new definition contradicts the historical evidence of women in ordained ministries up to the twelfth century. But the hierarchy has no problems with selective memory, as Macy explains: "The memory of ordained women has been nearly erased, and where it survived, it was dismissed as illusion or, worse, delusion. This was no accident of history. This is a history that has been deliberately forgotten, intentionally marginalized, and, not infrequently, creatively explained away."[391]

On the other hand, should the church really return to its ancient roots nearer to the time of Jesus, rather than just the church history that was cleansed of women in ordained service during and after the twelfth century, then women also could return to ordained service. The ancient church included them as deacons serving at the altar and even as priests and bishops. Interestingly, the Greek Orthodox Church also eliminated women as ordained ministers during the eleventh-twelfth centuries, but they decided to restore the female diaconate in October, 2008.[392] Further, unlike previous popes in the modern church, Pope Francis (2013-) appears open to increasing the role of women in providing sacred church services—he created a commission of six men and six women in August, 2016 to study the possibility of ordaining women as deacons in the Roman Catholic Church. But there were no public recommendations from this commission as of May, 2017.

9

REFORMING CHURCH FOR WEALTH, POWER, AND DEFENSE OF ITS TOLL ROAD TO SALVATION

Criticism of the church and its corruption was a persistent threat to the church's product credibility, wealth, and power by the eleventh century. Consequently, it responded in various ways, many of which it had used for centuries. It did this partly by more aggressively identifying and attacking 'evil others', particularly through the Inquisition and the crusades. But the church also introduced and implemented several reforms, some more successfully than others. The ones discussed here are those that clearly had economic incentives as main motives. These include:

• Incentives for reform.

- The problem of simony, the sale of spiritual services and religious posts/roles.
- Imposing celibacy on all priests to eliminate or at least reduce clerical marriage and concubinage.
- Imposing celibacy to prevent clerics from passing on church posts, wealth, and property to their heirs.
- Imposing celibacy to signal a 'purer' priesthood and help in reclaiming churches, church revenues, and church property from private parties.
- Imposing celibacy to signal a 'purer' priesthood in order to greatly reduce the power of lay rulers in appointing high clergy, especially powerful bishops and popes.
- Reducing the economic and political power of monasteries, while still retaining their role in enhancing the overall product credibility of the church.

Although the church attempted to force major reforms for hundreds of years, the first sweeping reforms began with the Gregorian Reforms, which were named after their originator, Pope Gregory VII (1073–85).[393] The church always has featured them as religious reforms, but major reform goals clearly involved wealth, power, and papal control of the church rather than religious 'purity' for the sake of the faith. Regardless of the main motives and given the corruption of the church and its churchmen, the notion of clerical reform and purity resonated across normally divided strata of society. However, it was difficult to fully implement the reforms for two related reasons. First, the papacy did not have enough power to successfully force the reforms down to the local level. Second, the local agents of the church typically had quite different incentives for implementing reforms, as their economic interests were not fully aligned with those of the central hierarchy—and that principal-agent problem is encountered in most large organizations. Consequently, many of the reforms reduced but did not eliminate the problems targeted. But the overall impact was to fundamentally alter many practices and, together with other strategies, largely defend the church's substantial monopoly power until Luther's successful revolt and the Protestant Reformation in the sixteenth century.

Incentives for Reform

The wealth, power, and corruption of the church and its leaders were the focus of critics, both inside and outside of the church. And those main criticisms were enhanced by: the diversity in Catholic practices that appeared to be heresy to many; and socioeconomic changes that resulted largely from the second commercial revolution, which started around the start of the tenth century.

The incentives for reforming church practices also came partly from religious concerns, especially among some monks concerned about ritual purity. But the other main motive—and one that was intertwined with religious concerns—clearly stemmed from concerns about the church's religious product credibility, wealth, and power. And those economic reform incentives are the ones emphasized here.

Reform Incentives from Enormous Changes In Social and Economic Conditions

Much of the momentum for reform came from the socioeconomic changes that resulted from the second commercial revolution during and after the tenth century. As the money economy began displacing the gift economy, there was a corresponding upheaval in social, economic, and power relations. Those changes affected religious attitudes and stimulated both heresies and calls for church reform. More informed and articulate laity and church opponents made it essential for the church to respond with reforms in order to maintain its product credibility, wealth, and power.

Diversity and Heresy as Incentives for Reform[394]

The Roman Catholic Church had very diverse approaches for worship and other religious practices into at least the eleventh century, and local bishops ruled supreme in determining how the faith was practiced in their dioceses. The considerable diversity made it more difficult to distinguish heresy when it again became such a concern in the eleventh and twelfth centuries—sometimes, orthodoxy and heresy were quite similar. The diversity of religious practices and the corruption within the church had eroded its product credibility to the point that competing religious movements were seen as holier than the church by many, including some of the church's own customers.

Reducing religious diversity to more closely follow uniform practices approved by the central hierarchy thus was intended to increase the church's product credibility, which is essential for any religious organization, especially one seeking wealth and power. Rome continued attempting to implement the Gregorian and related reforms for more than one hundred years and successfully began to impose much more uniformity on religious practices throughout the Roman Catholic domain, especially during the twelfth and thirteenth centuries and particularly during and after the papal monarchy of Pope Innocent III (1198-1216).

Attempted Reforms of Simony

Simony, the sale of spiritual services and religious offices or roles, completely contradicted the teachings of Jesus, who instead emphasized boundless love and free forgiveness.[395] And although simony was repeatedly condemned, it was a persistent problem that even was warned against by Jesus' first apostles.[396] Both Roman Emperors and church synods frequently condemned the practice. For example, Emperor Justinian (527-65), one of the important emperors in church history, outlawed simony and the sale or lease of church property. Frequent church condemnations of simony were included as part of Pope Gregory VII's (1073-85) Gregorian Reforms at synods in 1074, 1075, and 1078. And the condemnations were repeated by later church authorities, synods, and critics.

Despite repeated church attempts to bring simony under control, that form of church corruption thrived at all levels of the church both before and after the calls for reform.[397] A few notable examples of the corruption at the highest level of the church illustrate the point. Popes who engaged in the selling of church offices, roles, benefices, and spiritual benefits include:

- Pope Sergius II (844-47) increased his personal and family wealth by selling lucrative church offices to the highest bidders.
- Pope Clement IV (1265-68) required handsome payments or outright bribes for lucrative benefices (land grants intended to support priests in their work).
- Pope Boniface VIII (1294/95-1303) infamously devised the scheme of selling indulgences that supposedly remitted the punishments for the sins of *all* Christians who made a pilgrimage to Rome for the Jubilee year of 1300. This was a blockbusting

announcement because such indulgences previously had been almost exclusively for crusaders.

But the Avignon Papacy, which started around the turn of the fourteenth century and lasted for about seventy years, perhaps provides the strongest specific evidence of the magnitude of papal corruption—because evidence of the bribes paid by some popes for their posts is available.[398] For five of the Avignon popes, that evidence shows they paid huge bribes to *each* cardinal-elector who voted for them. These payments were 100,000 florins by both John XXII (1305-14) and Benedict XII (1334-42); 108,000 florins by Clement VI (1342-52); 75,000 florins by Innocent VI (1352-62); and 40,000 florins by Urban V (1362-70).[399] Thus, the approximate value of these payments in U.S. dollars as of October, 2017 by the winning popes to *each* cardinal ranged from a low of $5,746,000 by Urban V to a high of $15,513,000 by Clement VI.[400]

The church repeatedly tried to deal with the problem of simony, which nonetheless persisted. Further, this problem of succumbing to economic rather than spiritual incentives plagued the church from its very beginnings to well beyond the period covered here. In short, the church failed to solve its problem of selling spiritual services and religious roles.

Product Credibility, Economic Incentives, and Celibacy

Celibacy is another of those church concepts that has little or nothing to do with the teachings of Jesus. But ascetics were considered 'holier' than married men in popular thinking and philosophy from Greece and Rome. And there were calls for celibacy by church leaders from very early in church history, despite the fact that some, perhaps many, of Jesus' apostles were married, including St. Peter, as is known from Gospel stories. Nonetheless, there were many religious and economic incentives that led reformers to call for a celibate priesthood, especially during the eleventh-thirteenth centuries. And many of those religious and economic incentives were closely intertwined. Although many reasons were given, the focus here is on ones where product credibility and other economic incentives were major motives.[401]

Apart from any religious motives, the church's final push for celibacy had five strong and interconnected economic motivations. First, celibacy was a response to promote product credibility for its religious customers against widespread criticisms, including some especially effective ones by heretics, of the church's corrupt priests. Second, celibacy was seen by the reformers as essential in successfully demanding the return of proprietary churches and their revenues to church control. Third, celibacy was a way for the church to prevent the inheritance of church posts, property, and wealth that priests were leaving for their heirs. Fourth, because dealing with a central church authority was more efficient for secular rulers, the church's push for celibacy coincided with royal economic interests in also reigning in the property aspirations of men scattered throughout their realms. Fifth, celibacy and a 'purer' priesthood and church helped the church in greatly reducing the influence of lay powers over high church appointments that involved substantial wealth and power.

Ritual 'Purity' and Religious Product Credibility[402]

The push for a purer priesthood was not motivated just by religious concerns that focused on ritual purity. It also was an economically motivated incentive to enhance the church's product credibility with its religious customers by supposedly showing that clerics were interested in the next world, not this one. Partly, this impulse came from the fact that the dividing line between clergy and lay society was not nearly as firm in medieval society as it later became, especially after the Council of Trent in the 1500s. For example, the lowest class of clergy, who had small rural parishes, led nearly the same lives as their religious customers, and most of them were married before Pope Gregory VII's reign (1073-1085).

Celibacy and Economic Incentives of Church and Rulers Mesh

Another reason that celibacy probably was legally established in the eleventh and twelfth centuries is that it was in the economic interests of both the church hierarchy and rulers, because of how family control of churches deprived both of the ability to easily exercise control and extract wealth from scattered, private holdings.[403] The incentives to act grew through time as more church property was alienated to private owners, especially when that involved a network of closely related families and their associates who together had considerable power. Thus, the imposition of clerical celibacy at Lateran I (1123) and especially Lateran II (1139)—including the prohibition of the fairly common practice of clerics living with concubines who had to be cared for with church property—was in the economic interests of both secular rulers and the church.[404]

Celibacy Mandated for All Priests

Celibacy and chastity were held up as an ideal throughout the period covered, and celibacy finally was mandated as official church policy for all priests.[405] But there is no consensus on the exact date when mandatory celibacy was finalized. Regardless of the exact date, effectively implementing a policy of celibacy was a long affair, and there were repeated church threats against married clergy and concubinage—from Urban II in 1095, to Callixtus II in 1119, to the First and Second Lateran Councils in 1123 and 1139, and on to Gregory VII and the Third Lateran Council in 1179 (when married clergy no longer were mentioned but concubinage still was). Nonetheless, celibacy still was not observed by many churchmen. Instead, marriage and concubinage among clerics continued on a reduced scale after the reforms. Indeed, there probably were thousands of married priests and an unknown number who had concubines or prostitutes. In fact, the frequent condemnations by church councils of clergy with wives or concubines strongly indicate the practices continued for centuries.

Married Bishops and Popes Contradict Celibacy Ideal of Reformers [406]

There is substantial evidence that celibacy was not observed by all of the church's highest leaders, both before and after reforms were implemented. Little is known about most early popes and bishops, but some were married, as was St. Peter.[407] Because there were so many married bishops, the following top-twenty list focuses just on notable examples of married popes, popes who had children, and popes who were sons of popes, bishops, or priests:[408]

1. St. Peter (d. about 30-40 years after Jesus) was married, based on Gospel passages, but there was no bishop in Rome at that time, so he actually was not a pope according to the church definition of the pope as the only bishop of Rome (even though the church lists him as the first pope).

2. Bishop Sixtus I (ca. 116-125) was a married bishop of Rome, and he is listed as a pope in the church's official list, but he was not a pope in the sense of being the *only* bishop of Rome at that time. In the early church, there probably were many other married bishops, including men listed as popes in the church's official records, but historical records for the early years of the church are very sketchy.

3. Pope Damasus I (366-84) was married with a family before he ascended to the papal throne. But because of church concerns that a family man would leave church property to his family, he renounced his wife and family for the power and wealth of the papacy.

4. Pope Anastasius I (399-401) was a married man, whose son succeeded him as Pope Innocent I.

5. Pope Innocent I (401-417) was the son of the preceding pope, Anastasius I.

6. Pope Boniface I (418-422) was the son of a priest.

7. Pope Sixtus (Xystus) III (432-440) was the son of a priest.

8. Pope Felix III or II (483-492), was the son of a priest and ascended to the papacy as a widower with two children.

9. Pope Hormisdas (514-523) was married before ordination and fathered a son who became Pope Silverius.

10. Pope Agapitus (535-536) was the son of a priest.

11. Pope Silverius (536-37) was the son of Pope Hormisdas and also may have been married, but the evidence of his marriage is disputed.

12. Pope Theodore I (642-649) was the son of a bishop.

13. Pope Hadrian (Adrian) II (867-872) was married before his election.

14. Pope Marinus I (882-884) was the son of a priest.

15. Pope Boniface VI (896) was the son of a bishop. And he is the only pope who was elected after having been defrocked twice for immoral behavior, once as a subdeacon and later as a priest.

16. Pope Sergius III (904-911) is alleged to have fathered an illegitimate son, based on a chronicle of that era.[409]

17. Pope John XI (931-935/6) is the only pope reported to have been the illegitimate son of a prior pope (Pope Sergius III).

18. Pope John XVII (1003) was married before ordination and was the father of three sons.

19. Pope Clement IV (1265-1268) was a widower with two daughters when he was elected pope.

20. After the period covered in this book, records of the popes and their activities are more readily available, and they show that the practice of popes having children certainly did not end. For example, Williams reports that at least seven of the fifteen popes from 1471 to 1585 fathered children, most of whom were taken care of in high style.[410]

Celibacy to Prevent Inheritance of Church Property

'Hereditary' priests, who inherited their positions, churches, and church property from their fathers or other close relatives, were not at all unusual all the way up to the eleventh century.[411] The Rule of Aix provides an example that deals with large land holdings by churchmen. That rule, adopted in 816 under King Louis the Pious, relates primarily to large land endowments to cathedrals that then were divided up among the church's canons who served as lords over the parcels they supervised. This system meshed nicely with the hierarchical system of rural aristocracy that prevailed. The oldest son would inherit the family estate and younger sons could enter the church, closely connecting the interests of both. Further, clerical marriage encouraged the whole arrangement, and it also tended to result in church 'prebends' (assignments of land-revenues to churchmen) becoming family rather than church holdings.[412] One of the effective proponents for reforming marriage and inheritance practices was Abbo of Fleury (d. 1004), who was a strong advocate of celibacy for all clergy, not just monks.[413]

In addition to mandated celibacy, church leaders and rulers took other actions to prevent the children of clerics from inheriting property.[414] A 1022 church synod in Pavia prohibited clerical marriage even at the relatively low rank of subdeacon, and it also effectively disinherited children of clerical unions by changing their status to serfs, who could not legally inherit property.[415] This change created a disincentive for women to marry priests or live with them as concubines.

However, inheritances of church property did not end, so the church took additional steps at the Lateran II Council (1139).[416] All marriages of bishops, priests, deacons, subdeacons, canons regular, monks, and women religious were declared invalid, although the law was not fully enforced. Nonetheless, its success was increased by declaring that any who married would have concubines rather than legal wives, so any offspring would be defined as bastards, who could not inherit land or other wealth. This change was another large disincentive for women to marry churchmen or live with them as their concubines, and it effectively ended hereditary parishes and dioceses.

Reclaiming Church Property Controlled by the Laity

Into at least the tenth century, the institutional church had lost many churches or control of their wealth, even including altar donations, to private owners.[417] The sale and trade of churches as well as their lands and revenues, led to proprietary churches that were controlled by private owners, rather than the institutional church. And many churchmen, including Abbo of Fleury and Cardinal Humbert, were alarmed by the economic consequences for the church. For example, Cardinal Humbert painted a dark picture of the economic ruin of the Italian church in his *Libri tres adversus simoniacos* around 1054-58. Thus, although the Gregorian Reform movement was marketed as one focused on religious and spiritual renewal, it also clearly was motivated partly, if not largely, by the church's deteriorating economic position. Since there could be no convincing case for returning church properties to church control unless they would be in 'holy' hands when returned, celibacy was seen as a way of convincing the church's religious customers and opponents that now churchmen would be different. For celibate churchmen would have 'pure' intentions and no wives, concubines, or children to support.

Over a long period, the church's reforms allowed it to secure the return of privately owned and controlled churches and their revenues.[418] The church obtained its property back, partly by the threat of eternal damnation for holdouts who refused to turn over church property and revenues. Most of the restorations of churches and their revenues up to the twelfth century went to monasteries rather than bishops. The reason was that the monks were considered holier by most in society, even including many bishops. This made the monks better merchants than secular clergy for relieving suffering in purgatory on the church's toll road to salvation. Thus, persons generally favored the monasteries when they obtained some salvation insurance in exchange for their gifts of the churches and their revenues back to the institutional church.[419]

Church Reduces Lay Power over Appointments to High Church Offices

Celibacy was part and parcel of the Investiture Contest between the church and secular powers over the right to appoint high clergy to their offices. With a celibate priesthood, the church could more effectively argue that only the church had the power to appoint those to the holy orders of the church—because the church and secular society were different and should be kept separate. Of course, this was a new theory of the social order, for the church and state had been inextricably intertwined ever since Constantine made the church the chosen religion of imperial Rome in the fourth century. Nonetheless, the church eventually was able to reduce, if not eliminate, secular power over appointments to high church positions. Although secular rulers still had a heavy hand in church affairs, this was both a symbolic and practical victory for the power of the bishops and popes, since direct appointments were theoretically in the hands of the church, not rulers.

Monastic Reforms

Ascetics and monks were a feature of early Christianity, and they continued as a powerful force in the Catholic Church throughout the period covered here.[420] From the beginning, they were seen as holier than ordinary clergy because they had chosen to separate themselves from society for a life devoted to God. Consequently, the monasteries and their prayers were viewed as politically, economically, and religiously important in maintaining the stability, wealth, and military power of kingdoms and their rulers. But they were a double-edged sword for the church as both powerful signals of product credibility and strong competitors with the rest of the church hierarchy for wealth and power. Thus, the bishops and the popes had to deal with that competition, while also keeping the monks' product credibility as a sign for the church as a whole.

The bishops finally succeeded in imposing more control and order on monasteries by requiring that they follow the rule of St. Benedict of Nursia (d. 547/560). That rule required obedience to the abbot and a life divided into prayer, study, and manual labor *within* the monastery. Contact with the outside world required special permission of the abbot.[421] However, these rules could not be universally imposed, simply because bishops did not have enough authority and power. And the problems of controlling the monasteries increased when powerful laymen founded monasteries with themselves as abbots by obtaining papal approval and bypassing the control of the local bishops.

The church hierarchy also could not completely control some monasteries because their perceived holiness gave them substantial donations from their religious customers, so select monasteries had independent power and authority. Thus, regardless of the attempts of bishops to control them, wealthy monasteries and their powerful abbots still exercised substantial power and influence. In short, the medieval monasteries were powerhouses of prayer that attracted immense wealth from the church's religious customers. Eventually, however, that accumulated wealth and power ended up eroding their own religious credibility, wealth, and power. And reduced religious credibility for monasteries also reduced the church's overall religious credibility.

Renewed emphasis on ritual purity during the Early Middle Ages meant monasteries were again targeted by reformers, especially including the Carolingian rulers and reformers of the eighth and ninth centuries.[422] Those reforms were intended to make the monasteries sacred places apart from the world, but they continued as part of the world in hosting royalty, the rich and powerful, and royal prisoners. They also had some younger sons and daughters of royalty and the powerful as monastic members. In fact, the constant interactions between the monasteries and the outside world clearly helped the monasteries maintain their religious, economic, and political power. Moreover, select monasteries, most strongly exemplified by Cluny, heavily involved themselves in the money economy that began emerging during and especially after the tenth century. The resulting worldliness of such monasteries stimulated new reforming orders during the eleventh-thirteenth centuries that emphasized spiritual purity rather than direct involvement in the secular world.

Twelfth-Century Monastic Reforms[423]

Sacrum commercium flourished throughout the period covered in this book, and the fabulous wealth of the monasteries generated criticism within the church, as well as by 'heretics' outside of the church. The critics pointed out that ownership and wealth violated the vow of poverty. Around the turn of the twelfth century, the reform movement again attempted to end worldly monastic practices by introducing 'purer' orders devoted to poverty rather than wealth, especially including the Cistercians and the Order of Grandmont. For example and similar to the

Cistercians' initial goals, Stephen of Muret's (d. 1124) Order of Grandmont rejected the system of Cluny point by point. Instead, they would beg for alms, and there would be no ownership of land, no lucrative tithes or offerings, no paid-prayer confraternities, no documents to record the receipt or transfer of goods, and no fighting with heirs over contested bequests.

However, even the religious orders that began as reformers usually succumbed to the siren song of wealth, especially after their initial holiness attracted the type of wealth they originally criticized. Among others, Cluny and the Cistercians basically started as reform orders that were supposed to signal a purer church. But through the centuries, they and others ended up being transformed more into orders that emphasized wealth and power, after they became more strongly institutionalized to manage the wealth generated by their perceived holiness.

Erosion of Monks' Power by Competition from Mendicant Friars [424]

The power and authority of monks came from their perceived holiness associated with an ascetic life of withdrawal from the world. Starting early in the thirteenth century, new reforming orders of friars, the Dominicans and especially the Franciscans, renounced the wealth of the established monasteries by adopting a mendicant lifestyle that was centered on wandering and preaching in the world, rather than living in large and elaborate monasteries secluded from the world.[425] This change reversed nearly a thousand years of monastic history that had justified a life apart as a necessity for spiritual perfection. And the popularity of the new Franciscan and Dominican friars greatly reduced the influence, wealth, and power of older monastic movements.

However, as with other reforming orders in prior centuries, it was not too many years before the institutionalization of the Franciscans and the Dominicans also changed their focus into a more worldly one. For example, there were battles among the Franciscans over the right degree of evangelizing poverty for centuries, with several splits over the issue.[426] In short, the church tried but never could convincingly show over long periods that it had a large presence in the evangelizing poverty camp.

Difficulties in Fully Implementing Reforms

The difficulties in fully implementing the intended reforms resulted from limited central power and strong incentives for the agents of any hierarchy to resist change, unless it also is in their direct interests. And the local bishops and priests, as well as the monasteries and mendicant orders, simply had different incentives than the central hierarchy, as they were interested in their own wealth and power.

Pope Gregory VII (1073-1085) began the process of major reforms for the church, but he simply lacked the power to widely implement them.[427] A little more than a century later, Pope Innocent III (1198-1216) was more effectively the head of the entire society than any single secular ruler, and he made considerable progress in implementing many church reforms. All in all, the church succeeded in both separating itself from the world and taking its 'rightful' place above other worldly powers, at least in the conception of the church hierarchy. That conception endured for centuries without significant changes, even as reality changed dramatically, all the way up to the substantial revisions of Vatican II in the 1960s.[428]

Pope Innocent III was successful in greatly increasing the papacy's power, but he knew that it still would be difficult to enforce church reforms at the local level. The pope was determined to stress the papacy's power over church affairs because its power actually was so limited when it came to implementing policies at the local level, where entrenched local custom deterred even the most inspired pope, abbot, or bishop.[429] Thus, in an attempt to force the desired change down into local levels, Pope Innocent III announced the Fourth Lateran Council two years in advance and gathered together more than twelve hundred leading clerics in 1215. Although his attempt to fully establish central control was not entirely successful, it clearly increased hierarchical control over local church affairs.

Ownership and fabulous wealth by churches, bishops, and monasteries generated criticism within the church, as well as from 'heretics' outside of the church. However, apart from adopting various reforming monasteries and religious orders as signs of evangelizing poverty, very little was done to address widespread concerns about the wealth of the institutional church and its leaders, some churches, and some monasteries. Moreover, although the papacy was a frequent target of corruption concerns from both internal and external critics, it managed to avoid serious reforms of its own operations.[430] At the same time, the papacy actively led the attempted reforms of others. In fact, the papacy began issuing reform 'laws' for society and the church most notably under Pope Gregory VII in his *Dictatus pape* issued in 1075. In that document, he claimed the right to issue new laws as needed and demanded by the times. Although Gregory VII's claims were more bluster than reality, later popes often returned to his document as an ancient source of authority for the papacy's right to make universally applicable laws for others, even as it continued to ignore concerns about its own wealth, power, and corruption.

Conclusion

There were both religious and economic incentives for reforming many of the problems the church faced, but even the religious motives were intertwined with economic ones. And it is the economically motivated reforms discussed in this chapter. A problem never solved up to and well beyond 1350 was simony. The continuing problem of selling spiritual services and religious roles or posts before and after attempted reforms is most starkly illustrated by the deep corruption of the papacy.

There were many economic incentives for imposing celibacy on the priesthood, and the church was quite successful in suppressing the marriage and concubinage of priests. Yet notable exceptions continued and are clearly illustrated by married popes and bishops (and others who were not married but fathered children). Nonetheless, the widespread imposition of celibacy on the priesthood was very successful in eliminating the common practice of passing on church posts and property to the sons of clerics. The 'purer' priesthood signaled by celibacy also was very successful in helping the church reclaim church property and revenues that were in private hands. The return of church property to the church also was aided by the coincidence of the economic interests of the church and lay rulers. Finally, a 'purer' priesthood also was important in reducing the power of lay rulers to appoint high clergy, including powerful bishops and popes—theoretically, that reform was completely successful and it did reduce the actual power of rulers as well.

Ascetics, monks, and monasteries were a double-edged sword for the church. They were strong signals of product credibility for the church as a whole, but that also gave them independent power and wealth that sometimes caused problems for the church hierarchy. Although there were repeated reforms of monastic life, a recurring problem was that the perceived holiness of the monasteries made them highly effective merchants of salvation insurance for the church's religious customers. Perhaps it was inevitable that time and again, initially 'pure' spiritual communities were changed, once they themselves started accumulating wealth and power. It seems that the siren song of wealth and power in this world is hard to ignore, even in communities specifically founded with the intention of challenging it with evangelizing poverty.

Clearly, the church's reforms were not completely accomplished. Yet they and other strategies of the church—including attacks on 'evil others'—were successful enough that the Roman Catholic Church's extreme degree of monopoly power over Christianity in the West continued without any powerful and enduring competition into the sixteenth century. Then, Luther's successful revolt against the church and the Protestant Reformation substantially reduced the Roman Catholic Church's monopoly power.

Conclusion and Implications For Today

The Roman Catholic Church put salvation up for sale or trade and used an interrelated web of factors to create and defend its wealth and power. Altogether, its actions directly contradict Gospel passages that emphasize love and free forgiveness. What went wrong? The elite hierarchy that won control of early Christianity for the Catholic Church, as well as many of the following church leaders, simply responded to economic incentives for wealth and power. Although there were some exceptions, church leaders and churchmen repeatedly succumbed to the siren song of wealth and power. Regardless of the intentions of the early leaders of Christianity, the result of the consolidation of wealth and power within one large institution corrupted the early vision into an institution instead focused on its own power, wealth, and preservation. Perhaps the church's evolution is simply a natural one for many human institutions—not just the Catholic Church—that corrupt their initial vision as their wealth and power grows.

The church had so much power that it shaped not just religion, but culture, politics, and economic policies for more than a thousand years and well beyond the 1350 timeline for this study. The church's power has been substantially reduced, most notably by Luther and the Protestant Reformation. Nonetheless, vestiges of its ancient wealth and power continue to contaminate the church defined as the people of God rather than the Roman Catholic Church's hierarchical, male-dominated, and authoritarian institutional structure. And many church leaders, especially bishops and cardinals, still seem to see the church as their church. Other church workers and lay persons are supposed to be their obedient followers, who must accept church policies or face excommunication for what church leaders consider serious and publicly detected violations. In short, the once-mighty power of the church over an entire society and economy has been reduced to its attempted and much weaker control of its religious customers and workers.

Relevance of Reforms for the Modern Church

Prior chapters contain very few modern parallels and much more viable competition now exists in the religious marketplace than was the case up to 1350. Why project possible solutions for ancient problems into the twenty-first century? There are at least three reasons why many of the implications of this study still apply. First, economic incentives for wealth and power clearly motivate humans today, just as they did in the ancient world. Second, the faith monopoly of the church ended, but the church hierarchy still has substantial power, especially over church resources, policies, and actions. Third, although the exact nature of corruption and misguided, even disastrous, leadership decisions and actions or inactions have changed through the centuries, the interrelated web of factors used to create and defend the church's wealth and power still strongly affect it and its religious customers. That interrelated web of factors continues to directly or indirectly affect the hierarchy's attitudes, approaches, teachings, decisions, and policies in many ways, as discussed below.

Sin Rather Than Love

Whatever the initial motivations, church leaders used their basic theology of sin and redemption only through the church for wealth and power, even though that theology has no basis in the teachings of Jesus. Rather, Jesus' Gospel teachings emphasize that love of God and love of our neighbors are the two greatest commandments. But the church instead used its grim theology to mine the profits of guilt and sin from cradle to grave and beyond on its toll road to salvation. The emphasis on guilt and sin still permeates teaching and preaching in many quarters of the church (although that is in contrast to some parts of the church, such as the emphasis on love in Franciscan theology). There is a reason that Catholic guilt accurately describes so many Catholics—they are repeatedly exposed to the church's basic theology. In such a world, sin, guilt, and fear are lurking around every corner of daily life, thoughts, and dreams to trip up inherently sinful humans.

Payments on the Church's Toll Road to Salvation

In most countries, the church no longer has the power to force its religious customers to pay for its operations in various ways, even including a taxing power that the church had for centuries during the Middle Ages. Amazingly, however, that still is the case in Germany.[431] Germany's current religious tax was introduced in the nineteenth century and is collected by the government as a percentage of Germans' income tax payments and then transferred to German churches for a small transaction fee. The Roman Catholic Church's share of the tax recently has accounted for annual receipts of about six billion U.S. dollars, helping Germany's Catholic Church become one of the world's wealthiest churches.

However, many German church members have decided to stop paying the tax (by eliminating their designation as Catholics for tax purposes), and that has deeply concerned German bishops. Consequently, the German bishops have retaliated against their recalcitrant tax payers by refusing them the rights to the Eucharist, Catholic funerals, and other religious services. A German bishops' conference in September, 2012 confirmed that the Vatican had agreed with its new policy of imposing consequences on Roman Catholics who refuse to pay Germany's church tax.[432] In other words, Germany's Roman Catholic Church still engages in the church's ancient policy of explicitly charging for holy services—in clear contradiction of the teachings of Jesus and his apostles in the Gospels and Acts.

In other countries, the link between the church's holy services and payments to receive those services is not as strong as in Germany. Nonetheless, many of the church's religious customers throughout the world follow ancient customs, as illustrated by the following:

• Because of original sin, the importance of infant baptism and childhood education in the Catholic faith still is the norm in the church's brilliant marketing plan for recruiting, educating, and training the next generation to be good Catholics. This allows the church to recruit its next crop of customers before they reach the age of reason.

- Its religious customers routinely pay for religious services at every step of the way—for baptism and masses, for other holy services, and at death.
- The church no longer openly sells salvation via death bequests, but it subtly markets its powers to assist on the road to salvation for those approaching death through advice on wills and estate management to encourage significant donations to the institutional church. Purgatory still appears in the church's catechism, but most of the church's religious customers may be too skeptical to pay much to relieve suffering there.

Perhaps needless to say, the church usually features the payments of its religious customers as voluntary contributions, with Germany a notable exception. And both in Germany and other countries, the 'need' for financial support is linked to the church's supposed role in carrying out the mission of Jesus—despite his teachings that salvation is a free gift of God.

Church Wealth

Some obvious examples show how the church continues to treasure its worldly wealth, despite the warnings of Jesus against worldly wealth in the Gospels and his humble life and ministry:

- Jesus was born in a stable and lived a humble life. But cardinals and bishops continue to mimic imperial Rome's elaborate costumes and symbols, and many of them live like royalty. (Pope Francis is a notable exception.) Jesus did not suggest the aloof and wealthy hierarchy of the Roman Catholic Church. Rather, Jesus advocated a model of service, subservient leadership, and helping the poor and the least in the Gospels (again consistent with Pope Francis' emphasis, even if not with the emphasis of many others in the hierarchy).

- The Vatican complex (an estimated 11,000 rooms) and summer palace are enormous and hold vast stores of treasures. Jesus' life and teachings flatly contradict such extravagance and massive wealth.

- Jesus never raised money to build a church or synagogue, let alone an elaborate one. Yet the Roman Catholic Church glories in the enormous and hugely expensive churches it has built and continues to build. St. Peter's Basilica, the Sistine Chapel, and many other elaborately decorated churches are architectural and artistic marvels. But Jesus taught about the importance of help for the least, not opulence in worship spaces.

The Poor and Socioeconomic Justice

Many Gospel passages emphasize the importance of help for society's least and most overlooked. The modern church also emphasizes such help, but it does that more with writings and preaching than with substantial and concrete actions. The church clearly preaches a much more radical approach to the poor and the least than it exemplifies through its actions—despite many notable efforts that focus on the poor, such as St. Vincent de Paul Societies and various church charities and groups. Pope Francis (2013-) also has continued his emphasis on helping the poor and the least during his reign. Nonetheless, unless Pope Francis is able to make substantial changes in how the Vatican and local dioceses allocate personnel, money, and volunteers, the church will continue devoting what clearly has been a relatively small proportion of its total resources to concrete actions on Jesus' radical calls for socioeconomic justice.[433]

215

Regulating Celibacy, Sexual Behavior, and Procreation

The church has expended a tremendous amount of energy in attempting to control celibacy, the sexual behavior of its priests and religious customers, and procreation. The following illustrate these issues:

- St. Peter was married and other apostles of Jesus probably were as well. And married priests and bishops were a common feature of the Roman Catholic Church into at least the eleventh century. Then, celibacy was imposed as a strategic move during the eleventh-twelfth centuries to protect church wealth and provide more product credibility for its religious customers. Although the economic motives in creating the church's celibacy policy are abundantly clear, the church still packages celibacy as a 'religious' policy.

- The church normally does not allow married priests. However, it is interesting to note that celibacy and marriage restrictions can be waived when that serves the strategic interests of the church. Popes John Paul II (1978-2005) and Benedict XVI (2005-2013) waived the celibacy requirement in welcoming married priests of the Anglican Church and their religious followers into the Roman Catholic Church.[434] These married Anglican priests were allowed to remain married and serve as Roman Catholic priests.

- The church once had a profitable business line in regulating sexual dreams, thoughts, and behavior. Although its religious customers now pay much less attention to the church's sexual regulations, the following remnants of this business line continue into the modern church as part of its so-called moral authority:

- Sexual transgressions by women were punished much more severely than the same ones by men in the church's ancient sin manuals and policies. Although the booming business of collecting profits for such sinful behavior ended, the policies of the male hierarchy still focus on women for special attention in contraceptive policies and in proclaiming whether women are 'allowed' to terminate pregnancies, even if for incest or medical reasons.

- Church penalties for homosexual behavior were especially severe in the church's manuals that proscribed punishments for sexual transgressions. Although such penalties no longer can be collected, official church policies and attitudes continue to demean and sometimes demonize the LGBTQ people of God.

• The church took over the marriage market—including annulments and divorce—in the Middle Ages, at least partly to advance its wealth and power. At that time, it defined marriage as a sacred relation between a man and a woman and turned marriage into a church sacrament. The church continues to teach that marriage is a sacrament. Its church courts still rule on annulments, and the hierarchy still staunchly opposes marriage between same-sex couples, consistent with its long-standing discrimination against the gay and lesbian people of God.

Strategic Subordination of Women

The strategic subordination of women that includes overt discrimination against them began early in church history as part of its quest for wealth and power. The standard explanation for their subordination is that ancient societies and imperial Rome were patriarchal. Although that is part of the explanation, it alone would ignore the clear economic motives of male churchmen in subordinating women. Had the male leaders followed the example of Jesus, who was a notorious outsider in the Roman Empire, there would be no compelling reason to subordinate women—either in the early church or when women were finally defined out of ordained ministries by the male hierarchy during the twelfth century. Of course, that new definition contradicts abundant historical evidence of women in ordained ministries up to the twelfth century. But the hierarchy has no problems with selective memory.

On the other hand, should the church return to its ancient roots nearer to the time of Jesus, rather than just the church history that was cleansed of women in ordained service during and after the twelfth century, women also could return to ordained service. The Roman Catholic Church included them as deacons serving at the altar and even as priests and bishops all the way into the twelfth century. (Although the Greek Orthodox Church also eliminated women from ordained ministries during the eleventh-twelfth centuries, it restored the female diaconate in October, 2008.)

It is interesting to see how the issue of subordinating women has played out after 1350 in the Roman Catholic Church. Even with immense changes in society and the status/roles of women during the first two thousand years after Jesus, Popes Paul VI (1963-1978) and Bendict XVI (2005-2013) still strongly maintained the position against ordaining women, consistent with the policy of their male forefathers during and after the twelfth century. In contrast, Pope Francis (2013-) appears to be more open to increasing the role of women in providing sacred church services—in August, 2016, he created a commission of six men and six women to study the possibility of ordaining women as deacons in the Roman Catholic Church. However, the commission still had not made any public recommendations as of May, 2017. It also is very clear that even Pope Francis is not open to the idea of female priests.

Church Courts to Control its Workers and Religious Customers

The church set up a powerful court system that was used for wealth and power under the auspices of imperial Rome during the 300s. Initially, those courts applied only Roman law, as there was no body of church law. But as the centuries passed, the church decided it needed to go beyond the laws of imperial Rome to manage its affairs and rule over both secular and religious matters. Subsequently, complex laws that deal with a vast store of minutiae have been refined to the point that a fleet of canon lawyers are employed by the church to apply and interpret those laws.[435] Church courts still operate to judge whether persons comply with the church's religious doctrines.

Issues of Authoritarian Hierarchy

The hierarchical structure of the modern Roman Catholic Church leads to many issues, such as:

- The hierarchy still consists solely of males, who are mostly old and mostly white, even though the vast majority of the church's religious customers are not.
- The authoritarian control of the church by Rome and its power centers continues. Dissenters no longer can be burned at the stake, but they can be quashed, stripped of their authority to teach and preach, or even excommunicated.

- For centuries, the people and secular rulers had a strong voice in choosing bishops and popes. In a battle for power, the church finally succeeded in eliminating both by making: cardinals the sole electors of the pope; and the appointment of bishops the responsibility of the pope. The secrecy of the papal election process and the exclusion of the voice of the people continue.

- The church hierarchy still specializes in secrecy and lack of transparency in its decisions and finances. The people of God are basically excluded as the hierarchy zealously guards its ancient privileges of wealth and power.

- The medieval practice of kissing the church lord's (bishop's) ring as a sign of loyalty and obedience continues as part of priestly ordination ceremonies. Although some might dismiss this as an empty gesture from ancient times, it effectively conveys the fact that bishops are the supreme rulers of their dioceses, relative to both priests and the laity. Of course, the bottom rung on the ladder of authority in the male-dominated church is for religious women, who are under a vow of obedience to male churchmen.

- Religious corruption of various types has been analyzed from economic and legal viewpoints.[436] And there is a history of corruption and abuse at all levels of the church that has to be confronted with completely new measures never before effectively implemented. Such fundamental reforms require concrete and sustained actions that change the operations of both the hierarchy and local dioceses throughout the world. More policy guidelines that are widely ignored simply are window dressing for underlying, systemic problems.

Continuing Myth of Apostolic Succession
Versus Corrupt Leadership

The church has consistently maintained the myth that the pope is the direct representative of God and thus entitled to rule over the church. And the myth is supported by claiming apostolic succession from Pope Peter, even though St. Peter never was a pope, according to the church's own definition.[437] Further, the succession of popes includes some who: were leaders of the violence involved in the Inquisition and crusades; bought the papacy and continued selling holy services and posts during their reigns; were adulterers; fathered illegitimate children or gave up their legitimate wives and children to ascend to the papacy; and used church funds for extravagant lifestyles and to enrich their own families.

Language of Elitism

The church hierarchy adopted Latin as its official language, even though the texts of the New Testament were written in Greek and, according to historical records, Jesus spoke and read Aramaic and Hebrew. Imperial Rome collapsed, but the church still clings to the language of that ancient slave society for official business and pronouncements. Although it is not the spoken or written language of its religious customers, using Latin adds to the obscurity and elitism of the Roman Catholic Church hierarchy and its centers of power in Rome.

Additional Examples after 1350

Following the 1350 timeline for this book, there is widely known evidence of how the badly distorted decision-making of the hierarchy continued. A few examples include:

- In the seventeenth century, the church condemned the writings of Galileo, and the Inquisition imprisoned him. The church alleged that his scandalous theory—that the world revolved around the sun—was a major crime in contradicting church teaching. The church taught that the world was the center of the universe and the sun traveled around the world.

- Pope Innocent X condemned the 1648 Peace of Westphalia because it stated that, "Citizens whose religion differs from that of their sovereign are to have equal rights with his other citizens."[438] The papacy also condemned many other attempts at religious freedom as heresies.

- The church was dominated by the elite of society starting before the fourth century, and that domination continued through the entire timeline for this study and for centuries more. Thus, it perhaps is no surprise that the church's actions favored the rich and the elite for at least fifteen hundred years after Constantine made the Catholic Church the church of imperial Rome during the fourth century. The church often preached and still preaches a message of help for the least and the poor, but its concrete actions did not and still do not match its rhetoric. In any case, the first strong and official action of the church to speak out for justice for exploited workers came at the end of nineteenth century. The church's first official document on justice for exploited workers was issued in 1891 (*Rerum Novarum* or *On the Condition of Labor*). Of course, this enlightened position came centuries after the church had ended its own use of slaves on its property and many years after the exploitation of workers began in the factories of the industrial revolution—and years after other social reformers had called for justice for industrial workers.

- In the twentieth century, the church struck a deal with Hitler's future partner, Mussolini, to give up some of its property and wealth in exchange for recognition of Vatican City as an independent state within Rome. Yet a few years later, the church did not use its vast wealth to bribe Hitler into transferring the Jews to the church rather than to death camps. It also did not use its prestige and influence to strongly speak out against the Holocaust.[439] In addition, the church never took public action to individually excommunicate Hitler for his crimes against humanity (he supposedly excommunicated himself because of his actions).

- In the twentieth and twenty-first centuries, the Vatican failed to take seriously charges that Fr. Maciel, who was the founder and leader of the Legion of Christ for about fifty years, had repeatedly abused children sexually, had fathered children, and had misused the order's funds.[440] Finally, in 2010, after many accusations over many years, the Vatican condemned him for repeated sexual abuse of underage seminarians and for fathering at least three children with two women.[441] Perhaps his large pipeline of donations reportedly made to the Vatican explains the failure to act sooner.

- The clergy sexual abuse scandals widely reported at the end of the twentieth and beginning of the twentieth-first centuries reveal the consistent failure of church leaders to effectively and proactively respond to transgressions by their own clergy.

- Laity, priests, and certainly nuns have no say over bishops' authoritarian control. In fact, when a bishop chooses to convene a synod for his diocese, he is the only voting member of that synod—laity, nuns, and even priests have no votes. In short, within whatever constraints Rome and cardinals decide to impose, bishops rule their dioceses with substantial church power.[442]

- There is no way for the church's own religious customers to hold bishops accountable, except in rare cases when cardinals or the Vatican choose to intervene. Otherwise, the only recourse against bishops' actions or inactions is through legal systems when secular laws may be violated.

- Bishops sometimes make outrageous decisions that the church's own theologians and canon lawyers sharply question. Two of many excommunications imposed on persons involved in abortions illustrate the point.[443] During 2009 and 2010, bishops in Recife, Brasil and Phoenix, Arizona excommunicated persons involved in abortions undertaken because of extremely dangerous medical conditions or incest. Archbishop Cardoso Sobrinho of Recife declared the excommunication of the mother of a nine-year-old girl because she had arranged for an abortion for her daughter who was pregnant with twins after being raped by her stepfather. Although the mother was excommunicated, the rapist stepfather was not. In Phoenix, Bishop Olmsted asserted that Mercy Sister Margaret McBride had 'excommunicated herself' because she was on the ethics committee of St. Joseph's Hospital and had agreed with the decision to perform an abortion on a mother of four other children. The mother had severe pulmonary hypertension—and the medical opinion was that both she and the fetus would die without an abortion.

- Reported financial scandals involving the Vatican's own bank, which ironically is named the Institute for Works of Religion, resulted in the recent ouster of the bank's president.[444] (And Pope Francis has initiated additional reforms since then.)

- Modern examples that show how badly fundamental reform of the Roman Catholic Church is needed could be multiplied enormously, at least into a large book, if a detailed list of examples were provided.

Economics and Church Reform

The church's wealth and power depended on its monopoly power, so economic incentives created or at least substantially accentuated church problems. Thus, an economic 'solution' would involve two related steps:

1. The church's customers could withhold financial support, with or without leaving the church. Those staying in the church could insist on fundamental reform as a condition for continued or renewed financial support.

2. Much more competition could be created by breaking up the existing church into smaller competitors, thus greatly reducing the wealth and power that can be exercised by any one institutional entity. These new churches could even include the religious model of the early Christian followers of Jesus. They had no hierarchical structure, held services in house 'churches', alternated who led the services, and had women who presided over services.

Withhold Financial Support from the Hierarchy

Church leaders clearly understand that their wealth and power depends importantly on their economic resources, even though they often claim it depends on their spiritual authority. Starting with Constantine early in the fourth century, financial support and collaboration with secular powers allowed the institutional church to build its monopoly power to awesome proportions. Given that the church now has relatively limited influence over secular powers, its remaining power depends on its accumulated wealth, its customer base, and financial support from its religious customers. Without contributions, the institutional church would wither on the vine. Thus, one way to deal with unacceptable decisions and behavior is simply to withhold financial support or to direct that support to the beacons of hope still found within the larger church. The church's religious customers also could choose to use their finances in a way that requires church reform, but the coordinated effort that would require seems unlikely.

Alternatively, some people may choose to simply leave the church and take their financial support with them. In fact, the decline in religious participation in organized religions has been a notable development, especially in industrialized democracies.[445] Even in the United States in which religious affiliation has been the highest among industrialized democracies and much higher than in Europe, the decline in participation has accelerated, according to Pew survey findings.

More Competition

The one Roman Catholic Church could be subdivided into many competing churches.[446] In that case, the power of the church hierarchy would be reduced by more competition, as was dramatically provided by the Protestant Reformation. More competition, especially by smaller and Catholic-related churches under no the authority of the Vatican, would result in a variety of Catholic churches that would be more responsive to the wishes of their religious customers. For example, some of these churches could include married priests and women priests, harkening back to the situation in the ancient church.

At a global level, different churches might be divided along lines of religious orders or beliefs. That might include various versions of Dominican Catholic Churches, Jesuit Catholic Churches, Franciscan Catholic Churches, Benedictine Catholic Churches, Opus Dei Catholic Churches, and many others. For example, some church conservatives followed this path in 1970 by breaking away from Rome because of the church's liberalization following Vatican II.[447] More competition also might occur along country or regional lines, such as *much smaller:*

- European Catholic Churches (Europe has a large number of cardinals that made up over half of the electors in the 2013 election of Pope Francis, but it has relatively few practicing Catholics).
- Catholic-related churches in regions that include many Catholics but relatively few Cardinals. For example, these could include churches in Africa, the Americas, and Asia.
- Many other combinations along the above and other lines, including smaller regional groupings within or among regions and countries.

Perhaps women, younger men, Hispanics/Latinos, and Asians will lead reform since, as a group, they are the *overwhelming majority* in the Roman Catholic Church. In contrast, mostly older, mostly white males dominate the church hierarchy. Thus, some potential churches would favorably treat groups that currently are subordinated, even demonized, by the hierarchy (some offshoots of the institutional church already exist). The competition could be increased substantially, if more lay persons were to act, perhaps along with some religious orders, leaders, and individual priests.

Smaller, more competitive churches might even include some like the house churches of early Christianities that existed before church leaders managed to create the hierarchical structure of the Catholic Church. Smaller churches might not even have full-time leaders, as was the case for those early house churches. Some very small religious groups already have adopted this approach, but it may not be a viable one on a wide-scale basis.

Some smaller competitors also could increase cooperation with other Christian churches. For example, the hierarchy has precluded membership of the Roman Catholic Church in the World Council of Churches that was created to foster Christian cooperation. Further, smaller competitors also could be more serious about inter-religious dialogue and cooperation with other Christian faiths, Judaism, Islam, and many other non-Christian religions. The possibilities would be especially promising with smaller competitors focused on the life and teachings of Jesus rather than faith in the Roman Catholic Church and its hierarchy of authority.

Is Fundamental Reform Within the Church Possible?

It surely would be in the long-term interests of the institutional church to be more adaptive and responsive to its problems. But it may not be possible for the church's hierarchy to face them and reform because it has built such a strong culture of hierarchical and male control, secrecy, and cover-ups in attempting to defend its wealth and power. The clerical caste that controls the church reproduces itself by recruiting, training, mentoring, and monitoring other men before they are allowed entry into the highest leadership positions. In that way, the old men in charge in any era attempt to assure that like-minded men follow in their footsteps, so disagreements about church policies by men in top positions are minimized. An exception obviously slips through occasionally, as perhaps illustrated by Pope Francis, but other leaders tend to correct the behavior of those who seek too much reform. For example, Vatican II during the 1960s implemented some notable reforms in opening up the church. Yet, the counter-move against the liberalization of church rules by Vatican II was a strong force during the council. Since the council, the counter-movement continued under the following popes, up to and including Pope Benedict XVI, who resigned his position in 2013. The countermovement succeeded in restoring a more authoritarian and hierarchical structure that harkens back to the medieval church. Clearly, Pope Francis (2013-) has strongly advocated a church that transforms its customs, focuses on helping the poor and the least, and emphasizes evangelization. But how successful the new pope is in implementing his desired reforms in the hierarchy and at the local level probably will take some years after his rein to determine.

Given the above background on the church's leadership cult, it is not surprising that church leaders, who include a few thousand bishops and over two hundred cardinals, may not be able to conceive of a church controlled by the people of God rather than themselves. Further, the short-sighted failure to effectively respond is not unique to Roman Catholic Church leaders.[448] The inherent tendency of many centers of power in world history has been to cover up internal problems, especially when the leaders believe that publicly acknowledging those problems could threaten their personal credibility, power, and wealth. Also, such organizations tend to respond to scandal by placing the blame on individuals, without accepting institutional responsibility. These tendencies are pronounced in the Roman Catholic Church, as tragically illustrated by its failure to effectively and proactively deal with world-wide cases of sexual abuse that were allowed to continue and fester because of cover-ups by bishops, cardinals, and others in the church.

How could the possible reforms or any truly fundamental reform be accomplished? Most of those who choose to remain in the highest levels of the hierarchy are unlikely to have an open mind about institutional failings, so fundamental and wide-ranging reform led from the top seems questionable, despite Pope Francis' bold statements and some changes since 2013. In fact, Jesuit Fr. Tom Reese recently commented about the leadership's failure to deal with the church's sexual abuse scandals, but his comments bear directly on the unlikely chances that the church's leadership, including its bishops, will implement many fundamental reforms. Reese noted that, from his perspective within the church, reforms at the top are unlikely because:[449]

- The church has lost its ability to be a self-correcting institution.
- The hierarchy is focused on obedience and control, so it no longer can fix itself.
- There is no effective system for bringing bishops to account for problems in their dioceses.
- The Vatican has no problem investigating nuns and theologians, but investigating mismanagement by a bishop simply has not been a priority.
- Speaking truth to those in power about church mistakes can be a dangerous path for those within the church because of reprisals from the hierarchy.

Many others within the church also see little, if any, chance of the church reforming itself because of the hierarchy's resistance.

For example, Australian bishop Goeffrey Robinson argues in his 2008 book that the culture of the church leads it to crises and impedes reform.[450] As another example, Lasallian Br. Lous DeThomasis' 2012 book recounts problems that he observed during more than twenty years as President of St. Mary's University, a small Catholic university in Minnesota.[451] While he was there, his concerns mounted about how the institutional church was losing touch with its members, especially younger ones. Interestingly, DeThomasis thinks the death of the institutional church, which is so accustomed to ignoring its problems, is almost inevitable. However, he also believes that death could allow the church to turn into something that could 'carry out its original purpose.'

Despite the above pessimism for internal church reform, Pope Francis (2013-) certainly has made some calls for significant reform. In *Evangelii Gaudium*, his 224 page call to action released on November 26, 2013, the pope states in its opening lines: "I dream of a 'missionary option,' that is, a missionary impulse capable of transforming everything, so that the church's customs, ways of doing things, times and schedules, language and structures can be suitably channeled for the evangelization of today's world rather than for her self-preservation."

Hopefully, the pope will be successful in his early attempts to change the emphasis and focus of the church. However, truly fundamental change in the actual operations of the church and its hierarchy of authority will take much more than the early changes by the pope. And the old power structure of the church is still largely intact, although it has been put on notice, especially at the Vatican, by some of Pope Francis' decisions. Nonetheless, there are a few thousand bishops and more than two hundred cardinals who, as princes of the church, have substantial power in deciding how the church actually operates at the local level. Thus, any truly fundamental and long-lasting reform is a huge undertaking in the hierarchical and far-flung Roman Catholic Church.

Final Thoughts

In 1776, Adam Smith discussed some of the solutions suggested here when he pointed out that competition rather than monopoly power were good for consumers of bread, candlesticks, and religion. He emphasized that monopoly power tends to make churches ineffective, inefficient, unresponsive to their religious customers, and dangerous for social and religious freedom.[452] In many ways, the analysis in this book shows that nothing much has changed, so the solutions suggested so long ago are reaffirmed by a detailed study of the Roman Catholic Church's relentless quest for wealth and power.

Two thousand years after the worldly life of Jesus, perhaps the church's people of God will finally rise up and be in charge of smaller and more competitive churches or religious gatherings that could be created through their initiative, perhaps with the help of some priests, nuns, deacons, and religious workers who join them. In addition, some fundamental reforms might be implemented in the church, but it seems that probably would take intense pressure on the church hierarchy, including decisions by the church's customers to withhold financial support to force reforms. It also seems that the religious scholar, Marcus Borg, has it right when he contends that to be Christian and to be in a Christian church should mean working to transform one's life into the likeness of

Christ.[453] In that case, right belief is much less important than right behavior in following the way taught by Jesus. Christian churches then should exist not for their own sake but for the sake of a transformative process that could change the world. As Borg notes, God does not need a church, but Christians may to help them understand and follow Jesus.

Jesus' humble ministry perhaps was partly intended to serve as a strong warning about religious institutions. Jesus had no institutional or bureaucratic structure and no stockpile of enormous wealth, even though he lived when substantial wealth and power were the hallmarks of worldly success for religious organizations. Perhaps the warning from his approach for church reform is that any institutional entity that has such wealth and power simply cannot model fundamental spiritual truth. Otherwise, why did he not create such an entity in his earthly ministry? And that brings us back to the economic solution of smaller, more competitive groups that have limited worldly wealth and power. That path presumably would be rejected by most of the church's elite hierarchy, but it is open for the people of God to choose.

NOTES

1   In Roman Catholic teaching, purgatory is that intermediate state or 'place' where sinful souls destined for heaven go after bodily death for the purification through suffering necessary to enter heaven.

2   For more on using rational choice models, see: Stark, R., *The Rise of Christianity: How the Obscure, Marginal Jesus Movement Became the Dominant Religious Force in the Western World in a Few Centuries*, 1997, ch. 9; Stark R. and W. S. Bainbridge, *A Theory of Religion*, 1987; and Stark, R. and R. Finke, *Acts of Faith: Explaining the Human Side of Religion*, 2000. For a short discussion of the economics of religion, see McCleary, Rachel M., "The Economics of Religion as a Field of Study," in McCleary, Rachel M. (ed.), *The Oxford Handbook of the Economics of Religion*, 2011, pp. 3-36.

3   Economics also mainly takes belief systems as given, although other fields, such as the psychology of belief systems, focus on that area.

4   As discussed later, many writings of other versions of early Christianity and related religious beliefs have been rediscovered in the twentieth century. For example, the Gnostic gospels now are widely available, and scholars have compared them to the writings included in the New Testament.

5   Terrible weather resulted in the famine of 1315-1317 and then the plague of 1348-1351 combined with the famine to mark the end of that economic era. For example, see Roach, Andrew P., *The Devil's World: Heresy and Society 1100-1300*, 2005, pp. 170-78.

6   The scope of this book means that literally thousands of sources deal with its topics. Obviously, it is not based on all of those sources. However, to my knowledge from a cursory review of hundreds of other sources not referenced here, there is nothing that would fundamentally alter the structure, analysis, and concluding implications of the analysis. In almost all cases and certainly for all substantive arguments, the sources cited and used are from well recognized experts in their areas, such as history, sociology, political science, archaeology, church history, religious studies, medieval studies, theology and, of course, economics.

7   As noted earlier, The Roman Catholic and Greek Orthodox versions of the Catholic faith did not formally split until the eleventh century. And there were other offshoots from the Catholic Church during its early development.

8   I especially thank Keith Warner and others who wish to remain anonymous. Professor Warner noted that my analytical framework necessarily emphasizes the dark side of the church.

[9] For a discussion of the rational choice model, see see: See McCleary, Rachel M., "The Economics of Religion as a Field of Study," in McCleary, Rachel M. (ed.), *The Oxford Handbook of the Economics of Religion*, 2011, pp. 3-36; and Fox, Judith, "Secularization," in Hinnells (ed.), *The Routledge Companion to the Study of Religion*, 2010, pp. 306-321.

[10] For a detailed discussion of these and related issues, see see Ekelund Jr., Robert B., Robert F. Hébert, and Robert D. Tollison, *The Marketplace of Christianity*, 2006, pp. 48-62.

[11] Ekelund Jr., Robert B., Robert F. Hébert, and Robert D. Tollison, *The Marketplace of Christianity*, 2006, esp. pp. 1-14.

[12] For a much more detailed discussion of using economic models to analyze religious issues, see Ekelund Jr., Robert B., Robert F. Hébert, and Robert D. Tollison, *The Marketplace of Christianity*, 2006, esp. pp. 1-14.

[13] See: Iannaccone, Laurence R., "Introduction to the Economics of Religion," in *Journal of Economic Literature* 36 (September 1998), pp. 1465-1495; McCleary, Rachel M., "The Economics of Religion as a Field of Study," in McCleary, Rachel M. (ed.), *The Oxford Handbook of the Economics of Religion*, 2011, pp. 3-36; and Ekelund Jr., Robert B., Robert F. Hébert, and Robert D. Tollison, *The Marketplace of Christianity*, 2006, esp. ch. 2.

[14] For another study that covers a long sweep of history, see Ekelund Jr., R. B. and R. D. Tollison, *Economic Origins of Roman Christianity*, 2011.

[15] For much more on these ideas, see: Azzi, Basicy and Ronald Ehrenberg, "Household Allocation of Time and Religiosity: Replication and Extension," in *Journal of Political Economy*, 1975, pp. 415-23; and Innaccone, Laurence, R. and William Sims Bainbridge, "Economics of Religion," in Hinnells (ed.), *The Routledge Companion to the Study of Religion*, 2010, pp.461-476.

[16] For a detailed analysis of religious credence goods, see Iannaccone, Laurence R., "Risk, Rationality, and Religious Portfolios," in *Economic Inquiry* 38 (1995), pp. 285-295.

[17] For a discussion of some of these factors and others for religion in general, see Ekelund Jr., Robert B., Robert F. Hébert, and Robert D. Tollison, *The Marketplace of Christianity*, 2006, pp. 48-53.

[18]   Some of his major insights were laid out in: Becker, Gary S, *The Economic Approach to Human Behavior*, 1976; and Becker, Gary S., "A Theory of the Allocation of Time," in *Economic Journal* 65 (September 1965), pp. 493-508. For an application of the theory to religion, see Ekelund Jr., Robert B., Robert F. Hébert, and Robert D. Tollison, *The Marketplace of Christianity*, 2006, pp. 48-58.

[19]   'Club' goods or services satisfy the following conditions: one's use of them does not diminish the supply of them for others, non-members can be excluded from consuming them, and they are collectively produced by club members. Thus, many religious services, including many produced by the Catholic Church and discussed in the following chapters, are produced by team production and are club goods. Especially see: Iannaccone, Laurence R., "Introduction to the Economics of Religion," in *Journal of Economic Literature* 36 (September 1998), pp. 1465-1495; and Iannoccone, Laurence R., "Religious Markets and the Economics of Religion," in *Social Compass*, 1992, 39 (1), pp. 123-131.

[20]   See: Coleman, James, "Social Capital in the Creation of Human Capital," in *American Journal of Sociology*, 1994 Supplement, pp. s95-s120; Iannaccone, Laurence R., "Religious Participation: A Human Capital Approach," in *Journal for the Scientific Study of Religion*, September 1990, pp. 297-314; and Iannaccone, Laurence R., "Sacrifice and Stigma: Reducing Free-Riding in Cults, Communes, and Other Collectives," in *Journal of Political Economy*, 1992, pp. 271-291.

[21]   These basic concepts are applied in various ways to organized religions and their religious customers in some of the economic studies cited in this chapter. For example, see: Iannaccone, Laurence R., "Introduction to the Economics of Religion," in *Journal of Economic Literature* 36 (September 1998), pp. 1465-1495; Ekelund Jr., Robert B., Robert F. Hébert, and Robert D. Tollison, *The Marketplace of Christianity*, 2006; Iannaccone, L. R., "The Consequences of Religious Market Structure: Adam Smith and the Economics of Religion," in *Rationality and Society* 3.2 (1991); Ekelund Jr., R. B., R. F. Hébert, and R. D. Tollison, "An Economic Analysis of the Protestant Reformation," in *Journal of Political Economy* 110, no. 3 (2002); Ekelund Jr., R. B., R. F. Hébert, R. D. Tollison, G. M. Anderson, and A. B. Davidson, *Sacred Trust: The Medieval Church as an Economic Firm*, 1996; and Ekelund Jr., R. B. and R. D. Tollison, *Economic Origins of Roman Christianity*, 2011, especially Chapters 2-3.

[22]   The basics of supply and demand are easy to understand. Other things equal:

• Higher prices induce firms to bring more to the market, and lower prices induce the opposite response, so price and quantity supplied are positively related.

- On the demand side of the market, the incentives of price changes are the reverse. Consumers buy more at lower prices and less at higher prices, so price and quantity demanded are inversely related.

- In the competitive markets envisioned by Adam Smith, the interaction of many small buyers and sellers determines the equilibrium market outcome. Consumers 'rule' in such markets because sellers respond to provide what buyers are willing and able to buy at prices that cover sellers' costs and a 'normal' profit.

When other things are not equal, then buyers and sellers react to the changed circumstances. For example, higher material costs lead sellers to cut back the amount they are willing to sell at any price, tending to raise the market price. Or if buyers develop a stronger taste for a product or service, they are willing to pay more for the same amount than previously, tending to raise the market price. We see these effects on a daily basis in the demand, supply, and prices of food, clothing, housing, gasoline, and thousands of other goods and services.

[23] This effect is referred to as a more 'inelastic' demand curve in the relevant range. And a more inelastic demand curve allowed the Catholic Church to raise its prices as a profit-maximizing response.

[24] Of course, after the timeline for this book, the church's monopoly power was substantially reduced by Luther and the Protestant Reformation in the sixteenth century. As a result, the church lost market power, greatly reducing its pricing power and its ability to extract wealth from its customers.

[25] See Burgess, Paul L., *Popes, Corruption, and Holy Violence: The Early Catholic Church's Betrayal of Jesus*, 2015.

[26] A convenient and non-technical source that explains bargaining theory is Muthoo, Abhinay, "A Non-Technical Introduction to Bargaining Theory," in *World Economics* 1 (April-June 2000), pp. 145-166. This article is accessible on the web at http://privatewww.essex.ac.uk/~muthoo/simpbarg.pdf.

[27] Such bargaining between two (or few) parties, each of whom has some degree of monopoly power, can be analyzed with the tools of bilateral monopoly and bargaining theory. An early version of bargaining theory was conceived as a way to analyze employer-union negotiations, but it applies well to any situation of bilateral (or multilateral) negotiations. Bargaining theory also fits within the context of game theory.

[28] Rent-seeking has an enormous literature, and it has been used in studies of religion and the Catholic Church. For the theory of lobbying for government benefits, see: Peltzman, Sam, "Toward a More General Theory of Regulation," in *Journal of Law and Economics* 19 (1976), pp. 211-240; and Stigler, George, "The Theory of Economic Regulation," in *Bell Journal of Economics and Management Science* 2 (1971), pp. 3-21. For applications to religion and the Catholic Church see: Iannaccone, Laurence R., "Introduction to the Economics of Religion," in *Journal of Economic*

Literature 36 (September 1998), pp. 1465-1495; Ekelund Jr, Robert B., Robert F. Hébert, and Robert D. Tollison, *The Marketplace of Christianity*, 2006; and Ekelund Jr., R. B., R. F. Hébert, R. D. Tollison, G. M. Anderson, and A. B. Davidson, *Sacred Trust: The Medieval Church as an Economic Firm*,1996.

[29]   See: Ekelund Jr., Robert B., Robert F. Hébert, and Robert D. Tollison, *The Marketplace of Christianity*, 2006; and Ekelund Jr., Robert B., Robert F. Hébert, Robert D. Tollison, Gary M. Anderson, and Audrey B. Davidson, *Sacred Trust: The Medieval Church as an Economic Firm*, 1996;

[30]   Smith, Adam, *The Wealth of Nations*, pp. 740-766.

[31]   Contributions up to 1994 include: Smith, A. *The Wealth of Nations*, 1776 (1937); Stark, R. and W. S. Bainbridge, *A Theory of Religion*, 1987; Iannaccone, L. R., "A Formal Model of Church and Sect," in *American Journal of Sociology* 94 (1988); Iannaccone, L. R., "Religious Practice: A Human Capital Approach," in *Journal of Scientific Study of Religion* 29.3 (1990); Iannaccone, L. R., "The Consequences of Religious Market Structure: Adam Smith and the Economics of Religion," in *Rationality and Society* 3.2 (1991); Iannaccone, L. R., "Why Strict Churches Are Strong," *American Journal of Sociology* 99.5 (1994); Ekelund Jr., R. B. R. F. Hébert, and R. D. Tollison, " An Economic Model of the Medieval Church: Usury as a Form of Rent Seeking," in *Journal of Law, Economics, and Organization* 5 (Fall 1989); Ekelund Jr., R. B., R. F. Hébert, and R. D. Tollison, "The Economics of Sin and Redemption: Purgatory as a Market-Pull Innovation?" in *Journal of Economic Behaviour and Organization* 19 (September 1992); Ellison, C. D., "Religious Involvement and Subjective Well-Being," in *Journal of Health and Social Behavior* 32 (1991); Grief, A., "Cultural Beliefs and the Organization of Society: A Historical and Theoretical Reflection on Collectivist and Individualist Societies," in *Journal of Political Economy* 102.5 (1994); Redman, Barbara J., "An Economic Analysis of Religious Choice," in *Review of Religious Research* 21 (1980), pp. 330-342; Durkin J. T., Jr. and A. Greeley, "A Model of Religious Choice Under Uncertainty: On Responding Rationally to the Nonrational," in *Rationality and Society* 3.2 (1991), pp. 178-196; and Boulding, K. E., *Beyond Economics: Essays on Society, Religion, and Ethics*, 1968.

Others have made important contributions, including the much earlier hypothesis of M. Weber and R. Tawney that the Catholic Church impeded economic development. And there is the competing hypothesis of W. Sombart and J. Schumpeter that the Catholic Church advanced economic development. But these 'macro' studies of how religion may affect the overall trajectory of an economy deal with different impacts that are outside the focus of this book.

[32]   Contributions after 1994 include: Iannaccone, L. R., "Voodoo Economics? Reviewing the Rational Choice Approach to Religion," in *Journal for the Scientific Study of Religion* 34 (1995); Iannaccone, L. R., "Risk, Rationality, and Religious Portfolios," in *Economic Inquiry* 38 (1995); Young L. A. (ed.), *Rational Choice Theory*

and Religion: Summary and Assessment, 1997; Stark, R., *The Rise of Christianity: How the Obscure, Marginal Jesus Movement Became the Dominant Religious Force in the Western World in a Few Centuries*, 1997; Iannaccone, L. R., "Rational Choice: Framework for the Scientific Study of Religion," in L. A. Young (ed.), *Rational Choice Theory and Religion: Summary and Assessment*, 1997; Iannaccone, L. R., "Introduction to the Economics of Religion," in *Journal of Economic Literature* 36 (September 1998); Ekelund Jr., R. B., and R. D. Tollison, *Mercantilism as a Rent-Seeking Society*, 1981; Ekelund Jr., R. B. and R. D. Tollison, *Politicized Economies: Monarchy, Monopoly, and Mercantilism*, 1997; Ekelund Jr., R. B, F. G. Bion Jr., and R. W. Ressler, "Advertising and Information: An Empirical Study of Search, Experience and Credence Goods," in *Journal of Economic Studies*, 22 (1995); Ekelund Jr., R. B., R. F. Hébert, and R. D. Tollison, "An Economic Analysis of the Protestant Reformation," in *Journal of Political Economy* 110, no. 3 (2002); Ekelund Jr., R. B., R. F. Hébert, and R. D. Tollison, "The Economics of the Counter-Reformation: Incumbent Reaction to Market Entry," in *Economic Inquiry* 42 (October 2004); Ekelund Jr., R. B., R. F. Hébert, and R. D. Tollison, *The Marketplace of Christianity*, 2006; Ekelund Jr., R. B., R. F. Hébert, R. D. Tollison, G. M. Anderson, and A. B. Davidson, *Sacred Trust: The Medieval Church as an Economic Firm*,1996; Ekelund Jr., R. B. and R. D. Tollison, *Economic Origins of Roman Christianity*, 2011; McCleary, Rachel M., "The Economics of Religion as a Field of Study," in McCleary, Rachel M. (ed.), *The Oxford Handbook of the Economics of Religion*, 2011, pp. 3-36; Montgomery, J. D., "Contemplations on the Economic Approach to Religious Behavior," in *American Economic Review* 86.2 (1996), pp. 443-447; Hardin, Russell, "The Economics of Religious Belief," in *Journal of Institutional and Theoretical Economics* 153.1 (1997), pp. 259-278; Ellison, C. G., "Rational Choice Explanations of Individual Religious Behavior: Notes on the Problem of Social Embeddedness," in *Journal for the Scientific Study of Religion* 34 (1995); Grief, A., "Commitment, Coercion, and Markets: The Nature and Dynamics of Institutions Supporting Exchange," in Menard, C. and M. M. Shirley (eds.), *Handbook of New Institutional Economics*, 2005; and Grief, A., "Economic History and Game Theory: A Survey," in R. J. Aumann and S. Hart (eds.), *Handbook of Game Theory, V. 3*, 2002.

[33] Smith, Adam, *The Wealth of Nations*, 1776 (1937), Book V.

[34] Hull, Brooks B. and Frederick Bold, "Towards an Economic Theory of the Church," in *International Journal of Social Economics* 16 (1989), pp. 5-15.

[35] Ekelund Jr., R. B. and R. D. Tollison, *Economic Origins of Roman Christianity*, 2011.

[36] See: Iannaccone, Laurence R., "Introduction to the Economics of Religion," in *Journal of Economic Literature* 36 (September 1998), pp. 1465-1495; and Ekelund Jr., Robert B., Robert F. Hébert, and Robert D. Tollison, *The Marketplace of Christianity*, 2006, ch. 2.

[37] The main source for this section is Stark, *The Rise of Christianity: How the Obscure, Marginal Jesus Movement Became the Dominant Religious Force in the Western World in a Few Centuries*, 1997, pp. 1-13. For much more on the rise of Christianity, see Ekelund Jr., R. B. and R. D. Tollison, *Economic Origins of Roman Christianity*, 2011

[38] See: Stark, R., *The Rise of Christianity: How the Obscure, Marginal Jesus Movement Became the Dominant Religious Force in the Western World in a Few Centuries*, 1997; and Eilinghoff, C., "Religious Information and Credibility" in *German Working Papers in Law and Economics*, 2003.

[39] Hardin, Russell, "The Economics of Religious Belief," in *Journal of Institutional and Theoretical Economics* 153.1 (1997), pp. 259-278.

[40] Iannaccone, Laurence R., "Sacrifice and Stigma: Reducing Free Riding in Cults, Communes, and Other Collectives," in *Journal of Political Economy* 100.2 (1992), pp. 271-292.

[41] For those interested in exploring the topics in this section in much more depth, some additional sources include: Anderson, G. A., *Sin: a History*, 2009; and Wiley, T., *Original Sin: Origins, Developments, Contemporary Meanings*, 2002.

[42] For a related discussion of these salvation insurance issues, see Ekelund Jr., Robert B., Robert F. Hébert, and Robert D. Tollison, *The Marketplace of Christianity*, 2006, pp. 44-47.

[43] The main sources for this section are: Brown, *Augustine of Hippo: A Biography*, 1967 (2000), pp. 240-78 and 383-437; Casiday, "Sin and salvation: Experiences and reflections," in Casiday and Norris (eds.), *The Cambridge History of Christianity: Constantine to c. 600*, 2007, pp. 501-530; Delumeau, *Sin and Fear: The Emergence of a Western Guilt Culture, 13th-18th Centuries*, 1983 (1990), pp. 1-5, 9-25, 190-91, and 282-88; Greer, "Pastoral care and discipline," in Casiday and Norris (eds.), *The Cambridge History of Christianity: Constantine to c. 600*, 2007, pp. 567-584; Comby, *How to Read Church History: Book 1, From the beginnings to the fifteenth century*, 1985, pp. 52-3 and 77; Freeman, *The Closing of the Western Mind: The Rise of Faith and the Fall of Reason*, 2002, pp 288-91; Freeman, *A. D. 381: Heretics, Pagans, and the Dawn of the Monotheistic State*, 2008, pp. 160-61; and Freeman, *Egypt, Greece and Rome: Civilizations of the Ancient Mediterranean*, second edition, 2004, pp. 564-70 and 602-3.

[44] This paragraph is based mainly on Freeman, Egypt, *Greece and Rome: Civilizations of the Ancient Mediterranean*, second edition, 2004, pp. 564-70.

[45] Freeman, *The Closing of the Western Mind: The Rise of Faith and the Fall of Reason*, 2002, pp. 290-91.

[46]   Freeman, *The Closing of the Western Mind: The Rise of Faith and the Fall of Reason*, 2002, pp. 288-91.

[47]   However, some Gospel passages do have strong hints of a more pessimistic view of salvation. These include: Matthew 22:14 (many are called, but few are chosen); the parable of the wedding feast in Matthew 22:1-4 (the invited guests offend the host and are left out of the feast); Matthew 5:29-30 (pluck out your eye and cut off your hand if necessary); and the verses on how hard it is to enter the Kingdom of God in Matthew 7:13-14 and Luke 13:14. But, of course, there are many Gospel passages that have a very optimistic view of salvation, forgiveness, and the boundless love of a merciful God and Father.

[48]   Scriptural passages that might support a distinction between mortal and venial sins are an obscure passage in I John 5:16-17 and the identification of sins against the Holy Ghost in Matthew 12:31.

[49]   Augustine's theology of original sin and redemption could not be officially adopted by the church until it was formally stripped of his early and strong belief in predestination; that 'touch-up' of his theology was done at the conclusion of Second Synod of Orange (529).

[50]   Brown, *Augustine of Hippo: A Biography*, 1967 (2000), pp. 394-5.

[51]   This section is based on Delumeau, *Sin and Fear: The Emergence of a Western Guilt Culture, 13th-18th Centuries*, 1983 (1990), pp. 1-5, 25-31, 191-95, 215-25, 265-71, and 555-57; and Pelikan, *Christian Tradition, A History of the Development of Doctrine: V. 1, The Emergence of Catholic Tradition (100-600)*, 1971 (1975), pp. 320-331.

[52]   His discussion of sin occupies a significant portion of his famous *Summa*, and his *De Malo* focuses entirely on sin.

[53]   Hopkins, *A World Full of Gods: The Strange Triumph of Christianity*, (1999), 2001, pp. 124-5.

[54]   This section is based on: Ludlow, *The Early Church: The I.B.Tauris History of the Christian Church*, 2009, pp. 79-85; Gamble, "Marcion and the 'canon'," in Mitchell and Young (eds.), *The Cambridge History of Christianity, Vol. 1: Origins to Constantine*, 2006, pp. 195-213; Brown, *Augustine of Hippo: A Biography*, 1967 (2000), pp. 394-95; Borg, *Jesus: Uncovering the Life, Teachings, and Relevance of a Religious Revolutionary*, 2006, p. 175; Pagels, *The Origin of Satan*, 1996, pp. 171-78; and Freeman, *A. D. 381: Heretics, Pagans, and the Dawn of the Monotheistic State*, 2008, pp. 138-39 and 160-61.

[55]   Origen was a notable theologian of the early church, and he developed the idea that the Incarnation of Jesus was God's way of revealing Truth to man. Origen also

argued that God's love was so bountiful that it would allow everyone to achieve salvation eventually. Origen was one of the most respected theologians of his era, and he remains a notable theologian of the Greek Church. But once original sin took hold so firmly in the West, the Roman Catholic Church condemned him as a heretic many years after his death. Another early proponent of love was Marcion, but his works are known only through his detractors, because he too was declared a heretic by the Roman Catholic Church. For more on Marcion, see Gamble, "Marcion and the 'canon'," in Mitchell and Young (eds.), *The Cambridge History of Christianity, Vol. 1: Origins to Constantine*, 2006, p. 196.

56   Pagels, *The Origin of Satan*, 1996, pp. 171-73.

57   Freeman summarizes the consequences of rejecting a theology of love for one of sin. See: Freeman, *A. D. 381: Heretics, Pagans, and the Dawn of the Monotheistic State*, 2008, pp. 138-39.

58   Augustine was so powerful in Catholic theology and doctrine that it was 1690 before any pope (Alexander VII) overturned the formula that theologians used explicitly or implicitly over the centuries, namely that anything clearly based on Augustine could be defended and taught, regardless of any bull of a pontiff.

59   Dante's masterpiece was completed in the fourteenth century; then it was reprinted in fifteen editions in the fifteenth century and in thirty editions in the sixteenth century. The popularity of the *Comedy* shows how sin and guilt had become preoccupations of western culture. *The Canterbury Tales*, written in about 1308-1321 and then put together around 1386, further demonstrate the impact of sin and guilt in popular culture. The last of the *Canterbury Tales* (not always attributed to Chaucer) plumbs the depths of sin and guilt in detail in discussing penance and the road to salvation. However, England was not alone in producing detailed analyses of sin and guilt--France had the *Menagier de Paris* (1393), which has instructions to those in the last tale of *Cantebury* in how to seek confession and penance from the church for the Deadly Sins.

60   The main source for this paragraph is Bornstein, D., "How to Behave in Church and How to Become a Priest," in Rubin, M. (ed.), *Medieval Christianity in Practice*, 2009, pp. 109-115.

61   The contracts typically were drawn up by notaries who used standard legal forms to specify the legal duties of each party (such as the provision of instruction, lodging, and food by the priest in return for free services from the apprentice).

62   The main source for this paragraph is Angenendt, Arnold, "Sacrifice, gifts, and prayers in Latin Christianity," in Noble and Smith (eds.), *The Cambridge History of*

Christianity: Early Medieval Christianities, c. 600-c. 1100, 2008, pp. 463-64.

[63]   For an overview of economic issues and incentive pay for priests, see: Ekelund Jr., Robert B., Robert F. Hébert, and Robert D. Tollison, *The Marketplace of Christianity*, 2006, pp. 1-15 and 30.

[64]   Interestingly, Adam Smith also emphasized the effects of incentive pay on the efforts of Protestant and Roman Catholic clergy in *The Wealth of Nations*. He explained that the mendicant orders established by the Roman Catholic Church during the thirteenth century provided strong incentives for them to work hard in satisfying their customers, compared to clergy who received salaries, because donations to the mendicants depended on their own effort. See Smith, Adam, *The Wealth of Nations*, 1776 (1937), Book V.

[65]   Dominic led the way to careful training for priests/preachers when he realized that his order could not effectively combat heresy without theological training. That concern eventually led to a Dominican conventual school system to train preachers, and it was decided they could not engage in any preaching until they had completed at least three years of study under an experienced lector. The training was heavily influenced by the 'new' learning from Aristotle that had recently become available in the West through translations. Aristotle became the bedrock of training for the Dominicans and, a little later, for the entire church when the Domincan St. Thomas Aquinas was acknowledged as the master theologian for the Roman Catholic Church.

[66]   The main source for this paragraph is Little, *Religious Poverty and the Profit Economy in Medieval Europe*, 1978, ch. 11.

[67]   On a list of the ten fruits of good preaching by Humbert of Romans, the penitence of sinners was at the head of the list, just behind the conversion of infidels.

[68]   The main source for this section is Jansen, K. L., "A Sermon on the Virtues of the Contemplative," in Rubin, M. (ed.), *Medieval Christianity in Practice*, 2009, pp. 117-25.

[69]   See Wood, Ian, *The Missionary Life: Saints and the Evangelisation of Europe, 400-1050*, 2001, pp. 250-55.

[70]   Church leaders strongly emphasized that reverencing images and icons was acceptable--but they never could be worshiped, despite the contrary appearances in how religion actually was practiced. However, controversy continued within the church, especially between some bishops and monks.

71 For more on the iconoclast controversy, see Helvétius, Anne-Marie and Michel Kaplan, "Asceticisim and its institutions," in Noble and Smith (eds.), *The Cambridge History of Christianity: Early Medieval Christianities, c. 600-c. 1100*, 2008, pp. 282-88.

72 Nonetheless, the battle between bishops and monks continued into the eighth and ninth centuries, until the cults of images were firmly embedded in church law/customs in 843.

73 See Hen, Y., "The Early Medieval *Barbatoria*," in Rubin, M. (ed.), *Medieval Christianity in Practice*, 2009, pp. 21-25.

74 It is not clear why the rite died out in the Frankish kingdom and Francia but, after the time of Charlemagne (d. 814), the Franks apparently replaced it with the arming ceremony, which also was a church ceremony.

75 See Jones, P. M., "Amulets and Charms," in Rubin, M. (ed.), *Medieval Christianity in Practice*, 2009, pp. 194-201.

76 The main sources for this paragraph are: Smith, J. M. H., "Saints and their cults," in Noble and Smith (eds.), *The Cambridge History of Christianity: Early Medieval Christianities, c. 600-c. 1100*, 2008, pp. 581-86; and Helvétius, Anne-Marie and Michel Kaplan, "Asceticisim and its institutions," in Noble and Smith (eds.), *The Cambridge History of Christianity: Early Medieval Christianities, c. 600-c. 1100*, 2008, pp. 290-96.

77 The main source for this section is Angenendt, Arnold, "Sacrifice, gifts, and prayers in Latin Christianity," in Noble and Smith (eds.), *The Cambridge History of Christianity: Early Medieval Christianities, c. 600-c. 1100*, 2008, pp. 464-67.

78 See Morris, R., "The Problems of Property," in Noble and Smith (eds.), *The Cambridge History of Christianity: Early Medieval Christianities, c. 600-c. 1100*, 2008, p. 327.

79 The main source for this paragraph is Iogna-Prat, D., "Churches in the landscape," in Noble and Smith (eds.), *The Cambridge History of Christianity: Early Medieval Christianities, c. 600-c. 1100*, 2008, pp. 378-79.

80 The main sources for this paragraph are: Angenendt, Arnold, "Sacrifice, gifts, and prayers in Latin Christianity," in Noble and Smith (eds.), *The Cambridge History of Christianity: Early Medieval Christianities, c. 600-c. 1100*, 2008, p. 461; and Le Goff, Jacques (translated by Patricia Ranum), *Your Money or Your Life: Economy and Religion in the Middle Ages*, 2001, pp. 65-67.

81 The main source for this paragraph is Coon, Lynda L., "Gender and the body," in Noble and Smith (eds.), *The Cambridge History of Christianity: Early Medieval*

Christianities, c. 600-c. 1100, 2008, pp. 441-43.

82 Perhaps the Benedictines and other monks who abused small boys never read or believed Jesus' admonition in Matthew 18:5-6: *5 And he that shall receive one such little child in my name, receives me. 6 But he that shall scandalize one of these little ones that believe in me, it were better for him that a millstone should be hanged about his neck, and that he should be drowned in the depth of the sea.*

83 The main source for this paragraph is the detailed study of saintly missionaries by Ian Wood. See Wood, Ian, T*he Missionary Life: Saints and the Evangelisation of Europe, 400-1050*, 2001.

84 This paragraph and most examples are based on the detailed study of saintly missionaries by Ian Wood. See Wood, Ian, T*he Missionary Life: Saints and the Evangelisation of Europe, 400-1050*, 2001. Also see Warner, Keith D. and John E. Isom, J*ourney and Place: An Atlas of St. Francis*, 2008.

85 St. Francis' extensive travels for evangelization have been mapped in detail by Warner, Keith D. and John E. Isom, J*ourney and Place: An Atlas of St. Francis*, 2008.

86 The main sources for this paragraph are: Wood, Ian, T*he Missionary Life: Saints and the Evangelisation of Europe, 400-1050*, 2001, pp. 86, 124, and 262-63; and Duffy, *Saints and Sinners: A History of the Popes*, 2006, pp. 48-72.

87 Duffy, *Saints and Sinners: A History of the Popes*, 2006, pp. 48-72.

88 The recorded history of the church also makes it clear that miracles tended to proliferate when Catholics needed comfort, either because of natural disasters or military setbacks.

89 The main source for this paragraph is Abrams, Lesley, "Germanic Christianities," in Noble and Smith (eds.), *The Cambridge History of Christianity: Early Medieval Christianities, c. 600-c. 1100*, 2008, pp. 112-15.

90 Wood, Ian, T*he Missionary Life: Saints and the Evangelisation of Europe, 400-1050*, 2001, p. 86.

91 See Abrams, Lesley, "Germanic Christianities," in Noble and Smith (eds.), *The Cambridge History of Christianity: Early Medieval Christianities, c. 600-c. 1100*, 2008, pp. 118-21.

92 The main sources for this section are: Kraus, Henry, *Gold Was the Mortar: The Economics of Cathedral Building*, 1994; Duby, Georges (translated by Eleanor Levieux and Barbara Thompson), *The Age of Cathedrals: Art and Society, 980-1240*, 1983;

Duby, Georges (translated by Stuart Gilbert), *The Europe of the Cathedrals, 1140-1280*, 1966; Geary, Patrick J., *Furta Sacra: Thefts of Relics in the Central Middle Ages*, 1990; and Ekelund Jr., Robert B., Robert F. Hébert, and Robert D. Tollison, *The Marketplace of Christianity*, 2006, pp. 197-203 and 222-31.

[93]   The histories and some estimated costs are provided for many of these by Kraus, Henry, *Gold Was the Mortar: The Economics of Cathedral Building*, 1994.

[94]   Geary, Patrick J., *Furta Sacra: Thefts of Relics in the Central Middle Ages*, 1990.

[95]   Ekelund Jr., Robert B., Robert F. Hébert, and Robert D. Tollison, *The Marketplace of Christianity*, 2006, p. 222.

[96]   To the contrary, some economists have argued that cathedral building could be compared to government spending to stimulate a slack economy, but there always are opportunity costs involved. For a refutation of the stimulation argument, see Ekelund Jr., Robert B., Robert F. Hébert, and Robert D. Tollison, *The Marketplace of Christianity*, 2006, pp. 202-03.

[97]   See: Geary, Patrick J., *Furta Sacra: Thefts of Relics in the Central Middle Ages*, 1990; and Gimpel, Jean, *The Cathedral Builders*, 1983.

[98]   For example, see Duby, Georges (translated by Stuart Gilbert), *The Europe of the Cathedrals, 1140-1280*, 1966, p. 37.

[99]   A. Smith recognized this in his discussion of religion in his famous 1776 book, *The Wealth of Nations*.

[100]   The main source for this paragraph is Helvétius, Anne-Marie and Michel Kaplan, "Asceticisim and its institutions," in Noble and Smith (eds.), *The Cambridge History of Christianity: Early Medieval Christianities, c. 600-c. 1100*, 2008, pp. 290-96.

[101]   Although caring for the poor and sick was a traditional duty of bishops, monasteries sometimes assumed those duties, either by choice or necessity.

[102]   For a discussion of these groups, see Roach, *The Devil's World: Heresy and Society 1100-1300*, 2005, pp. 1-9.

[103]   Iannaccone, Laurence R., "Sacrifice and Stigma: Reducing Free Riding in Cults, Communes, and Other Collectives," in *Journal of Political Economy* 100.2 (1992), pp. 271-292.

[104]   For those interested in exploring the topics of this chapter in more detail, there are many additional sources. These include the following: Abulafia, D. (ed.),

The New Cambridge Medieval History: Vol. 5, c. 1198-c. 1300, 1999; Dunn, James D. G., *Christianity in the Making, Vol. 2: Beginning from Jerusalem*, 2009; Fouracre, P. (ed.), *The New Cambridge Medieval History: Vol. 1, c. 500-c. 700*, 2005; Fouracre, P. (ed.), *The New Cambridge Medieval History: Vol. 3, c. 900-c. 1024*, 2000; Jones, M. (ed.), *The New Cambridge Medieval History: Vol. 6, c. 1300-c. 1415*, 2000; Luscombe, D. and J. Riley-Smith (eds.), *The New Cambridge Medieval History: Vol. 4, c. 1024-c. 1198, Part 1*, 2004; Luscombe, D. and J. Riley-Smith (eds.), *The New Cambridge Medieval History: Vol. 4, c. 1024-c. 1198, Part 2*, 2004; Lynch, Joseph H., *The Medieval Church: A Brief History*, 1992; MacCulloch, D., *Christianity: The First Three Thousand Years*, 2009; McKitterick, R. (ed.), *The New Cambridge Medieval History: Vol. 2, c. 700-c. 900*, 1995; Reuter, T. (ed.), *The New Cambridge Medieval History: Vol. 3, c. 900-c. 1024*, 1999; Vidmar, John, *The Catholic Church through the Ages: A History*, 2005; Wickham, C., *Framing the Early Middle Ages: Europe and the Mediterranean, 400-800 (2005)*, 2006; and Young, Frances, Lewis Ayres, and Andrew Louth (eds.), *The Cambridge History of Early Christian Literature*, 2004.

[105]   See Rubin, "Sacramental Life," in Rubin and Simons (eds.), *The Cambridge History of Christianity: V. 4, Christianity in Western Europe c. 1100-c. 1500*, 2009, pp. 219-237.

[106]   The main source for this paragraph is Angenendt, Arnold, "Sacrifice, gifts, and prayers in Latin Christianity," in Noble and Smith (eds.), *The Cambridge History of Christianity: Early Medieval Christianities, c. 600-c. 1100*, 2008, pp. 458-60.

[107]   Further, bread no longer could be brought from household supplies, and only unleavened bread formed in coin-sized hosts that were specially prepared could be used. These changes also stimulated the thinking that only the finest golden chalices and patens were acceptable for the Eucharist.

[108]   Peter of Lombard (d. 1160) settled the disputed issue of exactly how many sacraments there were in the Roman Catholic Church--the seven of baptism, confirmation, ordination, marriage, confession, Eucharist, and 'extreme unction' for those nearing death.

[109]   The main sources for this paragraph are: Melody, J., "Commandments of the Church," in *The Catholic Encyclopedia*, retrieved May 28, 2012 from New Advent: http://www.newadvent.org/cathen/04154a.htm; and Holweck, F., "Ecclesiastical Feasts" in *The Catholic Encyclopedia*, retrieved May 28, 2012 from New Advent: http://www.newadvent.org/cathen/06021b.htm.

[110]   The main sources for this paragraph are: Melody, J., "Commandments of the Church," in *The Catholic Encyclopedia*, retrieved May 28, 2012 from New Advent: http://www.newadvent.org/cathen/04154a.htm; and Holweck, F., "Ecclesiastical

Feasts," in *The Catholic Encyclopedia*, retrieved May 28, 2012 from New Advent: http://www.newadvent.org/cathen/06021b.htm.

[111]   Resl, "Material support I: parishes," in Rubin and Simons, *The Cambridge History of Christianity: Christianity in Western Europe c. 1100-c. 1500*, 2009, pp. 102-3.

[112]   The main sources for this section are: Van Engen, John H., "Conclusion: Christendom, c. 1100," in Noble and Smith (eds.), *The Cambridge History of Christianity: Early Medieval Christianities, c. 600-c. 1100*, 2008, pp. 633-37; Pelikan, *Christian Tradition, A History of the Development of Doctrine: V. 1, The Emergence of Catholic Tradition (100-600)*, 1971 (1975), pp. 166-67; and Rubin, "Sacramental Life," in Rubin and Simons (eds.), *The Cambridge History of Christianity: V. 4, Christianity in Western Europe c. 1100-c. 1500*, 2009, pp. 219-237.

[113]   For a discussion of prayers for military victories, see Angenendt, Arnold, "Sacrifice, gifts, and prayers in Latin Christianity," in Noble and Smith (eds.), *The Cambridge History of Christianity: Early Medieval Christianities, c. 600-c. 1100*, 2008, pp. 467-68.

[114]   See: Payer, *Sex and the Penitentials: The Development of a Sex Code, 550-1150*, 1984; and Delumeau, *Sin and Fear: The Emergence of a Western Guilt Culture, 13th-18th Centuries*, 1983 (1990), esp. chs. 6-7.

[115]   As Delumeau explains: ". . . making the confession of sin a fundamental requirement . . . . lead[s] to . . . an almost collective quality . . . . This collective guilt complex is here defined as 'the religious and pathological deviance of a Christianity that focuses its message on the evocation of sin and which narrows its aim to the fight against sinning.' . . . . and the image of a destructive God . . ." See Delumeau, *Sin and Fear: The Emergence of a Western Guilt Culture, 13th-18th Centuries*, 1983 (1990), pp. 297-300.

[116]   See Smith, *The Wealth of Nations*, 1776 (1937), pp. 740-67, for his discussion of religion. Also see his small, companion book, Smith, *The Theory of Moral Sentiments*, 1759 (2004).

[117]   For more on the 'efficiency' of confession as a moral-authority and rent-seeking device, see: Ekelund Jr., Hébert, and Tollison, "An Economic Analysis of the Protestant Reformation," in *Journal of Political Economy* (2002), pp. 646-671; Ekelund Jr., Hébert, and Tollison, " An Economic Model of the Medieval Church: Usury as a Form of Rent Seeking," in *Journal of Law, Economics, and Organization* (Fall 1989), pp. 307-331; Ekelund Jr., Hébert, and Tollison, "The Economics of Sin and Redemption: Purgatory as a Market-Pull Innovation?" in *Journal of Economic Behaviour and Organization* (September 1992), pp. 1-15; and Arrunada, "Catholic

Confessions of Sin as Third Party Moral Enforcement", *The Gruter Institute Working Papers on Law, Economics, and Evolutionary Biology*: Vol. 3: Article 2 (2004).

[118]   Rent extraction simply means the costly but non-productive transfer of resources from one party to another, in this case from sinners to the church. It is a loss-generating activity, assuming that no gains are made by the confessing party because there are transaction costs in the form of money and time involved in extracting the confession and transferring the wealth. However, church authorities presumably would have argued that the spiritual gains more than justified the costs.

[119]   The main sources for this section are: Delumeau, *Sin and Fear: The Emergence of a Western Guilt Culture, 13th-18th Centuries*, 1983 (1990), chs. 6-7; Dunn, "Asceticism, and monasticism, II: Western," in Casiday and Norris (eds.), *The Cambridge History of Christianity: Constantine to c. 600*, 2007, pp. 669-690; Greer, "Pastoral care and discipline," in Casiday and Norris (eds.), *The Cambridge History of Christianity: Constantine to c. 600*, 2007, pp. 567-584; Payer, *Sex and the Penitentials: The Development of a Sex Code, 550-1150*, 1984; Rubin, M., "Sacramental Life," in Rubin and Simons (eds.), *The Cambridge History of Christianity: V. 4, Christianity in Western Europe c. 1100-c. 1500*, 2009, pp. 219-237; Langholm, *The Merchant in The Confessional: Trade and Price in the Pre-Reformation Penitential Handbooks*, 2003, pp. 1-12; Ekelund Jr. et al., *Sacred Trust: The Medieval Church as an Economic Firm*, 1996, pp. 60-71; Meens, Rob, "Remedies for sins," in Noble and Smith (eds.), *The Cambridge History of Christianity: Early Medieval Christianities, c. 600-c. 1100*, 2008, pp. 399-415; Geary, Patrick J., *Furta Sacra: Thefts of Relics in the Central Middle Ages*, 1990, pp. 110-28, 132-33, and 149-56; and Hamilton, S., "Doing Penance," in Rubin, M. (ed.), *Medieval Christianity in Practice*, 2009, pp. 135-43.

[120]   See: Ekelund Jr. et al., *Sacred Trust: The Medieval Church as an Economic Firm*, 1996, pp. 60-71; and Meens, Rob, "Remedies for sins," in Noble and Smith (eds.), *The Cambridge History of Christianity: Early Medieval Christianities, c. 600-c. 1100*, 2008, pp. 399-415.

[121]   The main sources for this paragraph are: Delumeau, *Sin and Fear: The Emergence of a Western Guilt Culture, 13th-18th Centuries*, 1983 (1990), ch. 6; Rubin, M., "Sacramental Life," in Rubin and Simons (eds.), *The Cambridge History of Christianity: V. 4, Christianity in Western Europe c. 1100-c. 1500*, 2009, pp. 219-237; and Langholm, *The Merchant in The Confessional: Trade and Price in the Pre-Reformation Penitential Handbooks*, 2003, pp. 1-12. Langholm explains that the rigorists insisted that absolution could not occur until 'perfect' contrition had occurred, and Thomas Aquinas (a Dominican) was the foremost authority of that group. Later, the non-rigorists claimed John Duns Scotus (a Franciscan) as their main authority, and their argument was that the absolution of the priest completed the process, even if 'perfect' contrition of the sinner had not yet been achieved. However, these two

positions did not perfectly separate the Franciscan and Dominican authors as a whole.

122   The mendicants had to be more subtle than local priests in determining the ability of their customers to pay because they usually did not personally know their customers.

123   This section is based on: Dunn, "Asceticism, and monasticism, II: Western," in Casiday and Norris (eds.), *The Cambridge History of Christianity: Constantine to c. 600*, 2007, pp. 669-690; Payer, *Sex and the Penitentials: The Development of a Sex Code, 550-1150*, 1984, pp. 55-114; Delumeau, *Sin and Fear: The Emergence of a Western Guilt Culture, 13th-18th Centuries*, 1983 (1990), chs. 6-7; Langholm, *The Merchant in The Confessional: Trade and Price in the Pre-Reformation Penitential Handbooks*, 2003, esp. chs. 1-3; Baun, Jane, "Last Things," in Noble and Smith (eds.), *The Cambridge History of Christianity: Early Medieval Christianities, c. 600-c. 1100*, 2008, pp. 619-21; and McDonnell, Kilian, "The *Summae Confessorum* on the Integrity of Confession as Prolegomena for Luther and Trent," in *Theological Studies* 54 (1993), pp. 405-26.

124   The main source for this paragraph is Baun, Jane, "Last Things," in Noble and Smith (eds.), *The Cambridge History of Christianity: Early Medieval Christianities, c. 600-c. 1100*, 2008, pp. 619-21.

125   For some periods, especially during the fourth century, it could be granted only once.

126   When the Irish monk, Columbanus, arrived in France in about 590, he preached repentance and used this new form of penance with great success. Although he was forced to leave in 612 due to opposition of the Frankish episcopal establishment and the royal family, the popularity of his approach changed penance practices in the monasteries and broader society forever. The penitentials from the early Middle Ages were mainly for monastic discipline; when they address laymen, they have an emphasis about sins of the flesh.

127   Various ones were considered the 'main' sins at different times, and all of them had many branches of sinful opportunities. The seven capital or deadly sins often were considered to be Anger or Wrath, Envy, Pride, Greed, Lust, Gluttony, and Sloth.

128   For example, the Third Council of Toledo (589) rejected the penitentials as a 'scandalous innovation', and a synod in 813 was outraged at the confusion spread by conflicting penitentials, some with dubious authorship.

129   Although the old penitentials were condemned in 813 and again in 829, essentially the same material continued to be written and used by circumventing the

prohibitions with the claim they were based on ancient sources (even though they obviously came from the 'condemned' penitentials). At least one avoided censure by claiming the sources were from a bookcase of the Roman Church. See: Payer, *Sex and the Penitentials: The Development of a Sex Code, 550-1150*, 1984, pp. 55-114; Delumeau, *Sin and Fear: The Emergence of a Western Guilt Culture, 13th-18th Centuries*, 1983 (1990), chs. 6-7; and Langholm, *The Merchant in The Confessional: Trade and Price in the Pre-Reformation Penitential Handbooks*, 2003, esp. chs. 1-3. Also see Roach, *The Devil's World: Heresy and Society 1100-1300*, 2005, pp. 92-96.

[130]   In many cases, these collections either did not cite the earlier penitentials as sources or provided incorrect citations. Buchard of Worm's *Decretum* came to be a famous source often cited as authoritative in the eleventh century. Then, Gratian's *Decretum* in the twelfth century also incorporated the issues of the earlier penitentials. It seems that the more systematic development of the church's canon law in the twelfth century led the sources away from the earlier penitentials, but that meant there was no practical guide for confessors. That gap was soon filled by new literature in the form of *summae confessorum* that provided detailed and specific guidance for dealing with the transgressions of the church's religious customers (without citation, these new works definitely continued the influence of the earlier penitentials). For details, see Payer, *Sex and the Penitentials: The Development of a Sex Code, 550-1150*, 1984, pp. 72-114.

[131]   This section is based on: Delumeau, *Sin and Fear: The Emergence of a Western Guilt Culture, 13th-18th Centuries*, 1983 (1990), chs. 6-7; Langholm, *The Merchant in The Confessional: Trade and Price in the Pre-Reformation Penitential Handbooks*, 2003, esp. chs. 1-3; and Payer, *Sex and the Penitentials: The Development of a Sex Code, 550-1150*, 1984, pp. 72-114. Also see Roach, *The Devil's World: Heresy and Society 1100-1300*, 2005, pp. 92-96.

[132]   This paragraph is based on Langholm, *The Merchant in The Confessional: Trade and Price in the Pre-Reformation Penitential Handbooks*, 2003, especially the introduction and ch. 1.

[133]   This paragraph is based on Langholm, *The Merchant in The Confessional: Trade and Price in the Pre-Reformation Penitential Handbooks*, 2003, especially the introduction and ch. 1. His study does not include all handbooks on sin, confession, and forgiveness (he concentrates solely on ones that deal with merchants).

[134]   Pope Gregory IX called him to Rome in 1230 as chaplain and 'papal penitentiary' and commissioned him to compile the collection of *Decretals* that is known by the name of that pope; this collection was completed in 1234. After completing the collection, Raymond returned to his own *Summa*, revised it, and brought it up to date, based on his work on the *Decretals*.

[135] The Dominican John of Freiburg's *Summa confessorum*, written in 1297-98, is the most complete guide for confessors written in the thirteenth century. He also composed his *Confessionale* for "simpler and less expert confessors". John does not so much popularize the church's famous theologian, Thomas Aquinas, as simply copy him verbatim in extensive passages. He also quotes other authorities and adds some original contributions.

[136] The Dominican and Franciscan handbooks drew on the earlier penitentials, and they provided detailed guidelines for interrogating sinners, using the shame of sinners to extract full confessions, and determining the corresponding penances for the sins revealed. See: Payer, *Sex and the Penitentials: The Development of a Sex Code, 550-1150*, 1984; and Delumeau, *Sin and Fear: The Emergence of a Western Guilt Culture, 13th-18th Centuries*, 1983 (1990), esp. chs. 6-7.

[137] The Great Schism put a temporary halt to the production of more handbooks, but the genre returned in huge numbers around 1500, including notable ones by Dominicans and Franciscans. (The Great Schism of 1378 refers to the period of 68 years during which two popes claimed jurisdiction over the Roman Church.) Partly, these handbooks and how they were used is what concerned Luther. He argued that confession had become the hierarchy's chief weapon in domination of God's people and in opposing God. In 1520, he burned at the stake both the Papal Bull *Esurge Domine* and Angelo de Chiavasso's *Summa angelica*, which he labeled diabolical. See Delumeau, *Sin and Fear: The Emergence of a Western Guilt Culture, 13th-18th Centuries*, 1983 (1990), esp. ch. 6.

[138] See Delumeau, *Sin and Fear: The Emergence of a Western Guilt Culture, 13th-18th Centuries*, 1983 (1990), esp. ch. 6.

[139] Some manuals also covered the eight beatitudes, the six or seven bodily acts of mercy, the six or seven acts of spiritual mercy, the four cardinal virtues, the three theological virtues, and other issues.

[140] The second edition of Marchant's *Compost et Kalendrier des bergiers* (1493) identifies eighty-seven branches of the Deadly Sins and has three offshoots for each, adding up to 261 branches; each of these branches also divide into three more 'bunches of foliage' for a total of 783 ways to fall prey to one of the Seven Deadly Sins. For the next three centuries, this encyclopedia of sin was repeatedly reprinted by publishers who specialized in popular literature. See Delumeau, *Sin and Fear: The Emergence of a Western Guilt Culture, 13th-18th Centuries*, 1983 (1990), ch. 6.

[141] The main source for this paragraph is Baun, Jane, "Last Things," in Noble and Smith (eds.), *The Cambridge History of Christianity: Early Medieval Christianities, c. 600-c. 1100*, 2008, pp. 619-21.

142   Many of the countless visions of apocalyptic terror can be understood in this context as possibly offering their readers and listeners consolation about their plights in the difficult situations and violent word they endured. This placed their personal sufferings in a broader context that offered hope in the next world, if not in this one. In the very end, God's justice would prevail, offering relief for current sufferings. This formed the bedrock of medieval Catholic sorrows and hope.

143   The main source for this section is McDonnell, Kilian, "The *Summae Confessorum* on the Integrity of Confession as Prolegomena for Luther and Trent," in *Theological Studies* 54 (1993), pp. 405-26.

144   This idea later evolved into that of the integrity of the confession that was essential for absolution—this idea was formalized by Raymond of Penafort, Albert the Great, Thomas Aquinas, and others during the thirteenth century.

145   McDonnell, Kilian, "The *Summae Confessorum* on the Integrity of Confession as Prolegomena for Luther and Trent," in *Theological Studies* 54 (1993), pp. 416-17.

146   For example, Thomas Chobham believed the confessor was in the mercy business and gave his *summa* the title, *Cum miserationes*, to connote that idea.

147   Although the modern church has abandoned a criminalized approach to confession, it still mandates confession of every grave sin. However, the burden of a full confession now is on the sinner, not on the father-confessor.

148   The main sources for this section are: Delumeau, *Sin and Fear: The Emergence of a Western Guilt Culture, 13th-18th Centuries*, 1983 (1990), chs. 6-7; Langholm, *The Merchant in The Confessional: Trade and Price in the Pre-Reformation Penitential Handbooks*, 2003, esp. chs. 1-3; Greer, "Pastoral care and discipline," in Casiday and Norris (eds.), *The Cambridge History of Christianity: Constantine to c. 600*, 2007, pp. 567-584; Little, *Religious Poverty and the Profit Economy in Medieval Europe*, 1978, ch. 2; and McDonnell, Kilian, "The *Summae Confessorum* on the Integrity of Confession as Prolegomena for Luther and Trent," in *Theological Studies* 54 (1993), pp. 405-26. Also see Roach, *The Devil's World: Heresy and Society 1100-1300*, 2005, pp. 92-96.

149   Little, *Religious Poverty and the Profit Economy in Medieval Europe*, 1978, ch. 2.

150   This policy was formally codified by St. Thomas Aquinas' treatment of the doctrine of penance that eventually became the official policy of the church. See Delumeau, *Sin and Fear: The Emergence of a Western Guilt Culture, 13th-18th Centuries*, 1983 (1990), ch. 6.

151   The main source for this paragraph's discussion of the church's justification for its wealth is González, Justo L., *Faith and Wealth: A History of Early Christian Ideas on*

the *Origin, Significance, and Use of Money*, 1990, pp. xiv, 22, and 73-76.

[152]   This section is based on: Newhauser, *The Early History of Greed: The Sin of Avarice in Early Medieval Thought and Literature*, 2000, pp. xi-xiv, 1-97, and 116-128; Langholm, *The Merchant in The Confessional: Trade and Price in the Pre-Reformation Penitential Handbooks*, 2003, pp. 256-71; and O'Brien, *An Essay on Mediaeval Economic Teaching*, 1920 (1968), pp. 74-79.

[153]   The main source for this paragraph is González, Justo L., *Faith and Wealth: A History of Early Christian Ideas on the Origin, Significance, and Use of Money*, 1990, pp. 132-34 and 173-93.

[154]   The main source for this paragraph is González, Justo L., *Faith and Wealth: A History of Early Christian Ideas on the Origin, Significance, and Use of Money*, 1990, pp. 173-93.

[155]   The main source for this paragraph is González, Justo L., *Faith and Wealth: A History of Early Christian Ideas on the Origin, Significance, and Use of Money*, 1990, pp. 124-28.

[156]   The main source for this paragraph is Smith, J. M. H., "Pilgrimage and Spiritual Healing," in Rubin, M. (ed.), *Medieval Christianity in Practice*, 2009, pp. 222-28.

[157]   The main source for this paragraph is Kleinberg, A. M., "The Possession of Blessed Jordan of Saxony," in Rubin, M. (ed.), *Medieval Christianity in Practice, 2009*, pp. 265-73.

[158]   Further, belief in demons was not just for the uneducated in early Christian history. For example, Jordon of Saxony was St. Dominic's thirteenth-century successor as Master General of the Dominican Order. He related an experience of how a simple brother of the order, Bernard, was possessed by a demon when he arrived at the Dominican convent at Bologna in 1221. Like all demons, Bernard's acted as a ventriloquist in using Bernard for his evil messages, but then a successful exorcism was performed.

[159]   The main source for this paragraph is Horden, P., "Sickness and healing," in Noble and Smith (eds.), *The Cambridge History of Christianity: Early Medieval Christianities, c. 600-c. 1100*, 2008, pp. 416-30.

[160]   The main source for this paragraph is Horden, P., "Sickness and healing," in Noble and Smith (eds.), *The Cambridge History of Christianity: Early Medieval Christianities, c. 600-c. 1100*, 2008, pp. 416-30.

[161]   Even when canon law dealt more directly with the issue after 1100, it led to

relatively few restrictions for priests and monks who practiced medicine.

162 The main sources for this paragraph are: Horden, P., "Sickness and healing," in Noble and Smith (eds.), *The Cambridge History of Christianity: Early Medieval Christianities, c. 600-c. 1100*, 2008, pp. 416-30; and Ziegler, J., "Fourteenth-Century Instructions for Bedside Pastoral Care," in Rubin, M. (ed.), *Medieval Christianity in Practice*, 2009, pp. 103-108.

163 Horden, P., "Sickness and healing," in Noble and Smith (eds.), *The Cambridge History of Christianity: Early Medieval Christianities, c. 600-c. 1100*, 2008, p. 430.

164 The main source for this paragraph is Ziegler, J., "Fourteenth-Century Instructions for Bedside Pastoral Care," in Rubin, M. (ed.), *Medieval Christianity in Practice*, 2009, pp. 103-108.

165 The main sources for this section are: Wood, *The Proprietary Church in the Medieval West*, 2006, pp. 459-62 and 478-86; Resl, "Material support I: parishes," in Rubin and Simons (eds.), *The Cambridge History of Christianity: V. 4, Christianity in Western Europe c. 1100-c. 1500*, 2009, pp. 99-106; Nelson, Janet L., "Law and its applications," in Noble and Smith (eds.), *The Cambridge History of Christianity: Early Medieval Christianities, c. 600-c. 1100*, 2008, pp. 299-300; and Helvétius, Anne-Marie and Michel Kaplan, "Asceticisim and its institutions," in Noble and Smith (eds.), *The Cambridge History of Christianity: Early Medieval Christianities, c. 600-c. 1100*, 2008, pp. 290-96.

166 For a discussion of these services, see: Rubin, "Sacramental Life," in Rubin and Simons (eds.), *The Cambridge History of Christianity: V. 4, Christianity in Western Europe c. 1100-c. 1500*, 2009, pp. 219-237; and Wood, *The Proprietary Church in the Medieval West*, 2006, pp. 478-86.

167 See Wood, *The Proprietary Church in the Medieval West*, 2006, pp. 478-86 and 754-75.

168 The main sources for this section are: Ekelund Jr., R. B. *et al.*, *Sacred Trust: The Medieval Church as an Economic Firm*, 1996; and Little, *Religious Poverty and the Profit Economy in Medieval Europe*, 1978. Other sources have similar ideas, including: Gilchrist, *The Church and Economic Activity in the Middle Ages*, 1969; Kaye, "Monetary and Market Consciousness in Thirteenth and Fourteenth Century Europe," in Lowry and Gordon (eds.), *Ancient and Medieval Economic Ideas and Concepts of Social Justice*, pp. 371-403; Lopez, *The Commercial Revolution of the Middle Ages, 950-1350*, 1976; Ekelund Jr., Hébert, and Tollison, " An Economic Model of the Medieval Church: Usury as a Form of Rent Seeking," in *Journal of Law, Economics, and Organization* (Fall 1989), pp. 307-331; Wood, *The Proprietary Church in the Medieval*

West, 2006, pp. 459-60; and Rubin, M., "Sacramental Life," in Rubin and Simons (eds.), *The Cambridge History of Christianity: V. 4, Christianity in Western Europe c. 1100-c. 1500*, 2009, pp. 219-237.

[169] Wood, *The Proprietary Church in the Medieval West*, 2006, pp. 459-60.

[170] For a detailed study of the medieval church as an economic firm, see Ekelund Jr. et al., *Sacred Trust: The Medieval Church as an Economic Firm*, 1996.

[171] See Kaye, "Monetary and Market Consciousness in Thirteenth and Fourteenth Century Europe," in Lowry and Gordon (eds.), *Ancient and Medieval Economic Ideas and Concepts of Social Justice*, pp. 371-403.

[172] See Ekelund Jr. et al., *Sacred Trust: The Medieval Church as an Economic Firm*, 1996.

[173] This paragraph is based on Rubin, M., "Sacramental Life," in Rubin and Simons (eds.), *The Cambridge History of Christianity: V. 4, Christianity in Western Europe c. 1100-c. 1500*, 2009, pp. 219-237.

[174] For those interested in exploring the topics in this chapter in much more depth, there are many additional sources that include the following: Boswell, J., *Christianity, Social Tolerance, and Homosexuality*, 1980; Botticini, M., "A Loveless Economy? Intergenerational Altruism and the Marriage Market in a Tuscan Town," in *Journal of Economic History* 59.1 (March 1999), pp. 104-121; Cochran, J. K. and L. Beeghley, "The Influence of Religion on Attitudes toward Nonmarital Sexuality," in *Journal of the Scientific Study of Religion* 30.1 (1991), pp. 45-62; d'Avray, D., "Annulment of Henry III's 'Marriage' to Joan of Ponthieu Confirmed by Innocent IV on 20 May 1254," in Rubin, M. (ed.), *Medieval Christianity in Practice*, 2009, pp. 42-51; d' Avray, D., *Medieval Marriage: Symbolism and Society* (2005), 2008; Donahue, C., Jr., "The Canon Law on the Formation of Marriage and Social Practice in the Later Middle Ages," in *Journal of Family History* 8 (1983), pp. 144-158; Duby, G. (translated by B. Bray), *The Knight, the Lady and the Priest: The Making of Modern Marriage in Medieval France* (1981), 1993; Duby, G. (translated by J. Dunnett), *Love and Marriage in the Middle Ages* (1988), 1996; Ekelund Jr., Robert B., D. R. Street, and and A. B. Davidson, "Marriage, Divorce, and Prostitution; Economic Sociology in Medieval England and Enlightenment Spain," in *European Journal of the History of Economic Thought* 3 (1996), pp. 183-199; Grossbard-Shechtman, S. A. and N. S. Neuman, "Economic Behavior, Marriage and Religiosity," in *Journal of Behavioral Science* 15 (Spring-Summer 1986), pp. 71-85; Houlbrooke, R., "The Making of Marriage in Mid-Tudor England: Evidence from the Records of Matrimonial Contract Litigation," in *Journal of Family History* 10 (1985), pp. 339-352; McGinn, T. A. J., "The Law of Roman Divorce in the Time of Christ," in Levine, Allison Jr., and Crossan (eds), *The Historical Jesus in Context*, 2006, pp. 309-22; Seward, D., "Marriage

Theory and Practice in the Conciliar Legislation and Diocesan Statutes of Medieval England," in *Medieval Studies* 40 (1978), pp. 408-460; and Smith, C. E., *Papal Enforcement of Some Medieval Marriage Laws*, 1940.

[175] For Augustine's sexual ideas and behavior, see Brown, P., *Augustine of Hippo: A Biography*, 1967 (2000).

[176] The main sources for the Council of Elvira are: *The New Advent* at http://www.newadvent.org/cathen/05395b.htm, March 13, 2010; and *The Catholic University of America* at http://faculty.cua.edu/pennington/Canon%20Law/ElviraCanons.htm, March 13, 2010.

[177] Other canons from the Council of Elvira include: "44. A former prostitute who has married and who seeks admission to the Christian faith shall be received without delay. . . . 78. If a Christian confesses adultery with a Jewish or pagan woman, he is denied communion for some time. If his sin is exposed by someone else, he must complete five years' penance before receiving the Sunday communion." See *The Catholic University of America* at http://faculty.cua.edu/pennington/Canon%20Law/ElviraCanons.htm, March 13, 2010.

[178] See Hunter, "Sexuality, marriage and the family," in Casiday and Norris (eds.), *The Cambridge History of Christianity: Constantine to c. 600*, 2007, p. 587.

[179] Pomeroy, S. B., *Goddesses, Whores, Wives, and Slaves: Women in Classical Antiquity*, (1975), 1995., p. 160.

[180] See Payer, *Sex and the Penitentials: The Development of a Sexual Code, 550-1150*, 1984, pp. 3-18.

[181] Payer, *Sex and the Penitentials: The Development of a Sexual Code, 550-1150*, 1984, pp. 19-122.

[182] Delumeau, *Sin and Fear: The Emergence of a Western Guilt Culture, 13th-18th Centuries*, 1983 (1990), p. 209.

[183] The main source for this section is Payer, *Sex and the Penitentials: The Development of a Sex Code, 550-1150*, 1984. Also see Delumeau, *Sin and Fear: The Emergence of a Western Guilt Culture, 13th-18th Centuries*, 1983 (1990), chs. 6-7.

[184] The first phase of the penitentials ended in 813 when they were explicitly condemned by a reform council. Nonetheless, when the use of the penitentials (or at least their detailed instructions on grilling religious customers) resumed within

one hundred years, the penalties relied heavily on those contained in the earlier penitentials for many sin-penance prices. Even though the penitentials analyzed by Payer and discussed below are for the period up to the early ninth century, all of the penitentials he examined for the period up to eleventh century had a strong emphasis on sexual behavior.For more on these issues, see Payer, *Sex and the Penitentials: The Development of a Sex Code, 550-1150*, 1984, pp. 40-71.

[185] This paragraph is based on Payer, *Sex and the Penitentials: The Development of a Sex Code, 550-1150*, 1984, pp. 72-114.

[186] Without citation, these new works definitely used the earlier penitentials.

[187] Payer, *Sex and the Penitentials: The Development of a Sex Code, 550-1150*, 1984, pp. 19-40. Payer also notes that a supposed letter of Pope Gregory I permits more leeway than some of the penitentials, but the authenticity of the letter included by Bede in his penitentials is doubtful.

[188] Payer, *Sex and the Penitentials: The Development of a Sex Code, 550-1150*, 1984, pp. 40-54.

[189] The sources for this section are: Payer, *Sex and the Penitentials: The Development of a Sex Code, 550-1150*, 1984, pp. 115-22 and Appendix C; and Delumeau, *Sin and Fear: The Emergence of a Western Guilt Culture, 13th-18th Centuries*, 1983 (1990), chs. 6-7.

[190] Delumeau, *Sin and Fear: The Emergence of a Western Guilt Culture, 13th-18th Centuries*, 1983 (1990), p. 202.

[191] This table is based on information in Payer, *Sex and the Penitentials: The Development of a Sex Code, 550-1150*, 1984, Appendix C.

[192] This section is based on Delumeau, *Sin and Fear: The Emergence of a Western Guilt Culture, 13th-18th Centuries*, 1983 (1990), ch. 7.

[193] Some other ecclesiastical writers (including Martin Le Maistre and John Mair) at the turn of the sixteenth century argued that common sense reveals that marriage partners were allowed to unite for pleasure, just as one can enjoy various foods without sin. However, these more reasonable positions did not seem to have much impact on other ecclesiastical attitudes.

[194] This paragraph is based on Hunter, "Sexuality, marriage and the family," in Casiday and Norris (eds.), *The Cambridge History of Christianity: Constantine to c. 600*, 2007, pp. 585-600.

[195] Osiek, "Family Matters," in Horsley (ed.), *A People's History of Christianity, Vol. 1: Christian Origins*, 2005, p. 201.

[196] Hunter, "Sexuality, marriage and the family," in Casiday and Norris (eds.), *The Cambridge History of Christianity: Constantine to c. 600*, 2007, pp. 591-92.

[197] The main source for this paragraph is Smith, J. M. H., "Pilgrimage and Spiritual Healing," in Rubin, M. (ed.), *Medieval Christianity in Practice*, 2009, pp. 226-28.

[198] This paragraph is based on: Roach, *The Devil's World: Heresy and Society 1100-1300*, 2005, pp. 17-27; and Van Engen, John H., "Conclusion: Christendom, c. 1100," in Noble and Smith (eds.), *The Cambridge History of Christianity: Early Medieval Christianities, c. 600-c. 1100*, 2008, pp. 625-31.

[199] A main argument for taking over the marriage market and making marriage a church sacrament was that the grace of the sacrament was understood to remove the inherent stain of marital sexual relations that resulted from original sin. The church gained it's definitive power over marriage and divorce, including many royal ones, in the eleventh century.

[200] This paragraph is based on Roach, *The Devil's World: Heresy and Society 1100-1300*, 2005, pp. 17-27.

[201] The main sources for this paragraph are: Roach, *The Devil's World: Heresy and Society 1100-1300*, 2005, pp. 17-27 and ch. 7; and Ekelund Jr. et al., *Sacred Trust: The Medieval Church as an Economic Firm*, 1996, ch. 5.

[202] For an economic analysis of the church's role in regulating marriage, see: Ekelund Jr. et al., *Sacred Trust: The Medieval Church as an Economic Firm*, 1996, ch. 5; and Ekelund Jr. et al., "The Political Economy of the Medieval Church," in McCleary, Rachel M. (ed.), *The Oxford Handbook of the Economics of Religion*, 2011, pp. 309-310.

[203] When the church took control of marriage and divorce, it used up some of society's scarce resources (labor, intellectual power, etc.) to simply transfer existing wealth from one owner to another. Thus, from society's point of view, the transfer involved a loss (costs without any new wealth).

[204] See: Ekelund Jr. et al., *Sacred Trust: The Medieval Church as an Economic Firm*, 1996, ch. 5; and Roach, *The Devil's World: Heresy and Society 1100-1300*, 2005, ch. 7.

[205] The main source for this paragraph is Ekelund Jr. et al., *Sacred Trust: The Medieval Church as an Economic Firm*, 1996, ch. 5.

[206] Between the fourth and thirteenth centuries, the church changed its regulations a few times. Marriage to second cousins was prohibited in the fourth century. The prohibitions were extended in the fifth century to include no marriages between aunts or uncles and nieces or nephews. In the sixth century, the prohibitions were extended to fifth cousins. In the ninth century, they were extended to sixth cousins. Under pressure, the church backed down in the thirteenth century to prohibiting marriages up to third cousins but not beyond.

[207] The main sources for this section are: Ekelund Jr. et al., *Sacred Trust: The Medieval Church as an Economic Firm*, 1996, ch. 5; Lunt, *Papal Revenues in the Middle Ages, Vols. I-II*, 1934; d'Avray, D., "Annulment of Henry III's 'Marriage' to Joan of Ponthieu Confirmed by Innocent IV on 20 May 1254," in Rubin, M. (ed.), *Medieval Christianity in Practice*, 2009, pp. 42-51; Duby, Georges (translated by Elbord Forster), *Medieval Marriage*, 1978; and Davidson, Audrey and Ekelund Jr., Robert, "The Medieval Church and Rents from Marriage Market Regulations," in *Journal of Economic Behavior and Organization* 32 (1997), pp. 215-245.

[208] Lunt, *Papal Revenues in the Middle Ages, Vols. I-II*, 1934.

[209] Lunt, *Papal Revenues in the Middle Ages, Vol. II*, 1934, pp. 524-26.

[210] Duby, Georges (translated by Elbord Forster), *Medieval Marriage*, 1978; and Davidson, Audrey and Ekelund Jr., Robert, "The Medieval Church and Rents from Marriage Market Regulations," in *Journal of Economic Behavior and Organization* 32 (1997), pp. 215-245.

[211] This paragraph is based on Ekelund Jr. et al., *Sacred Trust: The Medieval Church as an Economic Firm*, 1996, ch. 5.

[212] This paragraph is based on Ekelund Jr. et al., *Sacred Trust: The Medieval Church as an Economic Firm*, 1996, ch. 5.

[213] The *New Advent Online Bible* at http://www.newadvent.org/bible/joh008.htm.

[214] The main sources for this paragraph are: Angenendt, Arnold, "Sacrifice, gifts, and prayers in Latin Christianity," in Noble and Smith (eds.), *The Cambridge History of Christianity: Early Medieval Christianities, c. 600-c. 1100*, 2008, pp. 462-64; and Van Engen, John H., "Conclusion: Christendom, c. 1100," in Noble and Smith (eds.), *The Cambridge History of Christianity: Early Medieval Christianities, c. 600-c. 1100*, 2008, p. 633.

[215] For those interested in exploring the topics in this chapter in much more depth, there are many additional sources that include the following: Cornelison, S. J. and S. B. Montgomery (eds.), *Images, Relics, and Devotional Practices in Medieval and*

Renaissance Italy, 2006; Georgoudi, S., "Creating a Myth of Matriarchy," in Schmitt (ed.), *A History of Women in the West: From Ancient Goddesses to Christian Saints*, 1994, pp. 449-463; Nelson, J., "Royal saints and early medieval kingship," in Baker (ed.), *Sanctity and Secularity: The Church and the World*, 1973, pp. 39-44; Trout, D., "Saints, Identity, and the City," in Burrus (ed.), *A People's History of Christianity, Vol. 2: Late Ancient Christianity*, 2005, pp. 165-87; Webb, Diana, "A Saint and His Money: Perceptions of Urban Wealth in the Lives of Italian Saints," in Sheils, and Wood (eds.), *The Church and Wealth, Studies in Church History*, 1986, pp. 61-73; and Webb, Diana, "Saints and Cities in Medieval Italy," in *History Today* 43 (July 1993), pp. 15-22.

[216]   For Catholic veneration of the saints, see: Geary, Patrick J., *Furta Sacra: Thefts of Relics in the Central Middle Ages*, 1990, pp. xi-15 and 28-35; and Rapp, C., "Saints and holy men," in Casiday and Norris (eds.), *The Cambridge History of Christianity: Constantine to c. 600*, 2007, pp. 548-566.

[217]   This paragraph is based on: Cameron, R., *A Concise Economic History of the World: From Paleolithic Times to the Present*, 1989; Frank, G., "From Antioch to Arles: Lay devotion in context," in Casiday and Norris (eds.), *The Cambridge History of Christianity: Constantine to c. 600*, 2007, pp. 531-547; Thurston, "Relics," *The Catholic Encyclopedia*, retrieved January 2, 2009 from New Advent: http://www.newadvent.org/cathen/12734a.htm; and Tilley, M. A., "North Africa," in Mitchell and Young (eds.), *The Cambridge History of Christianity, Vol. 1: Origins to Constantine*, 2006, pp. 381-386.

[218]   A classic example is provided by a letter written in 156 about the death of St. Polycarp, who was burned at the stake. The saint's bones—considered more valuable than precious stones and finer than refined gold—were gathered up and deposited in a suitable place where his martyrdom could be celebrated annually. In North Africa, honoring local martyrs who died for the faith began during the late second and early third centuries. It is not clear how soon the veneration of minute fragments of bones, cloth, small packets of dust, and other items that had been in contact with the tombs of the saints or their relics were considered holy and venerated, but such practices were widespread by the early fourth century. St. Cyril confirms that the supposed wood of the Cross was distributed widely throughout the world before 350.

[219]   Although prominent theologians of the early church endorsed the veneration of saints' relics, official Roman Catholic confirmation of such a doctrine was not enunciated in a church council until the sixteenth-century Council of Trent, which was held largely in response to Protestant criticisms of Catholic practices and theology. The doctrine was further developed by the Roman Catechism written under instructions of the Council of Trent. That Catechism makes it abundantly

clear that no one should doubt the power of sacred ashes, bones, and other relics of the saints. Although official church teaching has strongly supported the reverencing of saints and their relics, the church has been very cautious in ever certifying the authenticity of particular relics. See Thurston, "Relics," *The Catholic Encyclopedia*, retrieved January 2, 2009 from New Advent at http://www.newadvent.org/cathen/12734a.htm.

[220] See Kemp, Eric W. *Canonization in the Western Church*, Oxford: Oxford University Press, 1948, pp. 44-45 and 138-140.

[221] Barro, Robert J., Rachel M. McCleary, and Axexander McQuoid, "The Economics of Sainthood (A Preliminary Investigation)," in McCleary, Rachel M. (ed.), *The Oxford Handbook of the Economics of Religion*, 2011, pp. 191-216.

[222] Young, "Prelude: Jesus Christ, foundation of Christianity," in Mitchell and Young (eds.), *The Cambridge History of Christianity, Vol. 1: Origins to Constantine*, 2006, pp. 1-34.

[223] See Freeman, *A. D. 381: Heretics, Pagans, and the Dawn of the Monotheistic State*, 2008, pp. 115-16.

[224] Horden, P. and N. Purcell, *The Corrupting Sea: A Study of Mediterranean History*, 2000, p. 429.

[225] This paragraph is based on: Brown, P., *The Cult of Saints: Its Rise and Function in Latin Christianity*, 1982, chs. 2-3; Angenendt, Arnold, "Sacrifice, gifts, and prayers in Latin Christianity," in Noble and Smith (eds.), *The Cambridge History of Christianity: Early Medieval Christianities, c. 600-c. 1100*, 2008, pp. 462-64; and Van Engen, John H., "Conclusion: Christendom, c. 1100," in Noble and Smith (eds.), *The Cambridge History of Christianity: Early Medieval Christianities, c. 600-c. 1100*, 2008, p. 633.

[226] Brown, P., *The Cult of Saints: Its Rise and Function in Latin Christianity*, 1982, pp. 41-43.

[227] Jones, A. H. M., *The Later Roman Empire, 284-602, A Social, Economic, and Administrative Survey: Books 1-2*, 1964, pp. 958-61.

[228] This paragraph is based on Holman, S. R., "Rich and Poor in Sophronius of Jerusalem's *Miracles of Saints Cyrus and John*," in Holman (ed.), *Wealth and Poverty in Early Church and Society*, 2008, pp. 103-124.

[229] Holman, S. R., "Rich and Poor in Sophronius of Jerusalem's *Miracles of Saints Cyrus and John*," in Holman (ed.), *Wealth and Poverty in Early Church and Society*, 2008, p. 107.

[230] Davies, J. G., *The Early Christian Church* (1965), 1995, p. 274.

[231] This paragraph is based on: Jones, A. H. M., *The Later Roman Empire, 284-602, A Social, Economic, and Administrative Survey: Books 1-2*, 1964, pp. 962-63; Louth, A., "Hagiography," in Young, Lewis, and Louth (eds.), *The Cambridge History of Early Christian Literature*, 2004, pp. 358-361; and Ehrman and Jacobs, *Chrsitianity in Late Antiquity, 300-450 C. E. : A Reader*, 2004, pp. 366-416.

[232] These miracles were performed both during and after the lifetimes of the saints. Most of the early saints are from the monastic tradition, and the emphasis on the holiness of monks rather than ordinary clergy continued through the Middle Ages. Bishop Athanasius's Life of Antony written around 360 usually is considered the account that became a pattern for other stories emphasizing the miracles performed by or because of the saints' power to intervene with God on behalf of their petitioners.

[233] The multitude of miracles contained in the stories of the saints makes them problematic for historians, but they can be used to help understand the beliefs of the times--the saints not only were present for the people, they directly intervened to perform miracles for their faithful petitioners. Adding to the supposed power of saints' relics, the recorded miracles almost always occurred because of direct contact with a saint's relic, shrine, or some object at the shrine. See: Louth, A., "Hagiography," in Young, Lewis, and Louth (eds.), *The Cambridge History of Early Christian Literature*, 2004, pp. 358-361; Ehrman and Jacobs, *Chrsitianity in Late Antiquity, 300-450 C. E. : A Reader*, 2004, pp. 366-416; Brown, P. *Augustine of Hippo: A Biography*, 1967 (2000), pp. 416-22; and Jones, A. H. M., *The Later Roman Empire, 284-602, A Social, Economic, and Administrative Survey: Books 1-2*, 1964, pp. 962-63.

[234] Bishop Athanasius used his *Life of Antony* for both purposes. For example, he portrayed Antony as a saint who was completely obedient to the wisdom of his bishops. Yet Antony never was part of the church's hierarchical establishment or known to have closely consulted bishops for guiding his life and community of monastic followers in the remote Egyptian desert. See: Ehrman and Jacobs, *Chrsitianity in Late Antiquity, 300-450 C. E. : A Reader*, 2004, pp. 366-416.

[235] The main source for this paragraph is Smith, J. M. H., "Saints and their cults," in Noble and Smith (eds.), *The Cambridge History of Christianity: Early Medieval Christianities, c. 600-c. 1100*, 2008, pp. 595-600.

[236] From the seventh to ninth centuries, the cults of relics increased in importance, as church leaders decided they were essential for all sacred spaces, including the altar. For example, Bede's history, which was written in the first half of the eighth century, records how the pope forwarded to his English representative the

'necessities' for worship and a church, including the supposed relics of the Holy Apostles. See Thurston, H., "Relics," *The Catholic Encyclopedia,* retrieved January 2, 2009 from New Advent at http://www.newadvent.org/cathen/12734a.htm.

[237] The main sources for this section are: Geary, Patrick J., *Furta Sacra: Thefts of Relics in the Central Middle Ages*, 1990, pp. xi-15 and 20-54, 50-59, and 65; Head, T., "Translation of the Body of St. Junianus," in Rubin, M. (ed.), *Medieval Christianity in Practice*, 2009, pp. 217-21; Smith, J. M. H., "Saints and their cults," in Noble and Smith (eds.), *The Cambridge History of Christianity: Early Medieval Christianities, c. 600-c. 1100*, 2008, pp. 581-605; Wood, S., *The Proprietary Church in the Medieval West*, 2006, pp. 86-108; Vauchez, André, "Saints and pilgrimages: new and old," in Rubin and Simons (eds.), *The Cambridge History of Christianity: V. 4, Christianity in Western Europe c. 1100-c. 1500*, 2009, pp. 327-34; Roach, *The Devil's World: Heresy and Society 1100-1300*, 2005, pp. 1-9, 17-27 and 178-81; Resl, "Material support I: parishes," in Rubin and Simons, *The Cambridge History of Christianity, V. 4*, 2009, pp. 102-3; Frankfurter, "Christianity and paganism, I: Egypt," in Casiday and Norris (eds.), *The Cambridge History of Christianity: Constantine to c. 600*, 2007, pp. 173-188; Frank, G., "From Antioch to Arles: Lay devotion in context," in Casiday and Norris (eds.), *The Cambridge History of Christianity: Constantine to c. 600*, 2007, pp. 531-547; and Schimmelpfennig, B., *The Papacy*, 1998, pp. 15-50.

[238] This paragraph is based on Brown, P., *The Cult of Saints: Its Rise and Function in Latin Christianity*, 1982, ch. 1 and pp. 124-27.

[239] The pagan religions found nothing unusual about worshiping the dead. However, the big difference was that the pagans never thought, as the Catholics did, that the saints could directly intercede on the behalf of humans with God. And the pagans were aghast at the thought of bringing the dead into the cities of the living.

[240] This paragraph is based on: Brown, P., *The Cult of Saints: Its Rise and Function in Latin Christianity*, 1982, ch. 1; Freeman, *A. D. 381: Heretics, Pagans, and the Dawn of the Monotheistic State*, 2008, p. 182; and Curtis, A. K., S. Lang, and R. Petersen, *The 100 Most Important Events in Christian History*, 1998.

[241] The main source for this paragraph is Smith, J. M. H., "Saints and their cults," in Noble and Smith (eds.), *The Cambridge History of Christianity: Early Medieval Christianities, c. 600-c. 1100*, 2008, pp. 601-05.

[242] The main source for this paragraph is Smith, J. M. H., "Saints and their cults," in Noble and Smith (eds.), *The Cambridge History of Christianity: Early Medieval Christianities, c. 600-c. 1100*, 2008, pp. 601-05.

[243] This paragraph is based on Wood, S., *The Proprietary Church in the Medieval West*, 2006, pp. 86-108.

[244] This paragraph is based on Rapp, C., "Saints and holy men," in Casiday and Norris (eds.), *The Cambridge History of Christianity: Constantine to c. 600*, 2007, p. 554.

[245] For example, by the late seventh century, the cloak shared by St. Martin with a beggar in his most famous miracle had become the most important relic used by the Merovingian kings in their military defense of what essentially amounts to ancient Gaul. This relic was tended by special church clergy and then carried into battles by the Merovingian and Carolingian kings during the seventh to ninth centuries.

[246] This paragraph is based on Wood, S., *The Proprietary Church in the Medieval West*, 2006, pp. 86-108.

[247] Frankfurter, "Christianity and paganism, I: Egypt," in Casiday and Norris (eds.), *The Cambridge History of Christianity: Constantine to c. 600*, 2007, pp. 181-82.

[248] This paragraph is based on: Vauchez, André, "Saints and pilgrimages: new and old," in Rubin and Simons (eds.), *The Cambridge History of Christianity: V. 4, Christianity in Western Europe c. 1100-c. 1500*, 2009, pp. 327-34; and Roach, *The Devil's World: Heresy and Society 1100-1300*, 2005, pp. 17-27.

[249] The main source for this paragraph is Roach, *The Devil's World: Heresy and Society 1100-1300*, 2005, pp. 17-27 and 178-81.

[250] The main source for this paragraph is Roach, *The Devil's World: Heresy and Society 1100-1300*, 2005, pp. 17-27 and 178-81.

[251] The main sources for this paragraph are: Roach, *The Devil's World: Heresy and Society 1100-1300*, 2005, pp. 17-27 and 178-81; and Resl, "Material support I: parishes," in Rubin and Simons, *The Cambridge History of Christianity, V. 4*, 2009, pp. 102-3.

[252] This paragraph is based on Roach, *The Devil's World: Heresy and Society 1100-1300*, 2005, pp. 1-9.

[253] This paragraph is based on Brown, P., *The Cult of Saints: Its Rise and Function in Latin Christianity*, 1982, chs. 2-3.

[254] This paragraph is based on Schimmelpfennig, B., *The Papacy*, 1998, pp. 15-50.

[255] There were only fourteen names included in the canon of the mass in 500, but

that later was expanded to thirty-nine.

[256] See Thurston, "Relics," *The Catholic Encyclopedia,* retrieved January 2, 2009 from New Advent at http://www.newadvent.org/cathen/12734a.htm.

[257] Resl, "Material support I: parishes," in Rubin and Simons, *The Cambridge History of Christianity, V. 4,* 2009, pp. 102-3.

[258] This was an unusual approach by the church in using ordinary laity in attempting to implement its policies, because they usually were not consulted on such matters.

[259] Many churchmen brought the revered relics of saints from their churches or monasteries, such as the relics of St. Junianus who attended the 989 meeting, courtesy of the monks who owned and controlled them.

[260] The main sources for this section are: Geary, Patrick J., *Furta Sacra: Thefts of Relics in the Central Middle Ages,* 1990, pp. xi-15, 20-54, 50-59, 65, 87-103, 110-28, 129-33, and 149-156; Head, T., "Translation of the Body of St. Junianus," in Rubin, M. (ed.), *Medieval Christianity in Practice,* 2009, pp. 217-21; Angenendt, Arnold, "Sacrifice, gifts, and prayers in Latin Christianity," in Noble and Smith (eds.), *The Cambridge History of Christianity: Early Medieval Christianities, c. 600-c. 1100,* 2008, pp. 462-64; Van Engen, John H., "Conclusion: Christendom, c. 1100," in Noble and Smith (eds.), *The Cambridge History of Christianity: Early Medieval Christianities, c. 600-c. 1100,* 2008, p. 633; and Rapp, C., "Saints and holy men," in Casiday and Norris (eds.), *The Cambridge History of Christianity: Constantine to c. 600,* 2007, pp. 548-566.

[261] The main sources for this section are: Geary, Patrick J., *Furta Sacra: Thefts of Relics in the Central Middle Ages,* 1990, pp. 33-54, 65, 87-103, 110-33, and 149-56; Rapp, C., "Saints and holy men," in Casiday and Norris (eds.), *The Cambridge History of Christianity: Constantine to c. 600,* 2007, pp. 548-566; and Thurston, "Relics," *The Catholic Encyclopedia,* retrieved January 2, 2009 from New Advent at http://www.newadvent.org/cathen/12734a.htm.

[262] The Fifth Council of Carthage (801 and 813) mandated that all altars without relics in the Frankish empire be replaced with ones that contained saints' relics. The Council of Chelsea in 816 mandated that relics be kept in all churches. In addition, new churches or ones being restored, chapels, shrines, and monasteries needed relics.

[263] The best known relic merchant of the ninth century evidently was a Roman Church deacon, who sold the bodies of Sts. Peter and Marcellinus to Einhard.

[264] For example, Pope Eugenius II gave away the body of St. Sebastian in 825, but

that did not prevent Pope Gregory IV (827-844) from conducting a solemn ceremony to translate the body of the same martyr from the catacombs to an altar in the chapel of Gregory the Great in St. Peter's.

[265]   The main sources for this section are: Geary, Patrick J., *Furta Sacra: Thefts of Relics in the Central Middle Ages*, 1990, pp. xi-15, 28-35, 87-103, 110-28, 129-33, and 149-156; Rapp, C., "Saints and holy men," in Casiday and Norris (eds.), *The Cambridge History of Christianity: Constantine to c. 600*, 2007, pp. 548-566; Kemp, Eric W., *Canonization in the Western Church*, 1948 for a detailed treatment, esp. pp.11-15, 38-39, 52, 61-69, 79-80, and 106; Catholic Encyclopedia, "Canonization and Beatification," http://www.newadvent.org/cathen/02364b.htm, downloaded November 9, 2012; Ferrero, Mario, "Competition for Sainhood and the Millennial Church," in Kyklos, August, 2002, pp. 335-60; and Barro, Robert J., Rachel M. McCleary, and Axexander McQuoid, "The Economics of Sainthood (A Preliminary Investigation)," in McCleary, Rachel M. (ed.), *The Oxford Handbook of the Economics of Religion*, 2011, pp. 193-95; and Thurston, "Relics," *The Catholic Encyclopedia*, retrieved January 2, 2009 from New Advent at http://www.newadvent.org/cathen/12734a.htm.

[266]   The church began attempting to centralize the saint-making process as early as the fifth century, when the fifth Council of Carthage (401 A.D.) declared that bishops were the primary ecclesiastical authority to determine the authenticity of martyrs and confessors who were to be made saints. However, there was no centralized control of the proliferation of questionable relics until the papacy attempted to take control of the saint-making market and the booming trade in relics by a decree of Lateran IV (1215) and a decree issued by Pope Gregory IX in 1234. Together these decrees stipulated that only the pope could designate anyone as a saint and that relics could not be bought or sold (or new relics venerated) without the approval of the pope. The discussion in this paragraph and note is based on: Kemp, Eric W., *Canonization in the Western Church*, 1948, pp. 11-15, 38-39, 52, 61-69, 79-80, and 106; Catholic Encyclopedia, "Canonization and Beatification," http://www.newadvent.org/cathen/02364b.htm, downloaded November 9, 2012; Ferrero, Mario, "Competition for Sainhood and the Millennial Church," in Kyklos, August, 2002, pp. 335-60; and Barro, Robert J., Rachel M. McCleary, and Axexander McQuoid, "The Economics of Sainthood (A Preliminary Investigation)," in McCleary, Rachel M. (ed.), *The Oxford Handbook of the Economics of Religion*, 2011, pp. 193-95.

[267]   The main source for this paragraph is Smith, J. M. H., "Saints and their cults," in Noble and Smith (eds.), *The Cambridge History of Christianity: Early Medieval Christianities, c. 600-c. 1100*, 2008, pp. 595-600.

[268]   The main source for this paragraph is Geary, Patrick J., *Furta Sacra: Thefts of*

Relics in the Central Middle Ages, 1990, pp. 110-28, 132-33, and 149-56.

[269] The main source for this paragraph is Geary, Patrick J., *Furta Sacra: Thefts of Relics in the Central Middle Ages*, 1990, pp. xi-15 and 28-35.

[270] Geary, Patrick J., *Furta Sacra: Thefts of Relics in the Central Middle Ages*, 1990, pp. 149-56.

[271] Frankfurter, "Christianity and paganism, I: Egypt," in Casiday and Norris (eds.), *The Cambridge History of Christianity: Constantine to c. 600*, 2007, p. 177.

[272] This paragraph is based on: Brown, P. *Augustine of Hippo: A Biography*, 1967 (2000), pp. 416-22; and Jones, A. H. M., *The Later Roman Empire, 284-602, A Social, Economic, and Administrative Survey: Books 1-2*, 1964, pp. 962-63.

[273] Rapp, C., "Saints and holy men," in Casiday and Norris (eds.), *The Cambridge History of Christianity: Constantine to c. 600*, 2007, p. 563. On this same point, also see Jones, A. H. M., *The Later Roman Empire, 284-602, A Social, Economic, and Administrative Survey: Books 1-2*, 1964, pp. 961-62.

[274] Vauchez, "Saints and pilgrimages: new and old," in Rubin and Simons (eds.), *The Cambridge History of Christianity: V. 4, Christianity in Western Europe c. 1100-c. 1500*, 2009, pp. 331-32.

[275] This paragraph is based on Trombley, F. R., "Christianity and paganism, II: Asia Minor," in Casiday and Norris (eds.), *The Cambridge History of Christianity: Constantine to c. 600*, 2007, pp. 189-209.

[276] At that time, the church was very concerned about baptized Christians reverting to pagan sacrifices, so severe penalties were imposed for such lapses and for consorting with magicians, sorcerers, or astrologers.

[277] The main sources for this section are: Vauchez, André, "Saints and pilgrimages: new and old," in Rubin and Simons (eds.), *The Cambridge History of Christianity: V. 4, Christianity in Western Europe c. 1100-c. 1500*, 2009, pp. 324-39; Thurston, "Relics," *The Catholic Encyclopedia*, retrieved January 2, 2009 from New Advent at http://www.newadvent.org/cathen/12734a.htm; Smith, J. M. H., "Saints and their cults," in Noble and Smith (eds.), *The Cambridge History of Christianity: Early Medieval Christianities, c. 600-c. 1100*, 2008, pp. 593-95; Perron, "The bishops of Rome, 1100-1300," in Rubin and Simons (eds.), *The Cambridge History of Christianity: V. 4, Christianity in Western Europe c. 1100-c. 1500*, 2009, pp. 27-28; Le Goff, *The Birth of Purgatory*, 1984, p. 320; and Roach, *The Devil's World: Heresy and Society 1100-1300*, 2005, pp. 1-9.

278   See Thurston, "Relics," *The Catholic Encyclopedia,* retrieved January 2, 2009 from New Advent at http://www.newadvent.org/cathen/12734a.htm.

279   Most historians agree that, by the time of Pope Innocent III (1198-1216) or perhaps Pope Gregory IX (1227-1241), only the pope had the power to canonize.

280   See Thurston, "Relics," *The Catholic Encyclopedia,* retrieved January 2, 2009 from New Advent at http://www.newadvent.org/cathen/12734a.htm.

281   This paragraph is based on: Fulton, Rachel, "Mary," in Rubin and Simons (eds.), *The Cambridge History of Christianity: V. 4, Christianity in Western Europe c. 1100-c. 1500,* 2009, pp. 283-96; and Vauchez, André, "Saints and pilgrimages: new and old," in Rubin and Simons (eds.), *The Cambridge History of Christianity: V. 4, Christianity in Western Europe c. 1100-c. 1500,* 2009, pp. 324-39.

282   Many have argued that St. Mary represented the inevitable 'return of the goddess' to Christianity and a response to deep emotional needs for maternal comfort and support not found through the male hierarchy and control of the church. Some even argue that Mary became a goddess like God and thus became the center of much devotional energy. It is undeniable that Mary did take on the attributes of earlier pagan goddesses of fertility, wisdom, and virginity.

283   The main source for this paragraph is Smith, J. M. H., "Saints and their cults," in Noble and Smith (eds.), *The Cambridge History of Christianity: Early Medieval Christianities, c. 600-c. 1100,* 2008, pp. 600-01.

284   The main sources for this section are: Paxton, F. S., "Birth and death," in Noble and Smith (eds.), *The Cambridge History of Christianity: Early Medieval Christianities, c. 600-c. 1100,* 2008, pp. 384-89; Wood, S. *The Proprietary Church in the Medieval West,* 2006, esp. pp. 224-26 and 478-86; Delumeau, *Sin and Fear: The Emergence of a Western Guilt Culture, 13th-18th Centuries,* 1983 (1990), esp. chs. 2-3; Smith, J. M. H., "Pilgrimage and Spiritual Healing," in Rubin, M. (ed.), *Medieval Christianity in Practice,* 2009, pp. 222-28; Paxton, F. S., "Agius of Corvey's Account of the Death of Hathumoda, First Abbess of Gandersheim, in 874," in Rubin, M. (ed.), *Medieval Christianity in Practice,* 2009, pp. 53-58; Roach, *The Devil's World: Heresy and Society 1100-1300,* 2005, pp. 170-78; Hopkins, *Death and Renewal: Sociological Studies in Roman History,* V. 2, 1983, (1985), pp. 243-52; Wood, D. *Medieval Economic Thought,* 2002, esp. pp. 224-26; Murphy, "The High Cost of Dying: an Analysis of *pro anima* Bequests in Medieval Dublin," in Sheils and Wood (eds.), *The Church and Wealth, Studies in Church History,* pp. 111-122; and Resl, B., "Bequests for the Poor," in Rubin, M. (ed.), *Medieval Christianity in Practice,* 2009, pp. 209-15.

285   This paragraph is based on Hopkins, *Death and Renewal: Sociological Studies in*

Roman History, V. 2, 1983, (1985), pp. 243-52.

[286] Such bequests were facilitated in the Roman legal code during the first century AD; this unintentionally proved to be a boon to the church after it was adopted by Constantine in the early fourth century. These first-century legal developments included the following: legally enforceable trusts were invented; and corporate entities, such as towns and the institutional church, acquired legal personalities, so they could receive bequests for public purposes.

[287] Tombs and gardens were reused or sold, despite legal restrictions. Rich tombs also were inviting targets for grave robbers.

[288] The main source for this paragraph is Paxton, F. S., "Birth and death," in Noble and Smith (eds.), *The Cambridge History of Christianity: Early Medieval Christianities, c. 600-c. 1100*, 2008, pp. 392-94.

[289] However, murderers, the excommunicated, heretics, and those who committed suicides had to be buried in unconsecrated ground that was away from both living and dead Catholics in good standing.

[290] The main sources for this paragraph are: Paxton, F. S., "Birth and death," in Noble and Smith (eds.), *The Cambridge History of Christianity: Early Medieval Christianities, c. 600-c. 1100*, 2008, pp. 384-89; and Smith, J. M. H., "Pilgrimage and Spiritual Healing," in Rubin, M. (ed.), *Medieval Christianity in Practice*, 2009, pp. 222-28.

[291] The Roman Catholic Church's development of the liturgy and ritual for death was several centuries in the making. But it was in a more or less definitive form by the 874 death of a count's wealthy daughter who was in the expensive process of forming an abbey in northwestern Europe. The ritual to accompany her death must have been an impressive one that was led by the local bishop. It began with anointing oil to cleanse the body of the effects of sin. It included a final confession, absolution for her sins, and a final communion of bread and wine. The ceremony ended with sung prayer to surround her as she was dying. Of course, such elaborate ceremonies for the laity were only for the rich. See Paxton, F. S., "Agius of Corvey's Account of the Death of Hathumoda, First Abbess of Gandersheim, in 874," in Rubin, M. (ed.), *Medieval Christianity in Practice*, 2009, pp. 53-58.

[292] It generally was viewed as impossible to repent and receive salvation on the death bed just because the Last Judgment was feared. The conversion was supposed to be more fundamental than that.

[293] See Wood, S. *The Proprietary Church in the Medieval West*, 2006, esp. pp. 478-86.

294   The main source for this paragraph is Paxton, F. S., "Birth and death," in Noble and Smith (eds.), *The Cambridge History of Christianity: Early Medieval Christianities, c. 600-c. 1100*, 2008, pp. 394-98.

295   The main source for this section is Resl, B., "Bequests for the Poor," in Rubin, M. (ed.), *Medieval Christianity in Practice*, 2009, pp. 209-15.

296   Interestingly, donations to Catholic hospital associations funded by a city's wealthy were more popular than those to the church itself during some periods, but those associations also guaranteed a stream of prayers for donors.

297   Paxton, F. S., "Birth and death," in Noble and Smith (eds.), *The Cambridge History of Christianity: Early Medieval Christianities, c. 600-c. 1100*, 2008, p. 395.

298   For more on the issues in this paragraph, see Roach, *The Devil's World: Heresy and Society 1100-1300*, 2005, pp. 170-78.

299   Needless to say, finding and examining such wills is a tedious and time-consuming process, but Murphy has examined 98 Irish wills from the period 1270-1500 and 1457-1483. See Murphy, "The High Cost of Dying: an Analysis of *pro anima* Bequests in Medieval Dublin," in Sheils and Wood (eds.), *The Church and Wealth, Studies in Church History*, pp. 111-122.

300   Unless otherwise noted, the following are based on Murphy, "The High Cost of Dying: an Analysis of *pro anima* Bequests in Medieval Dublin," in Sheils and Wood (eds.), *The Church and Wealth, Studies in Church History*, pp. 111-122.

301   See Wood, D. *Medieval Economic Thought*, 2002, pp. 224-26.

302   The main source for this paragraph is Delumeau, *Sin and Fear: The Emergence of a Western Guilt Culture, 13th-18th Centuries*, 1983 (1990), chs. 2-3.

303   Interestingly, there is nothing distinctly Catholic about the *danse* and the resumption of the focus on death during the thirteenth century. The increased concerns about death apparently reflected the disasters that struck Europe, beginning with the Black Death in the middle of the fourteenth century and continuing with bad harvests, increased internal revolts, foreign and civil wars, and the Great Schism that tore apart Latin Christianity.

304   For extensive discussions of St. Francis and his ideas, including his *Canticle of the Creatures*, see: Osborne, K. B., *The Franciscan Intellectual Tradition: Tracing Its Origins and Identifying Its Central Components*, 2003; Osborne, K. B. (ed.), *History of Franciscan Theology (Theology Series)*, 1994; Short, W., *Poverty and Joy: The Franciscan Tradition*, 1999; Flood, D. and A. Calogeras, *For People: An Introduction to Franciscan Life*, 1990;

Godet-Calogeras, J. F., "Evangelical Radicalism in the Writings of Francis and Clare of Assisi," in *Franciscan Studies* 64 (2006), pp. 103-121; Armstrong, R. J. and I. C. Brady (translation and introduction), *Francis and Clare: The Complete Works*, 1982; Cirino, A. and J. Raischl (eds.), *Franciscan Solitude*, 1995; Delio, I., *The Humility of God: A Franciscan Perspective*, 2005; and Hammond, J. M. (ed.), *Francis of Assisi: History, Hagiography, and Hermeneutics in the Early Documents*, 2004.

[305]   See Le Goff, Jacques (translated by Patricia Ranum), *Your Money or Your Life: Economy and Religion in the Middle Ages*, 2001, pp. 67-69.

[306]   See Pelikan, *Christian Tradition, A History of the Development of Doctrine: V. 1, The Emergence of Catholic Tradition (100-600)*, 1971 (1975), pp. 100 and 154-55.

[307] Le Goff, *The Birth of Purgatory*, 1984, pp. 1-14.

[308]   The Greek church fathers developed many of the initial ideas that much later led to Roman Catholic Purgatory. For example, both Clement of Alexandria (d. prior to 215) and Origen (d. 253/254) argued that purification of sinners after death should be viewed as 'education', as it contributed to their salvation. Clement and Origen also saw a kind of arithmetic in punishments that would match one's sins, and this idea passed into Roman Catholic Purgatory. Their ideas provided a basis for later churchmen to vary the prices for relief in Purgatory according to the severity of the sins. Of course, churchmen also could practice price discrimination by charging different prices for the same sins, with the price depending on the willingness and ability of their religious customers to pay.

[309] The main source for this paragraph is Le Goff, *The Birth of Purgatory*, 1984, pp. 52-95.

[310] This paragraph is based on: Le Goff, *The Birth of Purgatory*, 1984, pp. 85-95; and Pelikan, *Christian Tradition, A History of the Development of Doctrine: V. 1, The Emergence of Catholic Tradition (100-600)*, 1971 (1975), pp. 355-56.

[311] This paragraph is based on Le Goff, *The Birth of Purgatory*, 1984, pp. 15-51.

[312] This paragraph is based on Le Goff, *The Birth of Purgatory*, 1984, pp. 209-20. Also see Moore, R. I., *The Formation of A Persecuting Society: Authority and Deviance in Western Europe 950-1250*, 2007.

[313] This paragraph is based on Le Goff, *The Birth of Purgatory*, 1984, pp. 209-20. Also see Moore, R. I., *The Formation of A Persecuting Society: Authority and Deviance in Western Europe 950-1250*, 2007.

[314] The judicial feel of the system was not based on an image of the next world but

on legalistic structures of this world that were emerging strongly in the West by the end of the eleventh century.

[315] This paragraph is based on Le Goff, *The Birth of Purgatory*, 1984, pp. 220-234 and 320-30.

[316] This paragraph is based on: Bernstein, A. E., "Heaven, hell, and purgatory: 1100-1500," in Rubin and Simons (eds.), *The Cambridge History of Christianity: V. 4, Christianity in Western Europe c. 1100-c. 1500*, 2009, pp. 200-16; and Le Goff, *The Birth of Purgatory*, 1984, pp. 237-56.

[317] Despite including ghosts as proof, the scholastics (churchmen who were academics in the universities) still worked to come up with a logically consistent explanation of the afterlife. However, the church's use of suffrages and grants of indulgences for crusading made that extremely difficult.

[318] This paragraph is based on Le Goff, *The Birth of Purgatory*, 1984, pp. 256-78.

[319] This paragraph is based on Le Goff, *The Birth of Purgatory*, 1984, pp. 237-77.

[320] Even suffrages of sinners can benefit the souls of the dead, because their effect depends on the state of the dead, not that of the living (previously, many church writers argued that only holy ones could offer help).

[321] The devotion of the person celebrating the mass or causing it to be celebrated is essential to the effectiveness of the mass for the souls of the dead. This was an interesting twist because the church usually argued that the holiness of the priest did not matter, as long as proper church procedure was followed.

[322] The main sources for this paragraph are: Bernstein, A. E., "Heaven, hell, and purgatory: 1100-1500," in Rubin and Simons (eds.), *The Cambridge History of Christianity: V. 4, Christianity in Western Europe c. 1100-c. 1500*, 2009, pp. 200-16; and Le Goff, *The Birth of Purgatory*, 1984, pp. 283-88.

[323] The sources for this paragraph are: Bernstein, A. E., "Heaven, hell, and purgatory: 1100-1500," in Rubin and Simons (eds.), *The Cambridge History of Christianity: V. 4, Christianity in Western Europe c. 1100-c. 1500*, 2009, pp. 200-16; and Le Goff, *The Birth of Purgatory*, 1984, pp. 283-88.

[324] In all official pronouncements, the church hierarchy was very cautious in providing specifics about Purgatory. The official position was that It occurs between death and the Last Judgement, but there is nothing very concrete about the place or state, the exact nature of the punishments, or how many would be subject to purgatorial punishments as opposed to the eternal fire of Hell. It seems

that the church was worried about completely emptying out Hell into Purgatory. See Le Goff, *The Birth of Purgatory*, 1984, pp. 52-95 and 209-220.

[325] It also is quite clear that, given the church's emphasis on sin, fear, and guilt, the medieval imagination 'needed' an intermediate place where penance, hope, and salvation still could be attained after this life, even if at the cost of temporary suffering.

[326] This paragraph is based on Le Goff, *The Birth of Purgatory*, 1984, pp. 133-76 and 289-320. This 'bridge' between life on this earth and the final reckoning in the hereafter that was invented by the Roman Catholic Church never was duplicated in the Greek Orthodox Church.

[327] The main sources for this paragraph are: Bernstein, A. E., "Heaven, hell, and purgatory: 1100-1500," in Rubin and Simons (eds.), *The Cambridge History of Christianity: V. 4, Christianity in Western Europe c. 1100-c. 1500*, 2009, pp. 200-16; and Firey, " 'For I Was Hungry and You Fed Me': Social Justice and Economic Thought in the Latin Patristic and Medieval Christian Traditions," in Lowry and Gordon (eds.), *Ancient and Medieval Economic Ideas and Concepts of Social Justice*, pp. 333-370; and Le Goff, *The Birth of Purgatory*, 1984, pp. 278-83 and 330-33.

[328] The contemporary Catechism of the Roman Catholic Church commends the faithful to undertake almsgiving, penance, and indulgences on behalf of the dead in the section titled, "III. The Final Purification, or Purgatory." See *Catechism of the Roman Catholic Church* downloaded from http://www.vatican.va/archive/ENG0015/_P2N.HTM#1H, August 10, 2011.

[329] The main sources for this section are: Little, *Religious Poverty and the Profit Economy in Medieval Europe*, 1978, ch. 11; Le Goff, *The Birth of Purgatory*, 1984; Ekelund Jr., R. B., R. F. Hébert, and R. D. Tollison, "The Economics of Sin and Redemption: Purgatory as a Market-Pull Innovation?" in *Journal of Economic Behaviour and Organization* 19 (September 1992); Ekelund Jr., R. B., R. F. Hébert, and R. D. Tollison, *The Marketplace of Christianity*, 2006; Ekelund Jr., R. B., R. F. Hébert, R. D. Tollison, G. M. Anderson, and A. B. Davidson, *Sacred Trust: The Medieval Church as an Economic Firm*, 1996; and Bernstein, A. E., "Heaven, hell, and purgatory: 1100-1500," in Rubin and Simons (eds.), *The Cambridge History of Christianity: V. 4, Christianity in Western Europe c. 1100-c. 1500*, 2009, pp. 200-16.

[330] This paragraph is based on: Le Goff, *The Birth of Purgatory*, 1984, pp. 133-76 and 248-49; and Bernstein, A. E., "Heaven, hell, and purgatory: 1100-1500," in Rubin and Simons (eds.), *The Cambridge History of Christianity: V. 4, Christianity in Western Europe c. 1100-c. 1500*, 2009, pp. 200-16.

331   The role of the mendicants resulted in criticisms by some intellectuals, local priests, and bishops that the friars were usurping the clergy's functions. Interestingly, the friars (especially St. Francis) had been very supportive of priestly functions that the brothers could *not* perform but, soon after Francis died, the Friars began serving as priests, putting them into direct competition with local priests.

332   This paragraph is based on: Le Goff, *The Birth of Purgatory*, 1984, pp. 289-320; and Little, *Religious Poverty and the Profit Economy in Medieval Europe*, 1978, ch. 12.

333   Le Goff, *The Birth of Purgatory*, 1984, pp. 248-9.

334   This paragraph is based on: Le Goff, *The Birth of Purgatory*, 1984, pp. 289-320; and Little, *Religious Poverty and the Profit Economy in Medieval Europe*, 1978, ch. 12.

335   Little, *Religious Poverty and the Profit Economy in Medieval Europe*, 1978, p. 201.

336   Schmidtchen, Dieter and Achim Mayer, "Established Clergy, Friars and the Pope; Some Institutional Economics of the Medieval Church," in *Journal of Institutional and Theoretical Economics* 153 (1997), pp. 122-165.

337   Although their model is much more technical and narrowly focused than the other reasons discussed in this book for the rise of the mendicant orders, it still is completely consistent with those reasons.

338   This paragraph is based on Le Goff, *The Birth of Purgatory*, 1984, pp. 289-320.

339   This paragraph is based on: Bernstein, A. E., "Heaven, hell, and purgatory: 1100-1500," in Rubin and Simons (eds.), *The Cambridge History of Christianity: V. 4, Christianity in Western Europe c. 1100-c. 1500*, 2009, pp. 200-16; and Le Goff, *The Birth of Purgatory*, 1984, pp. 289-330.

340   This paragraph is based on Le Goff, *The Birth of Purgatory*, 1984, pp. 320-33.

341   Pope Boniface VIII was locked in a struggle with the king of France, Philip the Fair, over the allegiance of lay Catholic society. Undoubtedly, the Jubilee was conceived at least partly as a brilliant strategic move in this battle, as Boniface invited all Catholics to come to Rome on pilgrimage during 1300 for the remission of sins.

342   Although the Jubilee signaled the triumph of Purgatory in church doctrine, there still were many opponents, especially 'heretics' outside of the church.

343   This paragraph is based on Le Goff, *The Birth of Purgatory*, 1984, pp. 334-55.

344   Dante also: 1)Situated Purgatory on earth, not underground, and placed its entrance at the bottom of a mountain in the southern hemisphere (diametrically opposite Jerusalem). 2)Gave Purgatory seven circles that correspond to the seven deadly sins--in his order, they are pride, envy, wrath, sloth, avarice, gluttony, and lust (mainstream church teaching often was that only venial, not deadly, sins could be purged in Purgatory). 3)Had purgation accomplished in three ways: material punishment that instills virtue, meditation on the sin to be purged and its opposite virtue, and prayer. Love is the principle that governed the assignment of souls to a particular circle of Purgatory, because the common element of all sins is the absence of love of God. In Purgatory, lost souls had to make a climb back up into the love of God. In agreement with the church, he had far harsher punishments in Purgatory than on earth.

345   For a brief discussion of early house churches, see Ehrman, *After the New Testament: A Reader in Early Christianity*, 1999, pp. 317-19.

346   See Paxton, F. S., "Birth and death," in Noble and Smith (eds.), *The Cambridge History of Christianity: Early Medieval Christianities, c. 600-c. 1100*, 2008, pp. 383-85.

347   The main sources for this paragraph are: Cameron, *A Concise Economic History of the World: From Paleolithic Times to the Present*, 1989, pp. 148-51; and McLaughlin, "Women and men," in Rubin and Simons (eds.), *The Cambridge History of Christianity: V. 4, Christianity in Western Europe c. 1100-c. 1500*, 2009, pp. 196-99.

348   Alexandre, "Early Christian Women," in Schmitt (ed.), *A History of Women in the West: From Ancient Goddesses to Christian Saints*, 1994, pp. 438-40.

349   The main sources for this paragraph are: Cameron, *A Concise Economic History of the World: From Paleolithic Times to the Present*, 1989, pp. 148-51; and McLaughlin, "Women and men," in Rubin and Simons (eds.), *The Cambridge History of Christianity: V. 4, Christianity in Western Europe c. 1100-c. 1500*, 2009, pp. 196-99.

350   Torjesen, "Social and historical setting: Christianity as culture critique," in Young, Ayres, and Louth, *Early Christian Literature*, 2004, pp. 181-92.

351   Alexandre, "Early Christian Women," in Schmitt (ed.), *A History of Women in the West: From Ancient Goddesses to Christian Saints*, 1994, pp. 435-36.

352   For example, see: Pagels, *The Gnostic Gospels*, 1979; Alexandre, "Early Christian Women," in Schmitt (ed.), *A History of Women in the West: From Ancient Goddesses to Christian Saints*, 1994, pp. 409-444; and Freeman, *The Closing of the Western Mind: The Rise of Faith and the Fall of Reason*, 2002, pp. 233-50.

353   The main source for this paragraph is Nelson, Janet L., "Law and its

applications," in Noble and Smith (eds.), *The Cambridge History of Christianity: Early Medieval Christianities, c. 600-c. 1100*, 2008, p. 314.

354   It should be noted that many Bible scholars believe at least portions of these passages, which demean women, were not actually written by St. Paul. Although the Letter to the Corinthians was written by St. Paul, many scholars believe particular passages were added/modified by later writers. Further, Timothy may not have been written until the second century by someone other than Paul. However, for our purposes, the issue is not whether St. Paul actually wrote these passages, the point is they were included in the church's sacred canon of scripture for the New Testament in the fourth century.

355   All Bible quotes are from the online *New Advent Bible* at http://www.newadvent.org/bible/. For detailed discussions of the books in the Bible, see: Brown, Raymond, Joseph Fitzmyer, and Roland Murphy (eds.), *The New Jerome Biblical Commentary*, 1990; Ehrman Bart D., *Misquoting Jesus: The Story Behind Who Changed the Bible and Why*, 2005; and Ehrman, Bart D., *The New Testament: A Historical Introduction to the Early Christian Writings*, 2008.

356   For an in-depth study of the Gnostic Gospils, see Pagels, *The Gnostic Gospels*, 1979.

357   The main sources for this paragraph are: Van Engen, John H., "Conclusion: Christendom, c. 1100," in Noble and Smith (eds.), *The Cambridge History of Christianity: Early Medieval Christianities, c. 600-c. 1100*, 2008, pp. 637-39; and Macy, G., *The Hidden History of Women's Ordination: Female Clergy in the Medieval West*, 2008, ch. 5.

358   This paragraph is based on Freeman, *The Closing of the Western Mind: The Rise of Faith and the Fall of Reason*, 2002, pp. 233-50.

359   Pagels argues that another plank in the construction of the institutional church's mythical basis for apostolic, male succession is its emphasis on Matthew rather than either Mark or John for the resurrection story (Pagels, *The Gnostic Gospels*, 1979, pp. 6-25). Matthew has Peter (and another male) as the first witnesses of the empty tomb. In contrast, in the first Gospel written, Mark, and in the last Gospel written, John, Mary Magdalene is the first witness of the resurrection. But, according to Pagels, the orthodox position emphasizes Matthew to perpetuate the idea that Peter is the first witness of the resurrected Lord, laying the basis for the apostolic succession. Pagels contends that this argument is ingenious for, if accepted, it forecloses any other basis of authority or challenge to the church's male, hierarchical structure.

360   *The   Catholic   University   of   America   at*

http://faculty.cua.edu/pennington/Canon%20Law/ElviraCanons.htm, March 13, 2010.

361 Alexandre, "Early Christian Women," in Pantel (ed.), *A History of Women in the West: From Ancient Goddesses to Christian Saints*, 1994, p. 409.

362 Delumeau, *Sin and Fear: The Emergence of a Western Guilt Culture, 13th-18th Centuries*, 1983 (1990), pp. 265-71.

363 Alexandre, "Early Christian Women," in Schmitt (ed.), *A History of Women in the West: From Ancient Goddesses to Christian Saints*, 1994, pp. 438-40.

364 Rubin and Simons, "Introduction," in Rubin and Simons, *The Cambridge History of Christianity, V. 4,* 2009, p. 5.

365 Mclaughlin, "Women and Men," in Rubin and Simons, *The Cambridge History of Christianity, V. 4,* 2009, pp. 187-90.

366 See Mclaughlin, "Women and Men," in Rubin and Simons, *The Cambridge History of Christianity, V. 4,* 2009, pp. 192-95.

367 The main sources for this paragraph are: Macy, G., *The Hidden History of Women's Ordination: Female Clergy in the Medieval West*, 2008, chs. 3-5; and Macy, G., "Women Deacons: History," in G. Macy, W. T. Ditewig, and P. Zagano, *Women Deacons: Past, Present, Future*, 2011, pp. 9-36.

368 In contrast, even though Luther's Protestant Reformation in the early fifteenth century began with a male hierarchy and continued that way for many years, Protestant churches now affirm women as ministers and even bishops.

369 Goodstein, L., "Pope Francis Appoints a Panel to Study Women Deacons," *New York Times*, online ed., August 2, 2016.

370 There are several sources for this section, but many are from a leading expert on the ordination of women, Gary Macy, whose interest in women's ordination goes back several years in his academic career, for many years at the University of San Diego and continuing at Santa Clara University (as Chair of Religious Studies as of 2012); these include: Macy, G., *The Hidden History of Women's Ordination: Female Clergy in the Medieval West*, 2008; Macy, Gary, "Heloise, Abelard and the Ordination of Abbesses," in *Journal of Ecclesiastical History* 57, 2006 , pp. 16-32; Macy, Gary, "The Ordination of Women in the Early Middle Ages," in *Theological Studies* 61, 2000, pp. 502-7; and Macy, G., "Women Deacons: History," in G. Macy, W. T. Ditewig, and P. Zagano, *Women Deacons: Past, Present, Future*, 2011, pp. 9-36. Other major sources include the following in this note and the sources in the next note:

Madigan, Kevin and Carolyn Osiek (eds.), *Ordained Women in the Early Church: A Documentary History*, 2005; Miller, Maureen, "Masculinity, Reform, and Clerical Culture: Narratives of Episcopal Holiness in the Gregorian Era," in *Church History* 72, 2003, pp. 25-52; Wijngaards, J., *No Women in Holy Orders?, The Women Deacons of the Early Church*, 2002; Wijngaards, J., *The Ordination of Women in the Catholic Church, Unmasking a Cuckoo's Egg Tradition*, 2001; Martimort, A. G., *Deaconesses: An Historical Study*, 1986; Berman, C. (ed.), *Medieval Religion: New Approaches*, 2005; Warren, Nancy B., "The Ritual for the Ordination of Nuns," in Rubin, M. (ed.), *Medieval Christianity in Practice*, 2009, pp. 318-23; Lees, Clare (ed.), *Medieval Masculinities: Regarding Men in the Middle Ages*, 1994; McNamara, Jo Ann, "Canossa and the Ungendering of the Public Man," in Berman (ed.), *Medieval Religion: New Approaches*, 2005, pp. 102-22; McNamara, Jo Ann, "The Herrenfrage: The Restructuring of the Gender System, 1050-1150," in Lees (ed.), *Medieval Masculinities: Regarding Men in the Middle Ages*, 1994, pp. 3-29.

[371] Other main sources for this section include the following plus the ones in the prior note: Anatolios, "Discourse on the Trinity," in Casiday and Norris (eds.), *The Cambridge History of Christianity: Constantine to c. 600*, 2007, pp. 442-44; Gryson, Roger, *The Ministry of Women in the Early Church*, 1976; Van Dam, "Bishops and society," in Casiday and Norris (eds.), *The Cambridge History of Christianity: Constantine to c. 600*, 2007, pp. 350-53; Schillebeeckx, Edward, *Ministry: Leadership in the Community of Jesus Christ*, 1981; Eisen, Ute E., *Women Officeholders in Early Christianity: Epigraphical and Literary Studies*, 2001; Freeman, *The Closing of the Western Mind: The Rise of Faith and the Fall of Reason*, 2002, pp. 165-71 and 233-50; Alexandre, "Early Christian Women," in Schmitt (ed.), *A History of Women in the West: From Ancient Goddesses to Christian Saints*, 1994, pp. 431-35; Chadwick, Henry, *East and West: The Making of a Rift in the Church: From Apostolic Times until the Council of Florence*, 2005, pp. 13-28; Rossi, Mary Ann, "Priesthood, Precedent, and Prejudice: On Recovering the Women Priests of Early Christianity," (Translation with introduction of Giorgio Otranto of, "Note sul sacerdozio femminilie nell' antichità in margine a una testimonianza di Gelasio I," Vetera Christianorum,1982), in *Journal of Feminist Studies in Religion*, 1991, pp. 73-94; and Schimmelpfennig, *The Papacy*, 1998.

[372] This paragraph is based on: Macy, G., *The Hidden History of Women's Ordination: Female Clergy in the Medieval West*, 2008, pp. 26-43; and Alexandre, "Early Christian Women," in Schmitt (ed.), *A History of Women in the West: From Ancient Goddesses to Christian Saints*, 1994, pp. 431-35.

[373] The main source for this paragraph is Warren, Nancy B., "The Ritual for the Ordination of Nuns," in Rubin, M. (ed.), *Medieval Christianity in Practice*, 2009, pp. 318-23.

374   To emphasize the notions of chastity and their roles as brides of Christ, veils traditionally were used to cover up a nun's hair, because that was the long-time symbol of female sexuality. The presumed need to control nuns and protect their chastity resulted in very restrictive attempts to ensure that nuns were cloistered and protected from the outside world.

375   After the twelfth century, ordination came to be defined as requiring the laying on of hands by a bishop. However, earlier ordinations of both men and women did not always involve the laying on of hands. In fact, earlier ordinations were more likely to identify the *traditio instrumentorum* (instruments needed for the ministry, say a chalice for a priest) than the laying on of hands as essential for a valid ordination. See Macy, G., *The Hidden History of Women's Ordination: Female Clergy in the Medieval West*, 2008, esp. ch. 2.

376   The exact roles of women deacons are not known with certainty, but the evidence shows:
>They read the Gospels at Masses into the twelfth century, at least in the West. They also preached the Gospel, especially in places where men were not supposed to enter (e.g., women's quarters).
>They taught young women.
>They undressed and led female catechumens into the baptismal font, as explained in the *Apostolic Constitutions* of the fourth century.
>They were charged with the care of sick and poor women.

377   Also, it appears that women referred to as widows in the West may have performed the same functions as women deacons in the East, and widows are referred to as a specific order of the church in early western writings.

378   Van Dam, "Bishops and society," in Casiday and Norris (eds.), *The Cambridge History of Christianity: Constantine to c. 600*, 2007, pp. 350-53.

379   During the twelfth century the famous theologian Abelard, at the request of Heloise, his wife or former wife since the church forced their separation, wrote a history of women deacons. In this work, he asserted that abbess was the new name for the ancient order of women deacons.

380   Macy, G., *The Hidden History of Women's Ordination: Female Clergy in the Medieval West*, 2008, pp. 53-4.

381   Consistent with the view that women were ordained as priests because of a shortage of men, there is a much later example of a woman serving as a priest in Czechoslovakia in the twentieth century. Ludmila Javorová, a nun, was secretly ordained as a Roman Catholic priest in Czechoslovakia's underground church by

Bishop Davidek in 1970; some other unnamed women and married men of that underground church also were ordained as priests. However, once Ludmila Javorová's ordination became widely known after the fall of Czechoslovakian communism in 1989, she was barred by the Vatican from functioning as a priest. In February 2000, the Vatican declared the ordinations of both Bishop Davidek and priest Javorová invalid, even while recognizing the extreme circumstances under which they occurred. For the story of Javorová, see Winter, Miriam T., *Out of the Depths: The Story of Ludmila Javorová, Ordained Roman Catholic Priest*, 2001.

[382]   Macy, G., *The Hidden History of Women's Ordination: Female Clergy in the Medieval West*, 2008, p. 89.

[383]   As noted earlier, five references to presbyterae and deaconesses managed to find their way into the *Decretum*, and it was a key reference for the Roman Catholic Church's canon law until at least the Reformation in the sixteenth century. However, those references to ordained women simply were ignored by churchmen.

[384]   This argument actually was picked up in the twelfth century from a fourth-century writer referred to as Ambrosiaster.

[385]   The famous twelfth-century theologian, Abelard, nonetheless continued to strongly defend deaconesses as an ancient order of the church and abbesses as their more recent replacements. Abelard even argued that Mary Magdalene was an apostle to the apostles, for she first announced the resurrection of the Lord to the apostles.

[386]   Macy, G., *The Hidden History of Women's Ordination: Female Clergy in the Medieval West*, 2008, p. 99.

[387]   Macy, G., "Women Deacons: History," in G. Macy, W. T. Ditewig, and P. Zagano, *Women Deacons: Past, Present, Future*, 2011, p. 36.

[388]   The church's power struggle with lay lords (exemplified by the Investiture Contest over whether only bishops or lay lords could consecrate high clergy) continued into the early thirteenth century and Lateran IV (1215).

[389]   Nonetheless, churchmen had to deal with the fairly common perception that Mary Magdalene of the Gospels actually was an apostle, because she was the first witness to Jesus' resurrection in some Gospel accounts. The thirteenth-century Franciscan scholar, Duns Scotus, took on the task of discounting Mary Magdalene's status. He acknowledged that she may have been an apostle and preacher to women sinners, but he argued that she had been uniquely accepted by Christ and that acceptance did not pass on to other women. Of course, the church

had a different view for men, since privileges could be passed on for them, especially apostolic succession.

390   Macy, G., *The Hidden History of Women's Ordination: Female Clergy in the Medieval West*, 2008, pp. 125-27.

391   Macy, G., *The Hidden History of Women's Ordination: Female Clergy in the Medieval West*, 2008, p. 4.

392   Macy, G., *The Hidden History of Women's Ordination: Female Clergy in the Medieval West*, 2008, p. 17.

393   The main sources for this paragraph are: McBrien, *Lives of the Popes*, 1997; Collins, *Keepers of the Keys of Heaven: A History of the Papacy*, 2009; Kelly, *The Oxford Dictionary of Popes*, 2005; Lauret, B. (ed.), *Fifty Years of Catholic Theology: Conversations with Yves Congar*, 1988, esp. pp. 40-42; Frassetto, Michael, "Introduction," in Frassetto, Michael (ed.), *Medieval Purity and Piety: Essays on Medieval Clerical Celibacy and Religious Reform*, 1998, pp. xiv-xviii; and Beaudette, P., " 'In the World but not of It': Clerical Celibacy as a Symbol of the Medieval Church," in Frassetto (ed.), *Medieval Purity and Piety: Essays on Medieval Clerical Celibacy and Religious Reform*, 1998, pp. 35-40. Other sources are: Schimmelpfennig, *The Papacy*, 1998; Duffy, *Saints and Sinners: A History of the Popes*, 2006; De Rosa, *Vicars of Christ: the Dark Side of the Papacy*, 1988; Williams, *Papal Genealogy: The Families and Descendants of the Popes*, 1998; and Whalen, *Dominion of God: Christendom and Apocalypse in the Middle Ages*, 2009, pp. 9-41.

394   The main sources for this section are: Moore, R. I., *The Formation of A Persecuting Society: Authority and Deviance in Western Europe 950-1250*, 2007, pp. 64-65; and Lynch, *Simoniacal Entry into Religious Life from 1000 to 1260: A Social, Economic, and Legal Study*, 1976, ch. 3.

395   The main sources for this paragraph include: Jones, *The Later Roman Empire, 284-602*, Vols. 1-2, 1964, pp. 266-86; Cameron, *The Mediterranean World in Late Aniquity: AD 395-600*, 1993, pp 64-71 and 104-27; Norris, "Greek Christianities," in Casiday and Norris (eds.), *The Cambridge History of Christianity: Constantine to c. 600*, 2007, pp. 70-117; Schimmelpfennig, *The Papacy*, 1998, pp. Ch. III; McBrien, *Lives of the Popes*, 1997; Collins, *Keepers of the Keys of Heaven: A History of the Papacy*, 2009; and Kelly, *The Oxford Dictionary of Popes*, 2005.

396   Jesus' first apostles strongly warned against buying the gifts of God. For example, St. Peter was outraged that Simon Magus thought he could buy the power to confer the Holy Spirit on others, as recounted in Acts 8.18-22. This passage about Simon's attempt to buy holy gifts is the basis for the church's labeling the

sale and purchase of holy services as simony.

397   The main sources for this paragraph are: McBrien, *Lives of the Popes*, 1997; Collins, *Keepers of the Keys of Heaven: A History of the Papacy*, 2009; and Kelly, *The Oxford Dictionary of Popes*, 2005. In some cases, the above three sources are relied on so heavily that some passages are very close paraphrases of McBrien, Collins, or Kelly. Other sources for this section are: Bloch, *Feudal Society*, Vol. 2, 1961, pp. 145-62 and 394-407, 421-37; Gilchrist, *The Church and Economic Activity in the Middle Ages*, 1969, ch. 5; Perron, "The bishops of Rome, 1100-1300," in Rubin and Simons (eds.), *The Cambridge History of Christianity: V. 4, Christianity in Western Europe c. 1100-c. 1500*, 2009, pp. 22-38; Whalen, *Dominion of God: Christendom and Apocalypse in the Middle Ages*, 2009, pp. 9-41; Schimmelpfennig, *The Papacy*, 1998; Duffy, *Saints and Sinners: A History of the Popes*, 2006; De Rosa, *Vicars of Christ: the Dark Side of the Papacy*, 1988; Williams, *Papal Genealogy: The Families and Descendants of the Popes*, 1998; Wood, *The Proprietary Church in the Medieval West*, 2006, pp. 328-38; Freeman, *A. D. 381: Heretics, Pagans, and the Dawn of the Monotheistic State*, 2008, ch. XIII; and Lauret, B. (ed.), *Fifty Years of Catholic Theology: Conversations with Yves Congar*, 1988, esp. pp. 40-42.

398   The main sources for this paragraph are: McBrien, *Lives of the Popes*, 1997; Collins, *Keepers of the Keys of Heaven: A History of the Papacy*, 2009; and Kelly, *The Oxford Dictionary of Popes*, 2005. In some cases, the above three sources are relied on so heavily that some passages are very close paraphrases of McBrien, Collins, or Kelly. Other sources for this section are: Bloch, *Feudal Society*, Vol. 2, 1961, pp. 145-62 and 394-407, 421-37; Gilchrist, *The Church and Economic Activity in the Middle Ages*, 1969, ch. 5; Perron, "The bishops of Rome, 1100-1300," in Rubin and Simons (eds.), *The Cambridge History of Christianity: V. 4, Christianity in Western Europe c. 1100-c. 1500*, 2009, pp. 22-38; Whalen, *Dominion of God: Christendom and Apocalypse in the Middle Ages*, 2009, pp. 9-41; Schimmelpfennig, *The Papacy*, 1998; Duffy, *Saints and Sinners: A History of the Popes*, 2006; De Rosa, *Vicars of Christ: the Dark Side of the Papacy*, 1988; Williams, *Papal Genealogy: The Families and Descendants of the Popes*, 1998; Wood, *The Proprietary Church in the Medieval West*, 2006, pp. 328-38; Freeman, *A. D. 381: Heretics, Pagans, and the Dawn of the Monotheistic State*, 2008, ch. XIII; and Lauret, B. (ed.), *Fifty Years of Catholic Theology: Conversations with Yves Congar*, 1988, esp. pp. 40-42.

399   Williams, *Papal Genealogy: The Families and Descendants of the Popes*, 1998, p. 43.

400   From the middle to twelfth century into the first third of the sixteenth century, the metal content of the Italian florin was essentially unchanged, at 3.5 grams of pure gold. A gold content of 3.5 grams of pure gold and gold prices as of October 6, 2017 are used for the estimated values in the text. (One gram of gold was selling for $41.04, so one florin of theoretically pure gold from that era would translate

into roughly $143.64 dollars as of October, 6, 2017.) See any history of gold prices, such as that provided at http://goldprice.org/gold-price.html.

[401] Ritual purity also was a dominant incentive for some reformers, especially the reforming monks who at least theoretically, if not always in reality, practiced celibacy. Although chastity was a preoccupation of monks, it certainly was not for the secular clergy, who staffed most church altars. They were much less interested in giving up marriage and concubines than the monks who made professed celibacy an integral part of their lives.

[402] There are many sources for the historical information in this section. For example, see: Gilchrist, *The Church and Economic Activity in the Middle Ages*, 1969, pp. 27-39; and Bloch, *Feudal Society, Vol. 2*, 1961, pp. 345-55.

[403] The main sources for this paragraph are: Gilchrist, *The Church and Economic Activity in the Middle Ages*, 1969, pp. 27-39; Wood, *The Proprietary Church in the Medieval West*, 2006, pp. 292-311; and Leyser, "Clerical purity and the re-ordered world" in Rubin and Simons (eds.), *The Cambridge History of Christianity: V. 4, Christianity in Western Europe c. 100-c. 1500*, 2009, pp. 11-21. It was easier for rulers to deal with an established church bureaucracy than many different private owners to obtain benefits the rulers wanted from church property (lodging, military forces and provisions, and other privileges).

[404] Nonetheless, the church was dealing with the celibacy issue into the fourteenth century and beyond, especially in terms of whether men legally married before ordination could continue to live with their wives, even if theoretically in continence. The concubinage issue continued for even longer, into the sixteenth century. Further, as discussed in a later section, not even all of the popes observed celibacy after it was adopted as official church policy.

[405] This paragraph is based on: Gilchrist, *The Church and Economic Activity in the Middle Ages*, 1969, pp. 27-39; Little, *Religious Poverty and the Profit Economy in Medieval Europe*, 1978, pp. 99-112; Bloch, *Feudal Society, Vols. 1-2*, 1961, pp. 190-210; Leyser, "Clerical purity and the re-ordered world," in Rubin and Simons, *The Cambridge History of Christianity, V. 4*, 2009, pp. 11-21; Frassetto, Michael, "Introduction," in Frassetto, Michael (ed.), *Medieval Purity and Piety: Essays on Medieval Clerical Celibacy and Religious Reform*, 1998, pp. xiv-xviii; Beaudette, P., " 'In the World but not of It': Clerical Celibacy as a Symbol of the Medieval Church," in Frassetto (ed.), *Medieval Purity and Piety: Essays on Medieval Clerical Celibacy and Religious Reform*, 1998, pp. 35-40.

[406] For more on married popes and bishops or popes who were sons of priests, bishops, or popes, see reliable sources on the popes, especially including: Williams,

Papal Genealogy: The Families and Descendants of the Popes, 1998; Collins, *Keepers of the Keys of Heaven: A History of the Papacy*, 2009; Kelly, *The Oxford Dictionary of Popes*, 2005; McBrien, *Lives of the Popes*, 1997; **Schimmelpfennig**, *The Papacy*, 1998; and Duffy, *Saints and Sinners: A History of the Popes*, 2006. Also see: Leyser, "Clerical purity and the re-ordered world" in Rubin and Simons (eds.), *The Cambridge History of Christianity: V. 4, Christianity in Western Europe c. 100-c. 1500*, 2009, pp. 11-21; Gilchrist, *The Church and Economic Activity in the Middle Ages*, 1969, pp. 27-39; Macy, G., *The Hidden History of Women's Ordination: Female Clergy in the Medieval West*, 2008, pp. 54-8 and ch. 5; Bloch, *Feudal Society*, Vol. 2, 1961, pp. 145-62 and 394-407; De Rosa, *Vicars of Christ: the Dark Side of the Papacy*, 1988; and Wood, *The Proprietary Church in the Medieval West*, 2006, pp. 328-38. This section is based on these sources.

[407]   St. Peter actually was not a pope according to the church's definition (the pope is the sole bishop of Rome), even though he still is claimed as the first pope by the church.

[408]   Other sources also discuss the scandals of popes who were (allegedly or factually) sexually active during their papal reigns. But only a few of the relatively well documented cases of such popes are noted here.

[409]   However, an early-twentieth century scholar disputes the validity of that report. In any case, that son later became Pope John XI, whose mother, Marozia, was in a powerful Roman family that strongly supported Pope Sergius II.

[410]   Williams, *Papal Genealogy: The Families and Descendants of the Popes*, 1998, p. 168.

[411]   The main sources for this paragraph are: Leyser, "Clerical purity and the re-ordered world" in Rubin and Simons (eds.), *The Cambridge History of Christianity: V. 4, Christianity in Western Europe c. 100-c. 1500*, 2009, pp. 11-21; Dachowski, E., "*Teritus est optimus:* Marriage, Continence and Virginity in the Politics of Late Tenth- and Early Eleventh-Century Francia," in Frassetto (ed.), *Medieval Purity and Piety; Essays on Medieval Clerical Celibacy and Religious Reform*, 1998, pp. 117-130; Little, *Religious Poverty and the Profit Economy in Medieval Europe*, 1978, pp. 99-112; Bloch, *Feudal Society, Vols. 1-2*, 1961, pp. 190-210; and Gilchrist, *The Church and Economic Activity in the Middle Ages*, 1969, pp. 27-39.

[412]   For more on these issues, see: Little, *Religious Poverty and the Profit Economy in Medieval Europe*, 1978, pp. 99-112; and Bloch, *Feudal Society, Vols. 1-2*, 1961, pp. 190-210.

[413]   He believed that clergy could not live a holy life if they were begetting children and bequeathing church property to them, so he argued that clerical celibacy was the obvious solution. Despite Abbo's emphasis on the importance of religious

purity, the economic motives of reclaiming church property and preventing its loss to inheritances are apparent.

414 The main sources for this paragraph are: Gilchrist, *The Church and Economic Activity in the Middle Ages*, 1969, pp. 27-39; Wood, *The Proprietary Church in the Medieval West*, 2006, pp. 292-311; Leyser, "Clerical purity and the re-ordered world" in Rubin and Simons (eds.), *The Cambridge History of Christianity: V. 4, Christianity in Western Europe c. 100-c. 1500*, 2009, pp. 11-21; and McBrien, *Lives of the Popes*, 1997, pp. 168-69.

415 A main concern of Pope Benedict VIII and the emperor of the Romans at the 1022 synod was eliminating the loss of church property to the children of clerical wives and concubines.

416 The main source for this paragraph is Macy, G., *The Hidden History of Women's Ordination: Female Clergy in the Medieval West*, 2008, ch. 5.

417 The main sources for this paragraph are: Gilchrist, *The Church and Economic Activity in the Middle Ages*, 1969, pp. 27-39; Little, *Religious Poverty and the Profit Economy in Medieval Europe*, 1978, pp. 99-112; Bloch, *Feudal Society*, *Vols. 1-2*, 1961, pp. 190-210; and Leyser, "Clerical purity and the re-ordered world," in Rubin and Simons, *The Cambridge History of Christianity, V. 4*, 2009, pp. 11-21.

418 The main sources for this paragraph are: Gilchrist, *The Church and Economic Activity in the Middle Ages*, 1969, pp. 27-39; Wood, *The Proprietary Church in the Medieval West*, 2006, pp. 292-311; and Leyser, "Clerical purity and the re-ordered world" in Rubin and Simons (eds.), *The Cambridge History of Christianity: V. 4, Christianity in Western Europe c. 100-c. 1500*, 2009, pp. 11-21.

419 The monasteries also resisted the papacy's attempts to instead restore the control of many church revenues to the diocesan bishops. It seems that the laity generally paid their tithes, but there were many battles within the church over the proper owner of those tithes, especially between monasteries and bishops.

420 The main sources for this paragraph are: Frassetto, Michael, "Introduction," in Frassetto, Michael (ed.), *Medieval Purity and Piety: Essays on Medieval Clerical Celibacy and Religious Reform*, 1998, pp. xiv-xviii; and de Jong, M., "*Imitatio Morum.* The Cloister and Clerical Purity in the Carolingian World," in Frassetto (ed.), *Medieval Purity and Piety: Essays on Medieval Clerical Celibacy and Religious Reform*, 1998, pp. 49-80.

421 Those who did not follow these rules were supposed to accept clerical ordination and be subject to the authority of their bishops.

[422]   In particular, the emperor Louis the Pious convened church councils at Aachen in 816 and 817 to deal with monastic reform. The main source for this paragraph and note is Geréby, György, "The Life of the Hermit Stephen of Obazine," in Rubin, M. (ed.), *Medieval Christianity in Practice*, 2009, pp. 299-310.

[423]   The main sources for this section are: Angenendt, Arnold, "Sacrifice, gifts, and prayers in Latin Christianity," in Noble and Smith (eds.), *The Cambridge History of Christianity: Early Medieval Christianities, c. 600-c. 1100,* 2008, pp. 467-71; and Van Engen, John H., "Conclusion: Christendom, c. 1100," in Noble and Smith (eds.), *The Cambridge History of Christianity: Early Medieval Christianities, c. 600-c. 1100,* 2008, pp. 631-33.

[424]   The main sources for this section are: Angenendt, Arnold, "Sacrifice, gifts, and prayers in Latin Christianity," in Noble and Smith (eds.), *The Cambridge History of Christianity: Early Medieval Christianities, c. 600-c. 1100,* 2008, pp. 467-71; and Van Engen, John H., "Conclusion: Christendom, c. 1100," in Noble and Smith (eds.), *The Cambridge History of Christianity: Early Medieval Christianities, c. 600-c. 1100,* 2008, pp. 631-33.

[425]   St. Francis especially abhorred money, property, and ownership. The mendicants initially were wildly popular because of their emphasis on evangelizing poverty that contrasted so sharply with wealthy monasteries.

[426]   Interestingly, some in St. Francis' order began losing their zeal for evangelizing poverty even before he died.

[427]   The main sources for this paragraph are: Barrow, Julia, "Ideas and applications of reform," in Noble and Smith (eds.), *The Cambridge History of Christianity: Early Medieval Christianities, c. 600-c. 1100,* 2008, pp. 345-362; Frassetto, Michael, "Introduction," in Frassetto, Michael (ed.), *Medieval Purity and Piety: Essays on Medieval Clerical Celibacy and Religious Reform,* 1998, pp. xiv-xviii; and Beaudette, P., " 'In the World but not of It': Clerical Celibacy as a Symbol of the Medieval Church," in Frassetto (ed.), *Medieval Purity and Piety: Essays on Medieval Clerical Celibacy and Religious Reform,* 1998, pp. 35-40.

[428]   In this context, Vatican II can be interpreted as rejecting the separation of the church from the world that was implemented by the eleventh-thirteenth century reformers.

[429]   See Roach, *The Devil's World: Heresy and Society 1100-1300,* 2005, pp. 92-96.

[430]   See Van Engen, John H., "Conclusion: Christendom, c. 1100," in Noble and Smith (eds.), *The Cambridge History of Christianity: Early Medieval Christianities, c. 600-c. 1100,* 2008, pp. 633-35.

431   Information used in the text about the German church tax has been widely reported by international news organizations. For example, see the following articles: Luxmoore, J., "German bishops defend exclusion of Catholics who stop paying tax," *National Catholic Reporter* online edition, September 25, 2012, http://ncronline.org/search/site/johnathan%20Luxmoore%2C%20german%20bishops; Luxmoore, J., "German bishops defend exclusion of Catholics who stop paying tax," *National Catholic Reporter*, print edition, October 12-25, 2012; and Eddy, M., "German Catholic Church Links Tax to the Sacraments," *New York Times*, http://www.nytimes.com/2012/10/06/world/europe/german-church-ties-tax-to-sacraments-after-court-ruling.html?pagewanted=all&_r=0.

432   The German bishops also decreed that Roman Catholics who refuse to pay the tax no longer can receive: the sacraments of penance and confirmation (anointing of the sick also is prohibited, except for those facing death).

433   Although the actual proportion of church resources devoted to the poor and social justice issues cannot be determined because of the church's secrecy in accounting for its resources, especially its finances, observation of church activities shows that the proportion of human, physical, and financial resources devoted to such causes is a quite small proportion of total church resources.

434   Israely, J., "The Pope to Unhappy Anglicans: Come On In!" in *Time World*, at http://www.time.com/time/world/article0,8599,1931193,00.html#ixzz20RFg86VQ, October 20, 2009, downloaded July 12, 2012. The pope's decision to create a new structure for the Anglicans within the Roman Catholic Church follows earlier, ad-hoc decisions by Pope John Paul II to allow several married Anglican priests to convert, remain married, and serve as Roman Catholic priests.

435   Many of the church's ancient precedents were established when the church and secular powers colluded to control society for their mutual benefit.

436   For economic and legal analyses of corruption and religion, see: Paldam, M., "Corruption and Religion: Adding to the Economic Model," in *Kyklos*, 2001, pp. 383-414; and Koppelman A., "Corruption of Religion and the Establishment Clause," 50 Wm. & Mary L. Rev. 1831 (2009), http://scholarship.law.wm.edu/wmlr/vol50/iss6/2.

437   For example, see De Rosa, *Vicars of Christ: the Dark Side of the Papacy*, 1988, pp. 29-35.

438   De Rosa, *Vicars of Christ: the Dark Side of the Papacy*, 1988, p. 37.

439   Churchmen have justified the relative silence as a strategy that supposedly was best for Jesus' Jewish people, but the historical record strongly challenges that

claim.

[440] The details of the scandals are widely reported in the popular press, including *New York Times*, *National Catholic Reporter*, *Yahoo*, *Wikipedia*, and many blogs. For example, the *National Catholic Reporter's* March 14-23 edition includes extensive reporting on many details of the scandal, including charges of fraud, after thousands of pages of court documents were unsealed in February, 2013. Even longer versions of the story appear on NCR's website at http://ncronline.org/feature-series/legion-christ-investigation. The Vatican earlier had finally issued an official condemnation, and the new leaders of the Legion of Christ also have officially apologized. J. Paul Lennon, who left the Legion of Christ after 23 years, also has written a scathing first-hand account of the order (published in 2008, with further comments published in 2012).

[441] In 2006, his retirement to a life of prayer and penitence already had been ordered.

[442] The Jesuit Fr. Thomas Reese recently criticized the lack of accountability for bishops and questioned whether the hierarchy can fix itself because of its focus on obedience and control. See McElwee, J. J., "Unfinished work: Examining 10 years of clergy sex abuse," in *National Catholic Reporter*, May 11, 2012.

[443] For example, see: Modras, Ron, "Does excommunication do any good?" in *National Catholic Reporter*, July 9, 2010.

[444] There are many sources on the Vatican banking scandals. For one of these about the firing of the bank president, see the report by the *Catholic Free Press* posted at http://www.catholicfreepress.org/vatican/2012/05/25/vatican-bank-board-fires-president-citing-neglect-of-duties/.

[445] See Pew Research Center, *"Nones" on the Rise*, a survey report of the Pew Forum of Religion & Public Life, downloaded October 29, 2012 at http://www.pewforum.org/.

[446] For a discussion of strategic management issues for sustainable competitive advantage in religious organizations, see Miller, K. D. "Competitive Strategies of Religious Organizations," in *Strategic Management Journal*, May 2002), pp. 435-456.

[447] This conservative Catholic group formed the Society of St. Pius X in 1970 under the leadership of the French archbishop Marcel Lefebvre. The Vatican has made overtures for the group to return to the one 'true' church. See: Fournier, K., "Society of Pius X Responds Positively to Overture From the Vatican," *Catholic Online*, http://www.catholic.org/international/international_story.php?id=45778, April 20, 2012, downloaded July 19, 2012.

448   History is full of corrupt regimes (including the church's protectors in imperial Rome) and numerous commercial monopolies whose leaders continued to live in splendor, ignore internal problems, and fail to recognize changes that finally ended their economic and political power. In fact, a commercial monopoly never has lasted nearly as long as the church's monopoly reign of more than one thousand years (with continuing wealth and power up to this day). Of course, commercial monopolies never had salvation to sell or the long-time support of secular rulers, who collaborated with the Roman Catholic Church for their own wealth and power.

449   For Reese's comments at a May 2012 church conference in Santa Clara, California, see: McElwee, J. J., "Unfinished Work: 10 years of clergy sex abuse," in *National Catholic Reporter* online edition, May 11, 2012, http://ncronline.org/news/accountability/unfinished-work-examining-10-years-clergy-sex-abuse; and Reese, T. J., "Thomas J. Reese on Sex Abuse," in *America: The National Catholic Weekly*, online edition, posted May 10, 2012, http://www.americamagazine.org/blog/entry.cfm?blog_id=2&entry_id=5115.

450   Robinson was specifically addressing the sexual abuse crisis in the church, but his book shows that the church's culture applies to all church problems. See Robinson, G., *Confronting Sex and Power in the Catholic Church: Reclaiming the Spirit of Jesus*, 2008.

451   DeThomasis, L., *Flying in the Face of Tradition: Listening to the Lived Experience of the Faithful*, 2012. He believes the current church hierarchy is plagued by too many 'ideologues' who want no dialogue or questions raised about their decisions.

452   Smith, Adam, *The Wealth of Nations*, 1776 (1937), Book V.

453   See Borg, M., *Jesus: Uncovering the Life, Teachings, and Relevance of a Religious Revolutionary*, 2006, pp. 308-11.

BIBLIOGRAPHY

Abrams, Lesley, "Germanic Christianities," in Noble and Smith (eds.), **The Cambridge History of Christianity: Early Medieval Christianities, c. 600-c. 1100**, 2008, pp. 107-129.

Abulafia, A. S. **Christian-Jewish Relations 1000-1300: Jews in the Service of Medieval Christendom**, Great Britain: Pearson Education, 2011.

Abulafia, D. (ed.). **The New Cambridge Medieval History: Vol. 5, c.1198-c.1300**, Cambridge: Cambridge University Press, 1999.

Albert, Bat-Sheva, "Christians and Jews," in Noble and Smith (eds.), **The Cambridge History of Christianity: Early Medieval Christianities, c. 600-c. 1100**, 2008, pp. 159-177.

Allen, D. W., "A Review of R. B. Ekelund Jr. and R. D. Tollison, *Economic Origins of Roman Christianity*," **Journal of Economic Literature**, 2011, pp. 545-46.

Anderson, G. A. **Sin: a History**, New Haven, CN: Yale University Press, 2009.

Angenendt, Arnold, "Sacrifice, gifts, and prayers in Latin Christianity," in Noble and Smith (eds.), **The Cambridge History of Christianity: Early Medieval Christianities, c. 600-c. 1100**, 2008, pp. 453-471

Armstrong, R. J. and I. C. Brady (translation and introduction). **Francis and Clare: The Complete Works,** Mahwah, NJ: The Paulist Press, 1982.

Arnold, Benjamin. **Power and Property in Medieval Germany: Economic and Social Change c. 900-1300**, New York: Oxford University Press, 2004.

Arrunada, Benito, "Catholic Confessions of Sin as Third Party Moral Enforcement," **The Gruter Institute Working Papers on Law, Economics, and Evolutionary Biology: Vol. 3: Article 2** (2004). http://www.bepress.com/giwp/default/vol3/iss1/art2.

Atlante del Cristianesimo, ed. Roberto Rusconi, 2006 (revised English translation).
"The Church and the Jews: St Paul to Pius IX," in Kenneth R. Stow, **Popes, Church, and Jews in the Middle Ages: Confrontation and Response**, pp. I: 1-70.

Baker, Derek (ed.), **Sanctity and Secularity: The Church and the World**, New York: Barnes and Noble, for the Ecclesiastical History Society, 1973.

Barro, Robert J., Rachel M. McCleary, and Axexander McQuoid, "The Economics of Sainthood (A Preliminary Investigation)," in McCleary, Rachel M. (ed.), **The Oxford Handbook of the Economics of Religion**, 2011, pp. 191-216.

Barrow, Julia, "Ideas and applications of reform," in Noble and Smith (eds.), **The Cambridge History of Christianity: Early Medieval Christianities, c. 600-c. 1100**, 2008, pp. 345-362.

Bauer, Susan Wise. **The History of the Ancient World: From the Earliest Accounts to the Fall of Rome**, New York, NY: W. W. Norton, 2007.

Bauer, Susan Wise. **The History of the Medieval World: From the Conversion of Constantine to the First Crusade**, New York, NY: W. W. Norton, 2010.

Baun, Jane, "Last Things," in Noble and Smith (eds.), **The Cambridge History of Christianity: Early Medieval Christianities, c. 600-c. 1100**, 2008, pp. 606-624.

Beaudette, P., " 'In the World but not of It': Clerical Celibacy as a Symbol of the Medieval Church," in Frassetto (ed.), **Medieval Purity and Piety; Essays on Medieval Clerical Celibacy and Religious Reform**, 1998, pp. 23-46.

Becker, Gary S. **The Economic Approach to Human Behavior,** Chicago: The University of Chicago Press, 1976.

Becker, Gary S. **Human Capital: A Theoretical and Empirical Analysis, with Special Reference to Education**, New York: Columbia University, 2nd edition, 1975.

Becker, Gary S., "A Theory of Competition Among Pressure Groups for Political Influence," **Quarterly Journal of Economics** 97 (1983), pp. 371-400.

Becker, Gary S., "A Theory of the Allocation of Time," **Economic Journal** 65 (September 1965), pp. 493-508.

Becker, Gary S. and Kevin Murphy, "A Theory of Rational Addiction," **Journal of Political Economy** 96 (1988), pp. pp. 675-700.

Bernstein, Alan E., "Heaven, hell, and purgatory: 1100-1500," in Rubin and Simons (eds.), **The Cambridge History of Christianity: V. 4, Christianity in Western Europe c. 1100-c. 1500**, 2009, pp. 200-16.

Bloch, H., "The Pagan Revival at the end of the Fourth Century," in Momigliano (ed), **The Conflict between Paganism and Christianity in the Fourth Century**, 1963, pp. 193-218.

Bloch, Marc (translated by L. A. Manyon). **Feudal Society, Vol. I: The Growth of Ties of Dependence,** London: Routledge, originally published 1961, digital reprint 2003.

Bloch, Marc (translated by L. A. Manyon). **Feudal Society, Volume 2: Social Classes and Political Organization**, Chicago: The University of Chicago Press, originally published in English in 1961.

Borg, Marcus. **Jesus: Uncovering the Life, Teachings, and Relevance of a Religious Revolutionary**, New York: HarperSanFrancisco, 2006.

Bornstein, D., "How to Behave in Church and How to Become a Priest," in Rubin, M. (ed.), **Medieval Christianity in Practice**, 2009, pp. 109-115.

Boswell, J. **Christianity, Social Tolerance, and Homosexuality,** Chicago, IL: University of Chicago Press, 1980.

Botticini, M., "A Loveless Economy? Intergenerational Altruism and the Marriage Market in a Tuscan Town," **Journal of Economic History** 59.1 (March 1999), pp. 104-121.

Botticini, Maristella and Zvi Eckstein, "Religious Norms, Human Capital, and Money Lending in Jewish European History," in McCleary, Rachel M. (ed.), **The Oxford Handbook of the Economics of Religion**, 2011, pp. 57-80.

Bouchard, C. Brittain. **Holy Entrepreneurs: Cistercians, Knights, and Economic Exchange in Twelfth Century Burgundy.** Ithaca-London: Cornell University Press, 1991.
Boulding, Kenneth E. **Beyond Economics: Essays on Society, Religion, and Ethics**, Ann Arbor, MI: The University of Michigan Press, 1968.

Boulding, Kenneth E., "Religious Foundations of Economic Progress," in Boulding, **Beyond Economics: Essays on Society, Religion, and Ethics**, 1968, pp. 198-211.

Boulding, Kenneth E., "Religious Perspectives in Economics," in Boulding, **Beyond Economics: Essays on Society, Religion, and Ethics**, 1968, pp. 179-197.

Boulding, Kenneth E., "Some Contributions of Economics to Theology and Religion," in Boulding, **Beyond Economics: Essays on Society, Religion, and Ethics**, 1968, pp. 219-226.

Brams, S. J. **Biblical Games: Game Theory and the Hebrew Bible**, Cambridge, MA: MIT Press, 2002.

Brown, Peter. **Augustine of Hippo: A Biography**, London: University of California Press, 1967, new edition, 2000.

Brown, Peter. **The Cult of Saints: Its Rise and Function in Latin Christianity,** Chicago, IL: The University of Chicago Press, paperback edition, 1982.

Brown, Peter, "Introduction: Christendom, c. 600," in Noble and Smith (eds.), **The Cambridge History of Christianity: Early Medieval Christianities, c. 600-c. 1100**, 2008, pp. 1-18.

Brown, Peter. **The Rise of Western Christendom: Triumph and Diversity, 200-1000 AD**, Malden, Mass: Blackwell Publishing, 2nd edition, 2003.

Buchanan, James M., "An Economic Theory of Clubs," in **Economica** 32 (1965), pp. 1-14.

Bull, Marcus, "Crusade and conquest," in Rubin and Simons (eds.), **The Cambridge History of Christianity: V. 4, Christianity in Western Europe c. 1100-c. 1500**, 2009, pp. 340-52.

Burgess, Paul. **Early Church's Betrayal of Jesus: Popes, Corruption, and Holy Violence:**, Phoenix, AZ: working paper, 2015.

Cameron, Averil, "Constantine and the 'peace of the church'," in Mitchell and Young (eds.), **The Cambridge History of Christianity, Vol. 1: Origins to Constantine**, 2006, pp. 538-551.

Cameron, Averil. **The Mediterranean World in Late Antiquity, AD 395-600**, London: Routledge, originally published in 1993, digital reprint 2003.

Cameron, Rondo. **A Concise Economic History of the World: From Paleolithic Times to the Present**, New York, NY: Oxford University Press, 1989.

Cardman, Francine, "Poverty and Wealth as Theater: John Chrysostom's Homilies on Lazarus and the Rich Man," in Holman (ed.), **Wealth and Poverty in Early Church and Society**, 2008, pp. 159-175.

Casiday, Augustine, "Sin and salvation: Experiences and reflections," in Casiday and Norris (eds.), **The Cambridge History of Christianity: Constantine to c. 600**, 2007, pp. 501-530.

Casiday, Augustine and Frederick W. Norris (eds.). **The Cambridge History of Christianity: Constantine to c. 600**, Cambridge: Cambridge University Press, 2007.

Casiday, Augustine and Frederick W. Norris, "Introduction," in Casiday and Norris (eds.), **The Cambridge History of Christianity: Constantine to c. 600**, 2007, pp. 1-5.

Catechism of The Catholic Church, Liguori, MO: Liguori Publications for the United States Conference of Bishops, Inc., Engilsh edition, 1994.

Catholic Encyclopedia, "Canonization and Beatification," http://www.newadvent.org/cathen/02364b.htm, downloaded November 9, 2012.

Cirino, Andre and Josef Raischl (eds.), **Franciscan Solitude**, St. Bonaventure, NY: The Franciscan Institute, St. Bonaventure University, 1995.

Clark, Gregory. **A Farewell to Alms: A Brief Economic History of the World,** Princeton, New Jersey: Princeton University Press, 2007.

Cochran, J. K. and L. Beeghley, "The Influence of Religion on Attitudes toward Nonmarital Sexuality," **Journal of the Scientific Study of Religion** 30.1 (1991), pp. 45-62.
Coleman, James, "Social Capital in the Creation of Human Capital," **American Journal of Sociology**, 1994 Supplement, pp. s95-s120.

Collins, Roger. **Early Medieval Europe: 300-1000**, New York: Palgrave Macmillan, 3rd ed., 2010.

Collins, Roger. **Keepers of the Keys of Heaven: A History of the Papacy**, New York: Basic Books, 2009.

Comby, Jean (English translation by John Bowden and Margaret Lydamore). **How to Read Church History: Volume 1, From the beginnings to the fifteenth century**, New York, N. Y.: Crossroad, 1985.

Coon, Lynda L., "Gender and the body," in Noble and Smith (eds.), **The Cambridge History of Christianity: Early Medieval Christianities, c. 600-c. 1100**, 2008, pp. 433-452.

Cornelison, Sally J. and Scott B. Montgomery (eds.). **Images, Relics, and Devotional Practices in Medieval and Renaissance Italy**, Tempe, AZ: Arizona Center for Medieval and Renaissance Studies, Arizona State University, 2006.

Curtis, A. Kenneth J., Stephen Lang, and Randy Petersen. **The 100 Most Important Events in Christian History**, Grand Rapids, Michigan: Fleming H. Revell, 1998.

Dachowski, E., *"Teritus est optimus:* Marriage, Continence and Virginity in the Politics of Late Tenth- and Early Eleventh-Century Francia," in Frassetto (ed.), **Medieval Purity and Piety; Essays on Medieval Clerical Celibacy and Religious Reform**, 1998, pp. 117-130.

Davidson, Audrey, "The Medieval Monastery as Franchise Monopolist," **Journal of Economic Behavior and Organization** 27 (1995), pp. 119-128.

Davidson, Audrey and Ekelund Jr., Robert, "The Medieval Church and Rents from Marriage Market Regulations," in **Journal of Economic Behavior and Organization** 32 (1997), pp. 215-245.

Davies, J. G. **The Early Christian Church**, New York: Barnes & Noble (1965), 1995.

Davies, W. and P. Fouracre, "Conclusion," in Davies and Fouracre (eds.), **Property and Power in the Early Middle Ages** (1995), 2002, pp. 245-71.

Davies, W. and P. Fouracre, "Introduction," in Davies and Fouracre (eds.), **Property and Power in the Early Middle Ages** (1995), 2002, pp. 1-16.

Davies W. and P. Fouracre (eds.). **Property and Power in the Early Middle Ages**, Cambridge: Cambridge University Press (1995), 2002.

d'Avray, D., "Annulment of Henry III's 'Marriage' to Joan of Ponthieu Confirmed by Innocent IV on 20 May 1254," in Rubin, M. (ed.). **Medieval Christianity in Practice**, 2009, pp. 42-51.

d' Avray, D. **Medieval Marriage: Symbolism and Society**, Oxford: Oxford University Press (2005), 2008.

Day, John. **The Medieval Market Eonomy,** Oxford: Basil Blackwell, 1987.

de Jong, M., *"Imitatio Morum.* The Cloister and Clerical Purity in the Carolingian World," in Frassetto (ed.), **Medieval Purity and Piety; Essays on Medieval Clerical Celibacy and Religious Reform**, 1998, pp. 49-80.

Delumeau, Jean (translated by Eric Nicholson). **Sin and Fear: The Emergence of a Western Guilt Culture, 13th-18th Centuries**, New York: St. Martin's Press (1983), 1990.

De Roover, R., "The Concept of the Just Price: Economic Theory and Economic Policy," **Journal of Economic History** 18 (December, 1958), pp. 418-34.

De Rosa, Peter. **Vicars of Christ: the Dark Side of the Papacy**, New York, NY: Crown Publishers, 1988.

DeThomasis, L. **Flying in the Face of Tradition: Listening to the Lived Experience of the Faithful**, Chicago, IL: ACTA Publications, 2012.

Donahue, C., Jr., "The Canon Law on the Formation of Marriage and Social Practice in the Later Middle Ages," **Journal of Family History** 8 (1983), pp. 144-158.

Duby, Georges (translated by Eleanor Levieux and Barbara Thompson). **The Age of Cathedrals: Art and Society, 980-1240,** Chicago, IL: The University of Chicago Press, 1983.
Duby, G. (translated by A. Goldhammer), "The Courtly Model," in Klapisch-Zuber, C. (ed.). **A History of Women in the West: II. Silences of the Middle Ages** (1990), 1994, pp. 250-66.

Duby, Georges (translated by Stuart Gilbert). **The Europe of the Cathedrals, 1140-1280.** Geneva: Editions d' Art Albert Skira, 1966.

Duby, G. (translated by B. Bray). **The Knight, the Lady and the Priest: The Making of Modern Marriage in Medieval France.** Chicago: University of Chicago Press (1981), 1993.

Duby, G. (translated by J. Dunnett). **Love and Marriage in the Middle Ages.** Chicago: University of Chicago Press (1988), 1996.

Duby, Georges (translated by Elbord Forster). **Medieval Marriage,** Baltimore: John Hopkins University Press, 1978.

Duby, Georges (translated by Arthur Goldhammer). **The Three Orders: Feudal Society imagined,** Chicago: The University of Chicago Press, 1982.

Duffy, Eamon. **Saints and Sinners: A History of the Popes,** New Haven, CN: Yale Nota Bene Book, 2006.

Dulleck, Uweand Rudolf Kerschbamer, "On Doctors, Mechanics, and Computer Specialists: The Economics of Credence Goods," **Journal of Economic Literature** 44 (March 2006), pp. 5-42.

Dunn, James D. G. **Christianity in the Making, Vol. 2: Beginning from Jerusalem,** Grand Rapids, MI and Cambridge, U.K.: Eerdmans, 2009.

Dunn, Marilyn, "Asceticism, and monasticism, II: Western," in Casiday and Norris (eds.), **The Cambridge History of Christianity: Constantine to c. 600,** 2007, pp. 669-690.

Durkin John T., Jr. and Andrew Greeley, "A Model of Religious Choice Under Uncertainty: On Responding Rationally to the Nonrational," **Rationality and Society** 3.2 (1991), pp. 178-196.

Ehrman, Bart D. and Andrew S. Jacobs. **Chrsitianity in Late Antiquity, 300-450 C. E.: A Reader,** New York, NY: Oxford University Press, 2004.

Eilinghoff, C. "Religious Information and Credibility" in **German Working Papers in Law and Economics,** 2003, paper 8.

Ekelund Jr., Robert B., Franklin G. Bion Jr., and Rand W. Ressler, "Advertising and Information: An Empirical Study of Search, Experience and Credence Goods," **Journal of Economic Studies,** 22 (1995), pp. 33-43.

Ekelund Jr., Robert B., Robert F. Hébert, and Robert D. Tollison, "An Economic Analysis of the Protestant Reformation," **Journal of Political Economy** 110, no. 3 (2002), pp. 646-671.

Ekelund Jr., Robert B., Robert F. Hébert, and Robert D. Tollison, " An Economic Model of the Medieval Church: Usury as a Form of Rent Seeking," **Journal of Law, Economics, and Organization** 5 (Fall 1989), pp. 307-331.

Ekelund Jr., Robert B., Robert F. Hébert, and Robert D. Tollison, "The Economics of the Counter-Reformation: Incumbent Reaction to Market Entry," **Economic Inquiry** 42 (October 2004).

Ekelund Jr., Robert B., Robert F. Hébert, and Robert D. Tollison, "The Economics of Sin and Redemption: Purgatory as a Market-Pull Innovation?" **Journal of Economic Behaviour and Organization** 19 (September 1992), pp. 1-15.

Ekelund Jr., Robert B., Robert F. Hébert, and Robert D. Tollison. **The Marketplace of Christianity**, Cambridge, MA: MIT Press, 2006.

Ekelund Jr., Robert B., Robert F. Hébert, and Robert D. Tollison, "The Political Economy of the Medieval Church," in McCleary, Rachel M. (ed.), **The Oxford Handbook of the Economics of Religion**, 2011, pp.305-322.

Ekelund Jr., Robert B., Robert F. Hébert, Robert D. Tollison, Gary M. Anderson, and Audrey B. Davidson. **Sacred Trust: The Medieval Church as an Economic Firm,** New York: Oxford University Press, 1996.

Ekelund Jr., R. B., D. R. Street, and and A. B. Davidson, "Marriage, Divorce, and Prostitution; Economic Sociology in Medieval England and Enlightenment Spain," **European Journal of the History of Economic Thought** 3 (1996), pp. 183-199.

Ekelund Jr., Robert B. and Robert D. Tollison, **Economic Origins of Roman Christianity**, Chicago: University of Chicago Press, 2011.
Ekelund Jr., R. B. and R. D. Tollison, **Mercantilism as a Rent-Seeking Society,** College Station, TX: Texas A & M University Press, 1981.

Ekelund Jr., Robert B. and Robert D. Tollison. **Politicized Economies: Monarchy, Monopoly, and Mercantilism,** College Station, TX: Texas A & M University Press,1997.

Ellison, C. G., "Rational Choice Explanations of Individual Religious Behavior: Notes on the Problem of Social Embeddedness," **Journal for the Scientific Study of Religion** 34 (1995).

Ellison, C. G., "Religious Involvement and Subjective Well-Being," **Journal of Health and Social Behavior** 32 (1991).

Ehrenberg, Ronald, "Household Allocation of Time and Religiosity: Replication and Extension," **Journal of Political Economy**, 1975, pp. 415-23.

Ferrero, Mario, "Competition for Sainthood and the Millennial Church," **Kyklos**, August, 2002, pp. 335-60.

Finley, M. I. **The Ancient Economy.** Berkeley, CA: University of California Press (1973), 1999.

Firey, Abigail, " 'For I Was Hungry and You Fed Me': Social Justice and Economic Thought in the Latin Patristic and Medieval Christian Traditions," in Lowry and Gordon (eds.), **Ancient and Medieval Economic Ideas and Concepts of Social Justice**, 1998, pp. 333-370.

Flood, David and Athena Calogeras. **For People: An Introduction to Franciscan Life,** Chicago, IL: Haversack, Franciscan Federation, 1990.

Fouracre, P., "Introduction," in Fouracre, P. (ed.), **The New Cambridge Medieval History: Vol. 1, c. 500-c.700**, 2005, pp. 1-12.

Fouracre, Paul (ed.). **The New Cambridge Medieval History: Vol. 1, c. 500-c.700**, Cambridge: Cambridge University Press, 2005.

Fouracre, Paul (ed.). **The New Cambridge Medieval History: Vol. 3, c. 900-c.1024**, Cambridge: Cambridge University Press, 2000.

Fox, Judith, "Secularization," in Hinnells (ed.), **The Routledge Companion to the Study of Religion**, 2010, pp. 306-321.

Frank, Georgia, "From Antioch to Arles: Lay devotion in context," in Casiday and Norris (eds.), **The Cambridge History of Christianity: Constantine to c. 600**, 2007, pp. 531-547.

Frankfurter, David, "Christianity and paganism, I: Egypt," in Casiday and Norris (eds.), **The Cambridge History of Christianity: Constantine to c. 600**, 2007, pp. 173-188.

Frassetto, Michael. "Heresy, Celibacy, and Reform in the Sermons of Ademar of Chabannes," in Michael Frassetto (ed.), **Medieval Purity and Piety; Essays on Medieval Clerical Celibacy and Religious Reform**, 1998, pp. 131-148.

Frassetto, Michael. "Heretics and Jews in the Early Eleventh Century: The Writings of Rodulfus Glaber and Ademar of Chabannes," in Michael Frassetto (ed.), **Christian Attitudes Toward The Jews In The Middle Ages: A Casebook**, 2007, pp. 43-60.

Frassetto, Michael. "Introduction," in Michael Frassetto (ed.), **Medieval Purity and Piety; Essays on Medieval Clerical Celibacy and Religious Reform**, 1998, pp. ix-xviii.

Frassetto, Michael. "Introduction: Christians and Jews in the Middle Ages," in Michael Frassetto (ed.), **Christian Attitudes Toward The Jews In The Middle Ages: A Casebook**, 2007, pp. xiii-xviii.

Frassetto, Michael (ed.). **Medieval Purity and Piety; Essays on Medieval Clerical Celibacy and Religious Reform**, NY: Garland Publishing, Inc., 1998.

Freeman, Charles. **A. D. 381: Heretics, Pagans, and the Dawn of the Monotheistic State**, New York: Overlook Press, 2008.

Freeman, Charles. **The Closing of the Western Mind: The Rise of Faith and the Fall of Reason**, New York, NY: Vintage Books, 2002.

Freeman, Charles. **Egypt, Greece and Rome: Civilizations of the Ancient Mediterranean**, Oxford, England: Oxford University Press, 2004.

Freeman, Charles. **A New History of Early Christianity**. New Haven, CN: Yale University Press, 2009.

Fulton, Rachel, "Mary," in Rubin and Simons (eds.), **The Cambridge History of Christianity: V. 4, Christianity in Western Europe c. 1100-c. 1500**, 2009, pp. 283-96.

Gamble, Harry Y., "Marcion and the 'canon'," in Mitchell and Young (eds.), **The Cambridge History of Christianity, Vol. 1: Origins to Constantine**, 2006, pp. 195-213.

Geary, Patrick J. **Furta Sacra: Thefts of Relics in the Central Middle Ages**, Princeton, NJ: Princeton University Press (1978), 1990.

Georgoudi, Stella, "Creating a Myth of Matriarchy," in Schmitt (ed.), **A History of Women in the West: From Ancient Goddesses to Christian Saints**, 1994, pp. 449-463.

Gereby, Gyorgy, "The Life of the Hermit Stephen of Obazine" in Rubin, M. (ed.), **Medieval Christianity in Practice**, 2009, pp. 299-310.

Gilchrist, John. **The Church and Economic Activity in the Middle Ages.** New York: Macmillan, 1969.

Gill, Anthony, "Review of *Sacred Trust: The Medieval Church as an Economic Firm*," **Journal of Economic Literature** 36 (September 1998), pp. 1515-1526.

Gimpel, Jean. **The Cathedral Builders**. New York: Harper & Row, 1983.

Godet-Calogeras, Jean Francois, "Evangelical Radicalism in the Writings of Francis and Clare of Assisi," **Franciscan Studies** 64 (2006), pp. 103-121.

Gonzalez, Justo L. **Faith and Wealth: A History of Early Christian Ideas on the Origin, Significance, and Use of Money**, Eugene, OR: Wipf and Stock Publishers, 1990.

Goodstein, Laurie, "Pope Francis Appoints a Panel to Study Women Deacons: Q & A With a Member," **New York Times** online edition, August 2, 2016.

Greer, Rowan A., "Pastoral care and discipline," in Casiday and Norris (eds.), **The Cambridge History of Christianity: Constantine to c. 600**, 2007, pp. 567-584.

Grief, Avner, "Commitment, Coercion, and Markets: The Nature and Dynamics of Institutions Supporting Exchange," in Menard, C. and M. M. Shirley (eds.), **Handbook of New Institutional Economics**, 2005, pp. 727-786.

Grief, Avner, "Cultural Beliefs and the Organization of Society: A Historical and Theoretical Reflection on Collectivist and Individualist Societies," **Journal of Political Economy** 102.5 (1994), pp. 912-950.

Grief, Avner, "Economic History and Game Theory: A Survey," in Robert J. Aumann and Sorgiu Hart (eds.), **Handbook of Game Theory, V. 3,** Amsterdam: Elsevier, 2002.

Grosbard-Schechtman, S. A. and N. S. Neuman, "Economic Behavior, Marriage and Religiosity," **Journal of Behavioral Science** 15 (Spring-Summer 1986), pp. 71-85.

Hamilton, S., "Doing Penance," in Rubin, M. (ed.). **Medieval Christianity in Practice**, 2009, pp. 135-43.

Hammond, Jay M. (ed.). **Francis of Assisi: History, Hagiography, and Hermeneutics in the Early Documents.** Hyde Park, NY: New City Press, 2004.

Hardin, Russell, "The Economics of Religious Belief," **Journal of Institutional and Theoretical Economics** 153.1 (1997), pp. 259-278.

Head, T., "Translation of the Body of St. Junianus," in Rubin, M. (ed.). **Medieval Christianity in Practice**, 2009, pp. 217-21.

Hechter, Michael, "Religion and Rational Choice Theory," in Young, (ed.), **Rational Choice Theory and Religion: Summary and Assessment**, 1997, pp. 147-159.

Helvetius, Anne-Marie and Michel Kaplan, "Asceticisim and its institutions," in Noble and Smith (eds.), **The Cambridge History of Christianity: Early Medieval Christianities, c. 600-c. 1100**, 2008, pp. 275-298.

Hen, Y., "The Early Medieval *Barbatoria*," in Rubin, M. (ed.). **Medieval Christianity in Practice**, 2009, pp. 21-25.

Hinnells, John R. (ed.), **The Routledge Companion to the Study of Religion**, New York: Routledge, 2010, 2nd ed.

Hope

Hinnels, John R., "Why study religions?" in Hinnells (ed.), **The Routledge Companion to the Study of Religion**, 2010, pp. 5-20.

Holman, Susan R., "Rich and Poor in Sophronius of Jerusalem's *Miracles of Saints Cyrus and John*," in Holman (ed.), **Wealth and Poverty in Early Church and Society**, 2008, pp. 103-124.

Holman, Susan R. **Wealth and Poverty in Early Church and Society.** Grand Rapids, Mi: Baker Academic for Holy Cross Greek Orthodox School of Theology, 2008.

Hopkins, Keith. **Death and Renewal: Sociological Studies in Roman History, Volume 2**, Cambridge: Cambridge University Press (1983), 1985.

Hopkins, Keith. **A World Full of Gods: The Strange Triumph of Christianity**, New York: Plume (1999), 2001.

Horden, P., "The Confraternities of Byzantium," in Sheils and Wood (eds.), **Voluntary Religion**, 1986, pp. 25-45.

Horden, P., "Sickness and healing," in Noble and Smith (eds.), **The Cambridge History of Christianity: Early Medieval Christianities, c. 600-c. 1100**, 2008, pp. 416-432.

Horden, P. and N. Purcell. **The Corrupting Sea: A Study of Mediterranean History**, Oxford: Blackwell Publishing, 2000.

Houlbrooke, R., "The Making of Marriage in Mid-Tudor England: Evidence from the Records of Matrimonial Contract Litigation," **Journal of Family History** 10 (1985), pp. 339-352.

Hull, Brooks B. and Frederick Bold, "Towards an Economic Theory of the Church," **International Journal of Social Economics** 16 (1989), pp. 5-15.

Hunter, David, "Sexuality, marriage and the family," in Casiday and Norris (eds.), **The Cambridge History of Christianity: Constantine to c. 600**, 2007, pp. 585-600.

Iannaccone, Laurence R., "The Consequences of Religious Market Structure: Adam Smith and the Economics of Religion," **Rationality and Society** 3.2 (1991), pp. 156-177.

Iannaccone, Laurence R., "A Formal Model of Church and Sect," **American Journal of Sociology** 94 (1988), pp. S241-268.

Iannaccone, Laurence R., "Introduction to the Economics of Religion," **Journal of Economic Literature** 36 (September 1998), pp. 1465-1495.

Iannaccone, Laurence R., "Progress in the Economics of Religion," **Journal of institutional and Theoretical Economics** 150, no. 4 (1994).

Iannaccone, Laurence R., "Rational Choice: Framework for the Scientific Study of Religion," in Young, (ed.), **Rational Choice Theory and Religion: Summary and Assessment**, 1997, pp. 25-45.

Iannoccone, Laurence R., "Religious Markets and the Economics of Religion," **Social Compass**, 39 (1), pp. 123-131.

Iannaccone, Laurence R., "Religious Participation: A Human Capital Approach," **Journal of Scientific Study of Religion** 29.3 (1990), pp. 297-314.

Iannaccone, Laurence R., "Risk, Rationality, and Religious Portfolios," **Economic Inquiry** 38 (1995), pp. 285-295.

Iannaccone, Laurence R., "Sacrifice and Stigma: Reducing Free Riding in Cults, Communes, and Other Collectives," **Journal of Political Economy** 100.2 (1992), pp. 271-292.

Iannaccone, Laurence R., "Voodoo Economics? Reviewing the Rational Choice Approach to Religion," **Journal for the Scientific Study of Religion** 34 (1995), pp. 76-89.

Iannaccone, Laurence R., "Why Strict Churches Are Strong," **American Journal of Sociology** 99.5 (1994), pp. 1180-1211.

Iannaccone, Laurence, R. and William Sims Bainbridge, "Economics of Religion," in Hinnells (ed.), The Routledge Companion to the Study of Religion, 2010, pp.461-476.

Iannaccone, Laurence, R. and Feler Bose, "Funding the Faiths: Toward a Theory of Religious Finance," in McCleary, Rachel M. (ed.), The Oxford Handbook of the Economics of Religion, 2011, pp. 323-342.

Iannaccone, Laurence R., Roger Finke, and Rodney Stark, "Deregulating Religion: The Economics of Church and State," Economic Inquiry 35.2 (1997), pp. 1350-364.

Iogna-Prat, D., "Churches in the landscape," in Noble and Smith (eds.), The Cambridge History of Christianity: Early Medieval Christianities, c. 600-c. 1100, 2008, pp. 363-379.

Irani, K. D., "The Idea of Social Justice in the Ancient World," in Irani and Silver (eds.), Social Justice in the Ancient World, 1995, pp 3-8.

Irani, K.D. and Morris Silver (eds.). Social Justice in the Ancient World, Westport, CT: Greenwood Press, 1995.

Jansen, K. L., "A Sermon on the Virtues of the Contemplative," in Rubin, M. (ed.). Medieval Christianity in Practice, 2009, pp. 117-25.

Jones, A. H. M. The Later Roman Empire, 284-602, A Social, Economic, and Administrative Survey: Volume One. Baltimore: The John Hopkins University Press, reprint, 1964.

Jones, A. H. M. The Later Roman Empire, 284-602, A Social, Economic, and Administrative Survey: Volume Two. Baltimore: The John Hopkins University Press, reprint, 1964.

Jones, M., "Introduction," in Jones, M. (ed.). The New Cambridge Medieval History: Vol. 6, c. 1300-c.1415, 2000, pp. 3-16.

Jones, M. (ed.). The New Cambridge Medieval History: Vol. 6, c. 1300-c.1415, Cambridge: Cambridge University Press, 2000.

Jones, P. M.., "Amulets and Charms," in Rubin, M. (ed.). **Medieval Christianity in Practice**, 2009, pp. 194-201.

Kaye, Joel, "Monetary and Market Consciousness in Thirteenth and Fourteenth Century Europe," in Lowry and Gordon (eds.), **Ancient and Medieval Economic Ideas and Concepts of Social Justice**, 1998, pp. 371-403.

Kelly, J. N. D. **The Oxford Dictionary of Popes**, New York, NY: Oxford University Press, updated 2005.

Kemp, Eric W. **Canonization in the Western Church**, Oxford: Oxford University Press, 1948.

Kleinberg, A. M., "The Possession of Blessed Jordan of Saxony," in Rubin, M. (ed.). **Medieval Christianity in Practice**, 2009, pp. 265-73.

Koppelman A., "Corruption of Religion and the Establishment Clause," 50 **Wm. & Mary L. Rev.** 1831 (2009), http://scholarship.law.wm.edu/wmlr/vol50/iss6/2.

Kraus, Henry. **Gold Was the Mortar: The Economics of Cathedral Building**, New York: Barnes & Noble Books, originally published 1979, this edition 1994.

Lambert, M. **Medieval Heresy. Popular Movements from Bogomil to Hus**, London: Edward Arnold Publishers , 1977.

Lambert, Malcom. **Medieval Heresy: Popular Movements from the Gregorian Reform to the Reformation**, New York: Barnes and Noble (1977), 1998.

Langholm, Odd. **The Aristotelian Analysis of Usury.** Oslo, Norway: Norwegian University Press, 1984.

Langholm, Odd, "Economic Freedom in Scholastic Thought," **History of Political Economy** 14 (1982), pp. 260-283.

Langholm, Odd. **Economics in Medieval Schools: Wealth, Exchange, Value, Money and Usury According to the Paris Theological Tradition, 1200-1350.** Leiden, Netherlands: Brill, 1992.

Langholm, Odd. **The Merchant in the Confessional: Trade and Price in the Pre-Reformation Penitential Handbooks.** Leiden, Netherlands: Brill, 2003.

Langholm, Odd. **Wealth and Money in the Aristotelian Tradition: A Study in Scholastic Economic Sources.** Oslo, Norway: Norwegian University Press, 1983.

Lauret, B. (ed.). **Fifty Years of Catholic Theology: Conversations with Yves Congar.** Philadelphia: Fortress Press, 1988.

Lea, Henry Charles. **A History of the Inquisition of the Middle Ages: Volume I,** New York, NY: Cosimo Classics (1888), 2005.

Lea, Henry Charles. **A History of the Inquisition of the Middle Ages: Volume II,** New York, NY: Cosimo Classics (1888, 2005.

Le Goff, Jacques (translated by Janet Lloyd). **The Birth of Europe, 400-1500,** Oxford: Blackwell Publishing, paperback edition, 2007.

Le Goff, Jacques (translated by Arthur Goldhammer). **The Birth of Purgatory,** Chicago, IL: University of Chicago Press, paperback edition, 1984.

Le Goff, Jacques, "The Town as an Agent of Civilisation, 1200-1500," in C. Cipolla (ed.), **The Fontana Economic History of Europe, Vol. 1, The Town as an Agent of Civilisation, 1200-1500,** 1972, Section 2.

Le Goff, Jacques (translated by Julia Barrow). **Medieval Civilization 400-1500,** New York: Barnes and Noble (1964), 2000.

Le Goff, Jacques (translated by Patricia Ranum). **Your Money or Your Life: Economy and Religion in the Middle Ages.** New York: Zone Books (1986), 2001.

Leyser, Henrietta, "Clerical purity and the re-ordered world," in Rubin and Simons (eds.), **The Cambridge History of Christianity: V. 4, Christianity in Western Europe c. 1100-c. 1500,** 2009, pp. 11-21.

Limor, Ora, "Christians and Jews," in Rubin and Simons (eds.), **The Cambridge History of Christianity: V. 4, Christianity in Western Europe c. 1100-c. 1500**, 2009, pp. 135-48.

Little, Lester K., "Pride Goes Before Avarice: Social Change and the Vices in Latin Christendom," **American Historical Review** 76 (1971), pp. 16-49.

Little, Lester K. **Religious Poverty and the Profit Economy in Medieval Europe**, Ithaca, NY: Cornell University Press, 1978.

Lopez, Robert S. **The Commercial Revolution of the Middle Ages, 950-1350**, Cambridge: Cambridge University Press, 1976.

Lopez, R. S., "The Trade of Medieval Europe: The South," in Postan and Rich (eds.), **The Cambridge Economic History of Europe: Volume II, Trade and Industry in the Middle Ages**, Cambridge: Cambridge University Press, 1952, pp. 257-354.

Louth, Andrew, "Hagiography," in Young, Lewis, and Louth (eds.), **The Cambridge History of Early Christian Literature**, 2004, pp. 358-361.

Lowry, S. Todd, "Social Justice and the Subsistence Economy: From Aristotle to Seventeenth-Century Economics," in Irani and Silver (eds.), **Social Justice in the Ancient World**, 1995, pp. 9-24.

Lowry, S. Todd and Barry Gordon (eds.). **Ancient and Medieval Economic Ideas and Concepts of Social Justice**, Lieden and New York: Brill, 1998.

Lowry, S. Todd and Barry Gordon, "Introduction," in Lowry and Gordon (eds.), **Ancient and Medieval Economic Ideas and Concepts of Social Justice**, 1998, pp. 1-10.

Ludlow, Morwenna. **The Early Church: The I.B.Tauris History of the Christian Church**, London and New York: I. B. Tauris, 2009.

Lunt, William E. **Financial Relations of the Papacy with England to 1327**, Cambridge, MA: Mediaeval Academy of America, 1939.

Lunt, William E. **Financial Relations of the Papacy with England, 1327-1534,** Cambridge, MA: Mediaeval Academy of America, 1962.

Lunt, William E. **Papal Revenues in the Middle Ages, Vols. I-II,** New York: Columbia University Press, 1934.

Luscombe, D. and J. Riley-Smith, "Introduction," in Luscombe, D. and J. Riley-Smith (eds.), **The New Cambridge Medieval History: Vol. 4, c. 1024-c. 1198, Part 1,** 2004, pp. 1-10.

Luscombe, D. and J. Riley-Smith (eds.). **The New Cambridge Medieval History: Vol. 4, c. 1024-c. 1198, Part 1,** Cambridge: Cambridge University Press, 2004.

Luscombe, David and Jonathan Riley-Smith (eds.). **The New Cambridge Medieval History: Vol. 4, c. 1024-c. 1198, Part 2,** Cambridge: Cambridge University Press, 2004.

Lynch, Joseph H. **The Medieval Church: A Brief History,** London and New York: Longman, 1992.

Lynch, Joseph H. **Simoniacal Entry into Religious Life from 1000 to 1260: A Social, Economic, and Legal Study,** Columbus, OH: Ohio State University Press, 1976.

MacCulloch, Diarmaid. **Christianity: The First Three Thousand Years,** New York: Viking, 2009.

Macy, Gary. **The Hidden History of Women's Ordination: Female Clergy in the Medieval West,** Oxford: Oxford University Press, 2008.

Macy, Gary, "The Ordination of Women in the Early Middle Ages," **Theological Studies** 61, 2000, pp. 502-7.

Marcus, Joel, "Jewish Christianity," in Mitchell and Young (eds.), **The Cambridge History of Christianity, Vol. 1: Origins to Constantine,** 2006, pp. 87-102.

Mcbrien, Richard P. **The Church: The Evolution of Catholicism,** New York: HarperOne, 2008.

Mcbrien, Richard P. Lives of the Popes - reissue: The Pontiffs from St. Peter to Benedict XVI, New York, NY: HarperSanFrancisco, 2006.

McCleary, Rachel M., "The Economics of Religion as a Field of Study," in McCleary, Rachel M. (ed.), The Oxford Handbook of the Economics of Religion, 2011, pp. 3-36.

McCleary, Rachel M. (ed.), The Oxford Handbook of the Economics of Religion, New York: Oxford University Press, 2011.

McConnell, Michael W. and Richard A. Posner, "An Economic Approach to Issues of Religious Freedom," University of Chicago Law Review 56.1 (1989), pp. 1-60.

McDonnell, Kilian, "The *Summae Confessorum* on the Integrity of Confession as Prolegomena for Luther and Trent," Theological Studies 54 (1993), pp. 405-26

McElwee, Joshua J., "Bourgeois Dismissed from Order," in National Catholic Reporter 49, December 7-20, 2012.

McElwee, Joshua J., "Letter officially dismisses Bourgeois," in National Catholic Reporter, February 1-14, 2013.

McElwee, Joshua J., "Unfinished Work: 10 years of clergy sex abuse," in National Catholic Reporter online edition, May 11, 2012, http://ncronline.org/news/accountability/unfinished-work-examining-10-years-clergy-sex-abuse.

McGinn, T. A. J., "The Law of Roman Divorce in the Time of Christ," in Levine, Allison Jr., and Crossan (eds), The Historical Jesus in Context, 2006, pp. 309-22.

McGuckin, J. A., "The Vine and the Elm Tree: The Patristic Interpretation of Jesus' Teachings on Wealth," in Sheils and Wood (eds.), The Church and Wealth, pp. 1-14.

McKitterick, R., "Introduction," in McKitterick, (ed.), **The New Cambridge Medieval History: Vol. 2, c. 700-c.900**, 1999, pp. 3-17.

McKitterick, R. (ed.). **The New Cambridge Medieval History: Vol. 2, c. 700-c.900**, Cambridge: Cambridge University Press, 1995.

McMichael, Steven J. and Susan E. Myers (eds.), **Friars and Jews in the Middle Ages and Renaissance**, Boston, MA: Brill, 2004.

Meens, Rob, "Remedies for sins," in Noble and Smith (eds.), **The Cambridge History of Christianity: Early Medieval Christianities, c. 600-c. 1100**, 2008, pp. 399-415.

Miller, Kent D. "Competitive Strategies of Religious Organizations," **Strategic Management Journal** 23 (May 2002), pp. 435-456.

Mitchell, Margaret M. and Frances M. Young, "Conclusion: retrospect and prospect," in Mitchell and Young (eds.), **The Cambridge History of Christianity, Vol. 1: Origins to Constantine**, 2006, pp. 586-589.

Modras, Ron, "Does excommunication do any good?" in **National Catholic Reporter**, July 9, 2010.

Mokyr, Joel (ed.). **The Oxford Encyclopedia of Economic History: Volume 1**, New York, NY: Oxford University Press, 2003.
Mokyr, Joel (ed.). **The Oxford Encyclopedia of Economic History: Volume 2**, New York, NY: Oxford University Press, 2003.

Mokyr, Joel (ed.). **The Oxford Encyclopedia of Economic History: Volume 3**, New York, NY: Oxford University Press, 2003.

Mokyr, Joel (ed.). **The Oxford Encyclopedia of Economic History: Volume 4**, New York, NY: Oxford University Press, 2003.

Mokyr, Joel (ed.). **The Oxford Encyclopedia of Economic History: Volume 5**, New York, NY: Oxford University Press, 2003.

Montgomery, James D., "Contemplations on the Economic Approach to Religious Behavior," **American Economic Review** 86.2 (1996), pp. 443-447.

Moore, R. I. **The First European Revolution, c. 970-1215**, Malden, MA: Blackwell Publishing, 2000.

Moore, R. I. **The Formation of A Persecuting Society: Authority and Deviance in Western Europe 950-1250**, Malden, MA: Blackwell Publishing, second edition, 2007.

Moore, R. I., "New Sects and Secret Meetings: Associations and Authority in the Eleventh and Twelfth Centuries," in Sheils and Wood (eds.), **Voluntary Religion**, 1986, pp. 47-68.

Moore, R. I. **The Origins of European Dissent**, Toronto: University of Toronto Press (1977), 2005.

Moore, R. I., "Popular Violence and Popular Heresy in Western Europe 1000-1179," in Sheils, (ed.), **Persecution and Toleration, Studies in Church History, Volume 21,** pp. 43-50.

Morris, Ian and J. G. Manning, "Introduction," in Manning and Morris (eds.), **The Ancient Economy: Evidence and Models**, 2005, pp. 1-44.

Morris, R., "The Problems of Property," in Noble and Smith (eds.), **The Cambridge History of Christianity: Early Medieval Christianities, c. 600-c. 1100**, 2008, pp. 327-344.

Murphy, Margaret, "The High Cost of Dying: an Analysis of *pro anima* Bequests in Medieval Dublin," in Sheils, W. J. and Diana Wood (eds.), **The Church and Wealth, Studies in Church History**, 1987, pp. 111-122.

Muthoo, Abhinay, "A Non-Technical Introduction to Bargaining Theory," **World Economics** 1 (April-June 2000), pp. 145-166, http://privatewww.essex.ac.uk/~muthoo/simpbarg.pdf.

Neitz, Mary Jo and Peter R. Mueser, "Economic Man and the Sociology of Religion: A Critique of the Rational Choice Approach," in Young, (ed.), **Rational Choice Theory and Religion: Summary and Assessment**, 1997, pp. 105-118.

Nelson, Janet L., "Law and its applications," in Noble and Smith (eds.), **The Cambridge History of Christianity: Early Medieval Christianities, c. 600-c. 1100**, 2008, pp. 299-326.

Nelson, Janet L., "Royal saints and early medieval kingship," in Baker (ed.), **Sanctity and Secularity: The Church and the World**, 1973, pp. 39-44.

New Advent online Bible at http://www.newadvent.org/bible/mat001.htm.

Newhauser, Richard. **The Early History of Greed: The Sin of Avarice in Early Medieval Thought and Literature,** Cambridge: Cambridge University Press, 2000.

Nirenberg, David. **Communities of Violence: Persecution of Minorities in the Middle Ages**, Princeton, NJ: Princeton University Press, 1996.

Noble, Thomas F. X. and Julia M. H. Smith (eds.). **The Cambridge History of Christianity: Early Medieval Christianities, c. 600-c. 1100**, Cambridge: Cambridge University Press, 2008.

Norris, Frederick W., "Greek Christianities," in Casiday and Norris (eds.), **The Cambridge History of Christianity: Constantine to c. 600**, 2007, pp. 70-117.

O'Brien, George. **An Essay on Mediaeval Economic Teaching**, New York: Burt Franklin (1920), 1968.

Offer, Avner, "Between the Gift and the Market: The Economy of Regard," **Economic History Review** 50.3 (1997), pp. 450-476.

Ohrenstein, Roman A., "Talmud and Talmudic Tradition: A Socio-Economic Perspective," in Lowry and Gordon (eds.), **Ancient and Medieval Economic Ideas and Concepts of Social Justice,** 1998, pp. 209-68.

Olson, Mancur. **The Logic of Collective Action**. Cambridge, MA: Harvard University Press, 1965.

Osborne, K. B. **The Franciscan Intellectual Tradition: Tracing Its Origins and Identifying Its Central Components**, St. Bonaventure, NY: The Franciscan Institute, St. Bonaventure University, 2003.

Osborne, K. B. (ed.). **History of Franciscan Theology (Theology Series)**, St. Bonaventure, NY: The Franciscan Institute, St. Bonaventure University, 1994.

Osiek, Carolyn, "Family Matters," in Horsley (ed.), **A People's History of Christianity, Vol. 1: Christian Origins**, 2005, pp. 201-220.

Oslington, Paul (ed.). **The Oxford Handbook of Christianity and Economics**, New York: Oxford University Press, 2014.

Owen, Virginia Lee, "The Economic Legacy of Gothic Cathedral Building: France and England Compared," **Journal of Cultural Economics** (June 1989), pp. 89-100.

Pagels, Elaine. **The Origin of Satan**, New York, NY: Vintage Books, 1996.

Paldam, Martin, "Corruption and Religion: Adding to the Economic Model," **Kyklos** 54, nos. 2/3 (2001), pp. 383-414.

Schmitt Pantel, P. (ed.), **A History of Women in the West: From Ancient Goddesses to Christian Saints**, Cambridge, MA: Belknap Press, 1994.

Paris, Dov, "An Economic Look at the Old Testament," in Lowry and Gordon (eds.), **Ancient and Medieval Economic Ideas and Concepts of Social Justice**, 1998, pp. 39-103.

Paxton, F. S., "Agius of Corvey's Account of the Death of Hathumoda, First Abbess of Gandersheim, in 874," in Rubin, M. (ed.). **Medieval Christianity in Practice**, 2009, pp. 53-58.

Paxton, F. S., "Birth and death," in Noble and Smith (eds.), **The Cambridge History of Christianity: Early Medieval Christianities, c. 600-c. 1100**, 2008, pp. 383-398.

Payer, Pierre J. **Sex and the Penitentials: The Development of a Sex Code, 550-1150**, Toronto: University of Toronto Press, 1984.

Pelikan, Jarosalav. **Christian Tradition, A History of the Development of Doctrine: V. 1, The Emergence of Catholic Tradition (100-600)**, Chicago: The University of Chicago Press (1971), 1975.

Peltzman, Sam, "Toward a More General Theory of Regulation," **Journal of Law and Economics** 19 (1976), pp. 211-240.

Perron, Anthony, "The bishops of Rome, 1100-1300," in Rubin, Miri and Walter Simons (eds.), **The Cambridge History of Christianity: V. 4, Christianity in Western Europe c. 1100-c. 1500**, Cambridge: Cambridge University Press, 2009, pp. 22-38.

Pew Research Center, **"Nones" on the Rise**, downloaded October 29, 2012 at http://www.pewforum.org/.

Pomeroy, Sarah B. **Goddesses, Whores, Wives, and Slaves: Women in Classical Antiquity**, New York: Schocken Books (1975), 1995.

Rapp, Claudia, "Saints and holy men," in Casiday and Norris (eds.), **The Cambridge History of Christianity: Constantine to c. 600**, 2007, pp. 548-566.

Redman, Barbara J., "An Economic Analysis of Religious Choice," **Review of Religious Research** 21 (1980), pp. 330-342.

Reed, C. G., "The Ties That Bind: The Culture of Prejudice," Working Paper, Simon Fraser University, May 26, 2002.

Reed, C. G. and C. T. Bekar, "Religious Prohibitions against usury," **Explorations in Economic History**, 40 (2003), pp. 347-68.

Reese, Thomas J., "Thomas J. Reese on Sex Abuse," **America: The National**

Catholic Weekly, May 10, 2012,
http://www.americamagazine.org/blog/entry.cfm?blog_id=2&entry_id=5115.

Resl, B., "Bequests for the Poor," in Rubin, M. (ed.). Medieval Christianity in Practice, 2009, pp. 209-15.

Resl, B., "Material support I: parishes," in Rubin and Simons (eds.), The Cambridge History of Christianity: V. 4, Christianity in Western Europe c. 1100-c. 1500, 2009, pp. 99-106.

Reuter, T., "Introduction," in Reuter, (ed.), The New Cambridge Medieval History: Vol. 3, c. 900-c.1024, 1999, pp. 1-25.

Reuter, T. (ed.). The New Cambridge Medieval History: Vol. 3, c. 900-c.1024, Cambridge: The Cambridge University Press, 1999.

Reuter, T., "Property transactions and social relations between rulers, bishops and nobles in early elevenh-century Saxony: the evidence of the *Vita Meinwerci* Apendix 2: surviving notices of property transactions from Meinwerk's pontificate," in Davies and Fouracre (eds.), Property and Power in the Early Middle Ages (1995), 2002, pp. 165-99.

Roach, Andrew P. The Devil's World: Heresy and Society 1100-1300, Harlow, United Kingdom: Pearson Education limited, 2005.

Roberts, J. M. The New History of the World, New York, NY: Oxford University Press, 2003.

Robinson, G., Confronting Sex and Power in the Catholic Church: Reclaiming the Spirit of Jesus, Collegeville, MN: Liturgical Press, 2008.

Rosen, Sherwin, "The Economics of Superstars," American Economic Review 71 (December 1981), pp. 845-858.

Rubin, M. Gentile Tales: The Narrative Assault on Late Medieval Jews, Philadelphia, PA: University of Pennsylvania Press, 2004.

Rubin, M., "Introduction," in Rubin, M. (ed.). **Medieval Christianity in Practice**, 2009, pp. 1-3.

Rubin, M. (ed.). **Medieval Christianity in Practice**, Princeton, NJ; Princeton University Press, 2009.

Rubin, M., "Sacramental Life," in Rubin and Simons (eds.), **The Cambridge History of Christianity: V. 4, Christianity in Western Europe c. 1100-c. 1500**, 2009, pp. 219-237.
Rubin, M. and W. Simons (eds.). **The Cambridge History of Christianity: V. 4, Christianity in Western Europe c. 1100-c. 1500**, Cambridge: Cambridge University Press, 2009.

Rubin, M. and W. Simons, "Introduction," in Rubin and Simons (eds.), **The Cambridge History of Christianity: V. 4, Christianity in Western Europe c. 1100-c. 1500**, 2009, pp. 1-7.

Scheidel, Walter, Ian Morris, and Richard P. Saller (eds.). **The Cambridge Economic History of the Greco-Roman World,** Cambridge: Cambridge University Press, 2007.

Scheidel, Walter and Sitta Von Reden (eds.). **The Ancient Economy**, New York, NY: Routledge, 2002.

Schimmelpfennig, Bernhard. **The Papacy**, New York, NY: Columbia University Press, 1998.

Schmidtchen, Dieter and Achim Mayer, "Established Clergy, Friars and the Pope; Some Institutional Economics of the Medieval Church," **Journal of Institutional and Theoretical Economics** 153 (1997), pp. 122-165.

Seward, D., "Marriage Theory and Practice in the Conciliar Legislation and Diocesan Statutes of Medieval England," **Medieval Studies** 40 (1978), pp. 408-460.

Shahar, S., "Cathars and Baptism," in Rubin, M. (ed.). **Medieval Christianity in Practice**, 2009, pp. 14-19.

Sheils, W. J. and Diana Wood (eds.), **The Church and Wealth, Studies in Church History, Volume 24**, New York and Oxford: Basil Blackwell for the Ecclesiastical History Society, 1987.

Sheils, W. J. and Diana Wood (eds.), **Voluntary Religion, Studies in Church History, Volume 23**, New York and Oxford: Basil Blackwell for the Ecclesiastical History Society, 1986.

Sherkat, Darren E., "Embedding Religious Choices: Integrating Preferences and Social Constraints into Rational Choice Theories of Religious Behavior," in Young, (ed.), **Rational Choice Theory and Religion: Summary and Assessment**, 1997, pp. 66-86.

Short, William. **Poverty and Joy: The Franciscan Tradition**, Maryknoll, NY: Orbis Books, 1999.

Simons, W., "The Lives of the Beghards," in Rubin, M. (ed.). **Medieval Christianity in Practice**, 2009, pp. 238-45.

Simons, W., "On the margins of religious life: hermits and recluses, penitents and tertiaries, beguines and beghards," in Rubin and Simons (eds.), **The Cambridge History of Christianity: V. 4, Christianity in Western Europe c. 1100-c. 1500**, 2009, pp. 311-23.

Smith, Adam. **The Theory of Moral Sentiments**, Whitefish, MT: Kessinger Publishing (1759), 2004.

Smith, Adam. **The Wealth of Nations**, New York NY: Random House, The Modern Library (1776), 1937.

Smith, C. E. **Papal Enforcement of Some Medieval Marriage Laws**, University, LA: Louisiana State University Press, 1940.

Smith, J. M. H., "Pilgrimage and Spiritual Healing," in Rubin, M. (ed.). **Medieval Christianity in Practice**, 2009, pp. 222-28.

Smith, J. M. H., "Saints and their cults," in Noble and Smith (eds.), **The Cambridge History of Christianity: Early Medieval Christianities, c. 600-c. 1100**, 2008, pp. 581-605.

Snape, R. H. **English Monastic Finances In The Later Middle Ages,** Whitefish, MT: Kessinger Publishing's Rare Reprints, originally published by Cambridge University Press (1925), 2008.

Stark, Rodney, "Atheism, Faith, and the Social Scientific Study of Religion," **Journal of Contemporary Religion** 14 (1999), pp. 41-62.

Stark, Rodney, "Bringing Theory Back In," in Young, (ed.), **Rational Choice Theory and Religion: Summary and Assessment**, 1997, pp. 3-23.

Stark, Rodney, "Catholic Contexts: Competition, Commitment, and Innovation," **Review of Religious Research** 39 (1998), pp. 197-208.

Stark, Rodney, "Do Catholic Societies Really Exist?" **Rationality and Society** 4.3 (1992), pp. 261-271.

Stark, Rodney, "Micro Foundations of Religion: A Revised Theory," **Sociological Theory** 17 (1999), pp. 264-289.

Stark, Rodney. **The Rise of Christianity: How the Obscure, Marginal Jesus Movement Became the Dominant Religious Force in the Western World in a Few Centuries**, San Francisco: HarperCollins, 1997.

Stark, Rodney and William Sims Bainbridge. **A Theory of Religion,** New York and Bern: Peter Lang, 1987.

Stark, Rodney and William Sims Bainbridge, "Towards A Theory of Religion: Religious Commitment," **Journal for the Scientific Study of Religion** 19 (1980), pp. 114-128.

Stark, Rodney and Roger Finke. **Acts of Faith: Explaining the Human Side of Religion,** Berkeley, CA: University of California press, 2000.

Stark, Rodney, Laurence R. Iannaccone, and Roger Finke, "Religion, Science, and Rationality," **American Economic Review** 86.2 (1996), pp. 433-437.

Stark, Rodney and Lynne Roberts, "The Arithmetic of Social Movements: Theoretical Implications," **Sociological Analysis** 43 (1982), pp. 53-68.

Stigler, George, "The Theory of Economic Regulation," **Bell Journal of Economics and Management Science** 2 (1971), pp. 3-21.

Stow, K. R. **Popes, Church, and Jews in the Middle Ages: Confrontation and Response**, Aldershot, Great Britain: Ashgate Publishing, 2007, pp. IV: 1-81.

Stow, K. R. **Taxation, Community, and State: The Jews and the Fiscal Foundations of the Early Modern Papal State**. Stuttgart, Germany: Anton Hiersemann, 1982.

Stroumsa, Guy G., "Religious dynamics between Christians and Jews in late antiquity (312-640)," in Casiday and Norris (eds.), **The Cambridge History of Christianity: Constantine to c. 600**, 2007, pp. 151-172.

Thurston, Herbert, "Relics," **The Catholic Encyclopedia**. New York: Robert Appleton Company, New Advent, January 2, 2009, http://www.newadvent.org/cathen/12734a.htm.
Tilley, Maureen A., "North Africa," in Mitchell and Young (eds.), **The Cambridge History of Christianity, Vol. 1: Origins to Constantine**, 2006, pp. 381-386.

Todeschini, Giacomo. "Franciscan Economics and Jews in the Middle Ages: From a Theological to an Economic Lexicon," in McMichael and Myers (eds.), **Friars and Jews in the Middle Ages and Renaissance**, 2004, pp. 99-118.

Todeschini, Giacomo (translated by Donatella Melucci). **Franciscan Wealth: From Voluntary Poverty to Market Society**, St. Bonaventure, NY: The Franciscan Institute, St. Bonaventure University (2004), 2009.

Toynbee, Arnold. **An Historian's Approach to Religion**, London: Oxford University Press, second edition, 1979.

Trombley, Frank R., "Christianity and paganism, II: Asia Minor," in Casiday and Norris (eds.), **The Cambridge History of Christianity: Constantine to c. 600**, 2007, pp. 189-209.

Trout, D., "Saints, Identity, and the City," in Burrus (ed.), **A People's History of Christianity, Vol. 2: Late Ancient Christianity**, 2005, pp. 165-87.

Van Engen, John H., "Conclusion: Christendom, c. 1100," in Noble and Smith (eds.), **The Cambridge History of Christianity: Early Medieval Christianities, c. 600-c. 1100**, 2008, pp. 625-643.

Vauchez, A., "The church and the laity," in Abulafia, D. (ed.). **The New Cambridge Medieval History: Vol. 5, c. 1198-c.1300**, 1999, pp. 182-203.

Vauchez, Andre, "Saints and pilgrimages: new and old," in Rubin and Simons (eds.), **The Cambridge History of Christianity: V. 4, Christianity in Western Europe c. 1100-c. 1500**, 2009, pp. 324-39.

Vidmar, John. **The Catholic Church through the Ages: A History**, Mahwah, New Jersey: Paulist Press, 2005.

Warner, Keith D. and John E. Isom. **Journey and Place: An Atlas of St. Francis**, Cincinnati, Ohio: St. Anthony Messenger Press, 2008.

Waterman, A. M. C., "Economists on the Relation between Political Economy and Christian Theology: A Preliminary Survey," **International Journal of Social Economy** 14.6 (1987), pp. 46-68.
Webb, Diana, "Saints and Cities in Medieval Italy," **History Today** 43 (July 1993), pp. 15-22.

Webb, Diana, "A Saint and His Money: Perceptions of Urban Wealth in the Lives of Italian Saints," in Sheils, and Wood (eds.), **The Church and Wealth, Studies in Church History**, 1987, pp. 61-73.

Whalen, Brett Edward. **Dominion of God: Christendom and Apocalypse in the Middle Ages**, Cambridge, MA: Harvard University Press, 2009.

Wickham, C. **Framing the Early Middle Ages: Europe and the Mediterranean, 400-800**, New York: Oxford University Press (2005), 2006.

Wiley, T. **Original Sin: Origins, Developments, Contemporary Meanings**, New York: Paulist Press, 2002.

Williams, George L. **Papal Genealogy: The Families and Descendants of the Popes**, Jefferson, NC: MacFarland & Co., 1998.

Wills, Garry. **Papal Sin: Structures of Deceit**, New York, NY: Doubleday Image Books, 2001.

Winter, Miriam T., **Out of the Depths: The Story of Ludmila Javorová, Ordained Roman Catholic Priest**, New York, NY: The Crossroads Publishing Company, 2001.

Wood, Diana. **Medieval Economic Thought**. Cambridge: Cambridge University Press, 2002.

Wood, Ian. **The Missionary Life: Saints and the Evangelisation of Europe, 400-1050**, Essex, England: Pearson Education, 2001.

Wood, Susan. **The Proprietary Church in the Medieval West**, Oxford: Oxford University Press, 2006.

Young, Frances M., "Prelude: Jesus Christ, foundation of Christianity," in Mitchell and Young (eds.), **The Cambridge History of Christianity, Vol. 1: Origins to Constantine**, 2006, pp. 1-34.

Young, Frances, Lewis Ayres, and Andrew Louth (eds.). **The Cambridge History of Early Christian Literature**, Cambridge: Cambridge University Press, 2004.
Young, Lawrence A. (ed.). **Rational Choice Theory and Religion: Summary and Assessment**, New York: Routledge, 1997.

Zema, D. B., "Economic Reorganisation of the Roman See during the Gregorian Reform," **Studi gregoriani** 1, 1947, pp. 137-68.

Ziegler, J., "Fourteenth-Century Instructions for Bedside Pastoral Care," in Rubin, M. (ed.), **Medieval Christianity in Practice**, 2009, pp. 103-108.

Made in the USA
San Bernardino, CA
12 October 2018